# Special Effects

*Books by Harriet Frank, Jr.*

Single
Special Effects

# Special Effects

Harriet Frank, Jr.

Houghton Mifflin Company Boston
1979

*Library of Congress Cataloging in Publication Data*

Frank, Harriet.
Special effects.

I. Title.
PZ4.F824Sp [PS3556.R334] 78-11679
ISBN 0-395-27219-X

Printed in the United States of America

In loving memory of my mother

*"For God's sake hold your tongue and let me love."*

— John Donne

# Special Effects

# Chapter One

"You goddamn old bitch," the boy shouted as he banged into the side of Emma's car. "Why don't you get some goddamn glasses!"

Emma was thrown into the steering wheel, felt the car careen, thought what an ignoble end she would come to — hurled free like a rag doll — and was assailed by the first wave of self-pity she had felt since Charles left her. She ended up slamming into a palm tree, musing on how children were raised these days. The boy had unmistakably given her the finger as he tore off down Santa Monica Boulevard.

She climbed out of the car, awash with the injustice of it all. She was not old. She was not a bitch. She did need glasses but the need for them was recent, as were all the other unaccountable aches and pains that had appeared of late. She had never had a bunion. She had one now. Her digestion had been admirable. Of late, everything she ate seemed to lodge in her throat. Her ears rang like the insistent pealing of church bells and there was undoubtedly a new cavity in a back molar. Even now she felt its twinge.

She sat down on grass clearly posted with a NO TRESPASSING

sign and looked frantically for the cigarettes she had forsworn. They were there all right, crushed, fragrant, restorative. She snapped a match under her fingernail, thinking once again that it was a habit of Charles's. He always struck a match under his thumbnail. There was even a strange half-moon there. Charles was stigmatized by all kinds of odd scars and marks, as if his childhood had been a hazardous field, spiky with broken glass and rusted nails.

Emma examined herself carefully, licked a scratch on her arm and wondered at the callousness of a world that took no notice whatever of a woman sitting on a curb near a demolished car — an exceptionally tall and distraught woman at that. There was a time when people formed a circle around an accident, like petals surrounding the heart of a flower, awed and solicitous and secretly and profoundly grateful at being spared themselves. Charles, she recalled, would never let an occasion of mercy pass. He kept flares in his trunk and a first aid box, beautifully replete with splints and bandages, which he knew how to use, having gone to Red Cross classes as soon as the children were born. He carried lap robes and a flask of quite good brandy, and his voice, when he said, "Now just lie still, you'll be fine," promised life and surcease from pain and a large settlement from an insurance company with himself as judicious witness should there be a trial.

Suddenly she needed Charles. Charles was definitely what was needed now. She scrabbled in her untidy handbag, recalling how carefully Charles had instructed her on when and how he could be reached. Any time of day or night, he had said — that had to be understood between them. He implored her not to be prejudiced by their situation, not to turn away from him. He had had tears in his eyes and at the time she had patted his hand and said, "Of course," two or three times, as if he were hard of hearing.

When she found the number, she could not read it. Charles wrote in a crabbed, minuscule hand, and it was all too clear that she needed glasses. She wondered if she might stop the jogger running on the cinder path behind her and ask him to read it for her, but that would entail a long explanation about the dissolution of her marriage and how it had affected her eyesight and her digestion and even, in some mysterious way, had grown a bunion on her big toe.

Then there was the matter of small change. She had none. Nor any money at all. She wondered if the filling station on the corner would accept American Express or Diner's Club. She wondered what would happen if she simply collapsed into helpless tears, calling Charles's name aloud. Might he hear her halfway across town, might he raise his head from his typewriter like a buck scenting danger in the air and come to her? Charles believed in telepathy. She wished now she had not called it twaddle to his face.

She thought of walking up the street and knocking on one of those finely burnished doors on Maple Drive, but people these days were afraid of rapists and kidnapers and kept dogs and maids who did not speak English. She closed her eyes, thinking if she sat here till dark looking strange and stray someone might stop a police car or, failing that, a garbage truck. She saw herself being hoisted in its powerful claw along with broken eucalyptus branches and the bones of very expensive steaks. She spent the better part of an hour thinking about that, lying back in the grass, which smelled faintly of manure. All of Beverly Hills in early summer smelled of manure. Probably because the grass had to be greener here than anywhere else in the world. In a house overlooking the park she saw a man brushing his hair, first forward like a Roman general, then back into the severe baldness of an old nun.

Emma cried for help in a feeble voice replaced by a robust one when she saw she was ignored.

"Help," she said again, trying this time for a pleasant and undismayed tone. The man brushed his hair sideways and hated it.

"Help," Emma said.

He looked down upon her.

"I've had an accident," she said, waving cheerfully.

He closed the window and snapped down the shade.

You'll come to a toupee, even so, Emma thought malevolently and tried to stand. So far so good, although her steps were small and mincing, as if her feet were bound.

The gas station attendant would not lend her ten cents, pointing to a sign that read NO SOLICITING.

"I'll let you fix my wrecked car," she wheedled. "I'll let you overcharge me . . . more even than the Ford agency on Rodeo, and God knows they're thieves."

He brightened visibly, following her gesture. "You got a lotta body work there," he said, although the car was across the street and he had to be guessing.

"I just want to phone my husband," she said, then added hastily, "he doesn't know a thing about cars. I'm sure he'll tell you just to trundle it on in here and do your worst. I was on my way to the bank when this happened. Maybe you saw it and could be a witness."

"Don't send anybody in here to talk to me, lady. I'm up to my ass in litigation right this minute. Two divorces, two back alimonies, two child supports. Forget me."

He handed her the money. "Call your husband."

She knew she had summoned Charles away from a lettuce and tomato sandwich. He had one every day from the tomatoes he grew himself. They had been inundated by tomatoes throughout their marriage, with Charles sometimes asking her why she didn't pickle them, recalling wistfully his mother's shelves of quince jelly and green beans and piccalilli. She remembered telling him how lucky he had been to escape death by botulism, recalling jars from her mother-in-law she had opened that hissed and bubbled dangerously. The contents of one had killed their cat. Then she wished she hadn't said it, but by that time it was too late.

"Charles," she said, "it's Emma and I've wrecked the car."

"My God," he said. "Are you all right? Are you, Emma?"

She preened a little at the note of panic she heard.

"Charles," she said, "it's true what they say about your last thoughts before you die. You flashed before my eyes in your winter pajamas."

"I'm coming right there," he said. "Just sit down and breathe quietly." Then he bethought himself. "Where are you?"

"At the corner of Santa Monica Boulevard and Maple Drive. There's a big, fake Spanish house on the corner. I'm at the gas station. Charles," she said, "is this an imposition?"

"My God, no. What are you talking about? I'm coming. You could have been killed."

Even as he spoke, Emma thought of the chaos that would have attended her untimely demise. Everything would have surfaced — the terrible jumble of her bureau drawers, her passionate and explicit diary, her unpaid Saks bill, that silly record she made singing an aria from *Così Fan Tutte* out of sheer vanity in a decidedly thin soprano voice. How awful if she had died without telling her boys for one last time how wildly she loved them, how good their father was, how good life was.

She made a dozen instant resolves. She would take her boring cousin to lunch, an expensive lunch with wine. She would acknowledge God if He could be confined to nature worship and her own code of ethics. She would listen, listen, listen, with endless patience. She would not judge. She would be content with less, and half of that if need be. One side of her head began to ache. "Could I use your washroom, please?"

The gas station attendant gave her a sour look and a key.

The toilet was indescribably filthy and the water ran rusty brown from the tap. She had not seen Charles in six months and now he would see her with a bloodied nose and, yes, a chip in her front tooth.

It was uncharitable to think it, but Charles, when he arrived, looked no better than she. He looked like a traveler newly come from some infected port, eyes grainy, all membranes dry. His hair was longer than she remembered, a good nut-brown, recently washed. She could tell by the way it lifted in the breeze. He must be washing it every day, she conjectured, grooming himself with anxious care. He had had a mole near his mouth removed; there remained a small red scar. He wore a ring she had never seen before, a curious dark stone set into massive silver. He had lost weight. Unaccountably, she thought of autumn leaves, some still bright, some sere, burning into grayish dust, consumed.

He took her into a deep and silent embrace. He said her name in a muffled and solemn voice. No one else sounded those notes of farm-bred, Calvinist-indoctrinated probity in quite the same way.

"Are you all right?"

"No," she said. "I've wrenched something in my back, my head aches, my car's wrecked and my insurance rates will go through the roof. Also, I feel like a fool, calling you away from your work."

"I was working the *New York Times* crossword. I hadn't written a word all morning. I sewed a button on my shirt. I phoned the weather bureau."

"In that case . . ." she said, unworthily glad that he was arid and voiceless.

"You cut your hair," he told her.

She ran her fingers through the close crop, which had cost her fifty dollars without tip and which she felt made her look like Gertrude Stein.

"It was in lieu of my throat," she said mildly and then, when she saw his dismay, she offered a soothing pat on the arm.

"Would you buy me a cup of coffee?"

"I'd rather take you to the doctor. I'd like you to be looked over."

"Charles," Emma said, "do not mother me or I will burst into tears and embarrass both of us. I would like a cup of coffee and a cheese Danish, even if I am on a diet. Maybe even a corned beef sandwich although it's only eleven o'clock in the morning."

He nodded. "I'll just arrange about your car." He handed her into his shabby Plymouth, shoving aside stacks of library books. "All right?"

"Fine," she said.

She watched him as he spoke with the attendant — Charles listening solemnly as he was being cheated out of his boots. He was of that stringy, hardy breed that had crossed prairies, felled forests, scaled mountains, turned dark stubborn faces into the setting sun. Charles believed that if a man looked you squarely in the eye and shook your hand with a certain firmness, he could be trusted. Nothing had ever abraded that belief, although magazine subscriptions he had ordered from door-to-door salesmen never arrived and loans made to friends went unpaid. He never checked a restaurant bill or a bank statement, never counted his change. Honor loomed so large in his scale of things that when he fell from it new lines appeared on his face and he sought help from doctors and priests and wept in his sleep.

They went to Nate 'n Al's Delicatessen because Emma liked the huge sandwiches and took the extra bread and rolls away in her handbag. The big, bare room was redolent with the smell of dill pickles, full of the ear-assaulting din of deal making and bartering. The restaurant had the roar and clatter of a marketplace. The litany of business rose around them.

"He's looking for ten percent of the gross. I said what the fuck is left for me? Who needs him? I can get Kraut money. I should pay for his tennis court off my picture?" And: "I said I don't want her. She's old. She's a boozer. Faye Dunaway is what we're shooting for. Or maybe Fonda." And: "Harold Pinter. He says use Harold Pinter. I don't fall on my ass over Harold Pinter. Short sentences my secretary can write."

Cigars jutting, the men faced each other across the littered tables, ticking off grosses, tabulating costs, wolfing down sour cream and lox and pastrami.

Charles found the only clean table in the room. He guided her into her seat, first sweeping the crumbs from it with the sleeve of his jacket. Then he took his own place, studied her intently as if seeking something from her.

Emma shifted one way and then another. His gaze made her aware of the pin in her bra strap, her scuffed shoes, her next-tooldest skirt. She thought of his new love, his Carla of the white skin and wide amber eyes, the light, boneless look of her, and wished that she had not eaten so many donuts with midnight greed and that she had creamed her skin instead of falling into bed with a dirty face. Then she sniffed, audibly, disdainfully. Hadn't the man seen her with chicken pox caught from the kids, seen her with head colds, with eyes narrowed to slits from allergy? Hadn't he held her head while she heaved, felled by ptomaine, seasickness, pregnancy? He had seen stretch marks and appendectomy scars and hair going gray at the roots. Take me or leave me, she thought, then winced, then grinned. He had left her.

And yet . . . and yet . . . there was an eagerness about him. Damned if it wasn't typical of Charles to create an island of intensity and emotion amidst chicken soup and stuffed cabbage.

"You're never home, Emma. I've called. Where are you these days?"

She slouched on the base of her spine. Charles had often admonished her to stand tall, to do justice to her full six feet, but she still ducked her head and hunched her shoulders and jackknifed in chairs.

"Where am I? Well, sometimes in bed with the covers up over my head and the cat on my stomach keeping me warm. Sometimes watching an old Carole Lombard movie with the phone off the hook. Sometimes at my sister's drinking beer with her in the kitchen and talking about men and misery. Sometimes in bad company, sometimes in good."

"Emma, you are much on my mind. Do you believe that?"

"Not really," she said dryly.

"Every day and most nights. Except when there's a Lakers game." He peered at the menu and Emma saw with a pang that he did not use his reading glasses. "I write to the boys twice a week. I'm lucky if I get a postcard a month. Both of 'em send one postcard between 'em."

"That's about what I get. If they phone, they reverse the charges. Charles, listen. They're seventeen years old. They're up at Santa Barbara watching their friends burn down the Bank of America and getting crabs and living life. Mo writes terrible poetry. Adam's made the dean's list. They work Saturdays in a shoe store. They go to Buddhist prayer meetings on Sunday. They're fine. They're happy."

"Emma," he said suddenly, "I want to buy you something. A blouse. A parakeet. Some earrings."

"Are you flush all of a sudden?"

"No, but when I heard you say you'd been in an accident, I got very grim. I want to take note of your being alive with some kind of gesture."

"Maybe you'll pay half my doctor's bill. I'd certainly like that."

"I'll pay half of half of it — my cupboard's pretty bare." He laid his hand on hers for a moment and then withdrew it.

"Charles," Emma said, looking at him. "What is it? Are you in the dark night of the soul or what? Is your stomach bothering you? Are you worried about money? Is your new girl a fizzle? Why are you so conciliatory? Tell me."

"I miss you, Emma."

"Well, that's not surprising. My goodness, Charles, we were as hot as firecrackers once. I'd take it very hard if I hadn't left some kind of an impression on you. We were lovely in bed. We liked the same toothpaste. I gave up smoking for you, though I've started up again. You gave up Jockey shorts for me."

"Emma, Emma, Emma," he said.

"That's my name."

"I'm full of doubts."

Emma resisted an impulse to reach across the table and comfort him with a touch. It seemed perverse not to; it seemed cold and unfamiliar and remote. But weren't they, truly, now cold and unfamiliar and remote?

She put her elbows on the table instead.

"I'd like to see you once in a while, Emma. I'd like to hang out with you, as the kids say. I'd like to talk to you."

"What about?"

"Me," he said, and laughed.

"Nothing's changed," Emma said, but without rancor.

"We've always been friends," he told her, as if anything else were incomprehensible.

"We've been more and we've been less," Emma said, righting the account with some asperity. She marveled at his complacency, envied it, wondered that he could sustain it.

"Charles," she said, "you left me for another woman. And a younger one to boot. You can't trot back and forth between us, getting fed scraps at the back door."

"Lady, you hand out a stiff sentence."

"The punishment fits the crime."

"Unrelenting Emma."

She mulled that. I did see you through pneumonia and writer's block, she thought, and the fall of the stock market and the inexorable departure of youth. And I *was* reduced by your going, my friend, oh, yes, I was battered and baffled, with sweat on my upper lip and strange palpitations of the heart and a feeling of winter in my bones. "If I owe you anything for your coming today, I'll have to discharge the obligation in some other way. I'll send you some pesticide for the tomato plants or something."

"What harm could lunch do?"

Of all the consolations I require, Emma thought, a midday meal is not one of them. Recant, forswear, return — and we'll see. "Pride forbids," she said.

Charles was not without grace. He submitted, nodding his head as if he heard a door closing very far away.

Emma glanced at her watch. "I have to go. No, finish your coffee," she said as he started to rise. "Lend me two dollars. I'll call a cab. I have to drop a script off at the studio."

"Just one thing, Emma," he told her. "Get glasses. You need em. I don't want you driving a car when you can't see."

She looked down at him, thinking that she liked his hair the old way, that she liked the disfiguring mole that had been sacrificed and that he needn't have discarded his wedding ring which had been her grandfather's.

"You wear yours," she said. "You need 'em too and you look fine in them." They touched hands briefly and she was gone.

Emma's office was at the back of the building where all the other drones labored. The big, buff, plaster structure had seen better days. Now, with its long, rugless corridors, the aggressive flush of its toilets and its chipped paint, it resembled a Great Depression boarding house. The writers were housed on the second story with an unpleasant view of the parking lot. As they were a nomadic tribe, bolted metal nameplates had been dispensed with and a painter appeared instead with frightening regularity to inscribe and remove their names. Here lies one whose name is writ in water.

The story analysts were relegated downstairs, where some attempt had been made at permanence. The walls were hung with blown-up photos of actors embalmed in bright, seductive, virile poses. There was an occasional frisson along Emma's nerves at the realization that a number of them were dead. Conversation in the hall tended to be muted. The old, drunken, exuberant conviviality of the heyday was gone.

Emma had made a lair for herself in her cramped quarters. Plants grew in a green, unkempt tangle in her window. An old paisley shawl draped the couch whose springs had burst forth in wiry tendrils; a battered coffee pot stood on her pitted and gouged desk. Much of the havoc she had wrought herself, with careless cigarette burns, spilled tomato juice and yogurt, and a general disregard of order. She never threw anything away and now towers of papers and magazines rose on every side. Sometimes a sluggish domestic stirring would result in her sweeping her arm across her desk toward the wastebasket, but at once she thought the better of it and scrambled to retrieve what she had just thrown out. She had been reared in a Spartan atmosphere of scrupulously polished furniture, Lysol, and naphtha cleanliness, somberly disposed family photos, clocks and candlesticks and Victorian ornaments standing like soldiers.

It had made her wild. Ever after, where Emma lived there was distinction and chaos. Her sons thrived on it. Her dogs, two or three, reveled in it. Charles loathed it. After he had left, she spent some time musing on their life together. Yes, he had definitely abhorred her housekeeping, and it was quite true that meals were often slapdash affairs, that clothes lay where they dropped, that beds often went unmade for unforgivable days at a time, but there were roses in all the rooms and Vivaldi on the record player and a good fire on a wet afternoon and great coffee on the stove night and day.

As for money. She was superb with money. Tight, Charles said. Maybe so, but they owned the house they lived in and didn't owe a dime. It was a matter of pride. "We've got 'fuck you' money," she would say, and Charles would shake his head and look away as if he did not know who she was when she haggled with the grocers and the antique dealers. "C'mon . . . throw in the soup bones. I've been shopping here for twelve years." "The leg's been replaced on that Hepplewhite chair. I'll take it off your hands but at a price."

"Listen," she had told Charles while she sat over the monthly bills, chewing on her pen, "everybody in this town is up to his ears in debt. Ask in Hermès, they'll tell you. Ask in Hunter's Book Shop; Saks; Jurgenson's. Ask the doctors on Bedford. If the local merchants blew the whistle, this town would empty out tomorrow."

Charles had ducked behind his newspaper. She had not let it go. Solvency was an article of faith with her.

"Elegance," she declaimed, "is paying your Mexican maid on time. Elegance is paying your bills. And incidentally, Charles, I would appreciate it if you could do without the new Oxford unabridged for a while. It costs a fortune."

"I'm a writer. Books are the tools of my trade."

"You can use my old Funk and Wagnalls. It's got all the

words in it." She smiled sweetly as she always did when she was affecting small economies.

"Emma," he had said, "you put me in mind of those hard-faced women sitting behind their cash boxes in French bistros."

"Salt of the earth," she had replied.

Echoes of that conversation still rang in her head, overlaid, even at this distance, with satisfaction. The new freezer, paid for in cash; the power mower likewise. The bathroom tiles on time but only on a six-months' contract. The boys' braces . . . well, nobody could handle that without selling the family jewels.

"Any calls?"

Her secretary, Mavis, was black, beautiful, feisty, and devoted to her boss. She spelled atrociously, thought quickly, and was a conduit for all the rumors, gossip, backbiting and slaughter in the business. She slept with women and would have liked to include Emma; she sensed that Emma was lenient but without interest.

"Mr. Bolen would like you to come up. He's been waiting half an hour. I told him you were at the doctor's."

"Anything else?"

"Yeah. Mo called from Santa Barbara. Let's see. I wrote down the message . . . here it is. 'Maw, I'm not sure the best is yet to be, but hang in there. Happy Birthday. Moses.' " She looked up at Emma. "That's a fresh kid."

Emma smiled. "That's a good kid. Nothing from his twin brother?"

"Not so far."

"One love, one lemon," Emma said. "All right, I'm going up to Bolen's. Call William Morris and ask them to pick up the two scripts on my desk. There's no interest here. I've attached a note. Also, call Mr. Jessup on the set and ask if he'd like to talk to me sometime this afternoon about the Casey book. He's expecting to hear from me. Did you eat lunch?"

"I had two martinis. I'm feelin' down today."

"How does that differ from yesterday? Go take a nap on the couch. Put the calls on the switchboard."

Mavis yawned and stretched, showing her firm little breasts, two hazelnuts. "What birthday is it, Mrs. Howard, or aren't you saying?"

"The evil birthday," Emma said. "Forty."

"You don't look it."

"I feel it. Through and through."

Stewart Bolen's hands shook and his eyes did not meet Emma's as he beckoned her into his office. They had worked together for ten years. Bolen had been at the studio for twenty. He looked like a man who lived alone, ate sparingly, slept in a narrow bed, voiced prayers in the night. In fact, he had a wife who had twice been hospitalized for nervous disorders and who called him daily at the studio to weep over the phone until he would cry out, "Stop, Evelyn, stop. We both have to get through the day," and hang up on her. Emma liked him. He loved books, read them carefully, annotating erudite comments in tiny script in the margins. He had gone to Yale and had known Robert Frost. He ran the story department as if it was some kind of a shabby exclusive school and he the headmaster.

"I've just been fired," he said, "just this morning." He sat slack, aged, dismissed. "I'm to clean out my desk sometime this week. At my convenience."

Emma shook her head. "It isn't possible," she said. "Even in this place."

Stewart Bolen rearranged the papers on his desk. He was given to small nervous fidgetings, adjusting his glasses, fiddling with the Phi Beta Kappa key on his watch chain, interlacing his fingers, filling in pauses with a dry, apologetic cough.

"I've been conscientious," he said. "No one, I think, more so. My work has had all my energies. Not that I have a great deal anymore. I should have spent more time with Evelyn." He paused. "You know about my wife, Evelyn, don't you, Emma?"

Emma nodded.

"She's considerably older than I, but she's been a delight to me. She reads Hebrew, you know. She was a superb scholar.

When she's herself, she's wonderful to be with. I rely on her judgment as much as my own. We've been married forty years. Forty years this spring." He looked uncertain, bereft. "You must forgive this discussion of my personal affairs, Emma."

He seemed ashamed of being so visible in his anxiety, like a patient, cringing and naked before the verdict of his doctor.

Emma was used to physical solutions to pain. She swept her children into fierce embraces, strained them against her. Clutch and kiss mended most things with them. With Charles, it had been another kind of comfort, bed comfort, the shelter of her arms. This shabby old man with his liverish complexion and trembling hands required something else of her.

"Stewart," she exhorted, "don't let them put you out. Go up to the front office and speak your piece. You've worked at this studio for twenty years. Don't get turned out. Get *thrown* out. Those idiots up there have been using your taste and your opinions and palming them off as their own ever since you've been here. At least get severance pay. Get your pension. Get a lawyer if you have to."

He took out a large linen handkerchief and mopped his forehead. Someone had initialed it with a beautiful monogram and had rolled the edges by hand. The scent of cedar wafted toward her. She saw then, in her mind's eye, how he was cared for. She saw the old-fashioned bedroom he shared with Evelyn, his shabby dressing gown laid on the counterpane, a cut glass vase of pinks on the nightstand, medicine bottles arranged to hand, resting on a table. She saw Evelyn, with long girlish plaits, lying beside him, placing an elegant, blue-veined hand over his in the dark. Then they would sleep, the light, insecure sleep of old people, sleep that would bring hard-won courage to start another day.

"I would like to make a dignified departure," he said heavily.

Emma was impatient. "All right. *I'll* go upstairs. There's no toilet paper in the ladies' room. I want to tell someone."

"Emma, don't be rash."

"I'm never rash," she said, smiling at him. "That's my trouble.

There's a fifth of bourbon in my office. No, I'm not a secret drinker, Stewart, it's there for menstrual cramps and occasional black moods. Go help yourself."

Emma knew very well what she was up to. It was an old pattern with her. Her desk at home was littered with appeals to Help Christian Children, Save the Herons, dance in informal dress for multiple sclerosis. Whenever her household rocked, whenever Charles retreated to his study, inward and deeply silent, whenever her mother called with age and imminent death in her voice, whenever she herself was humbled by the threat of illness (her doctor discovered a cyst on her ovary, her white count rose), Emma found and espoused a cause. She marched and phoned and solicited and petitioned, placating fate, righting the scales in her favor. If she planted trees in Israel, Moses would not have mononucleosis. If she kept sewage out of the Pacific Ocean, her mother would live another year. If she saved the whales, Charles's flagging spirts would be revived. Even as she crossed to the executive building, she drove a hard bargain with a mediator she did not altogether believe in. I'll get him back his job, you get me . . . She stopped. She did not care to formulate a desire just yet.

She came into a paneled anteroom and smiled at a secretary who glanced up at her indifferently.

"Mrs. Howard," she said.

"May I ask what you wish to see him about?"

"No, you may not ask what I wish to see him about!" Emma emphasized her reply by leaning forward and bringing her face close to the girl's. "Just let him know I'm here."

"One moment."

The girl flicked the intercom. "Mrs. Howard would like to see you, Mr. Mason."

"Who?"

Emma raised her voice. "One of your lowly minions, Mr. Mason. Emma Howard from the story department."

There was silence for a moment, then the man's voice, sounding hollow and metallic, said, "Come on in, Emma."

The man behind the desk did not get up. He had suffered a lower lumbar displacement which kept him off the tennis courts, out of women's beds and in considerable pain. His arena narrowed, he had become bullish and slightly dangerous. Emma liked him.

"Sit down, Emma. If it's about a raise, don't bring it to me. I won't give it to you."

"It's not money." She sat on the couch, disdaining the chair in front of his desk. He had to turn to face her.

"I never see you unless you come up here to grouse about something." He examined her with the sour gaze of an unwell man. She was as tall as a basketball player, slender, with a big mouth and beautiful eyes. But sloppy. A long thread dangled from her skirt. A seam was open in her jacket. He shot his immaculate cuffs and was offended.

"How long you been working here, Emma?"

"Twelve years."

"I'm going to do something for you. Trot yourself over to makeup. Let 'em fix your face. Fix your hair. It wouldn't hurt you to sharpen up." He held up his hands before she could protest. "Nothing personal. I know I'm never gonna get in bed with you. With this back, I'm probably never gonna get in the hay again — but that's not your problem. What do you want from me, Emma?"

"I want to talk to you about Stewart Bolen."

"Yeah," he said heavily, "that's a shame. All the old faces are going. They get cancer. They put their hands in the till. One way or another . . . they all go."

"He's been here longer than you have."

"Naw . . . we came the same year. I left William Morris. He left Rogers and Cowan. Fifty-six, it was. So what does that prove? His arteries are hardening. It's in his insurance report. What can I do? He forgets my name half the time."

"He hasn't saved any money."

"Who has in this town? You think I'm well off? My lawyer has it all and my doctor, not to mention my second wife. Incidentally, I heard you and Charlie were separated. True?"

She nodded.

"Somebody else? He's crazy."

"Thank you," she said dryly.

"He's *crazy*. I'm gonna tell you something, Emma. I don't like women. I'm not queer. Everybody knows that I've been a big swordsman in my time, so I don't have to make a case. Believe me, if I don't like 'em, I've got reasons. I make an exception of you. And my mother, God bless her. Who's the girl? Somebody younger? He should talk to me about picking green apples. Send him in here to talk to me."

"Talk to me," Emma said. "About Stewart."

"Finished," Mason said. "Over. Kaput. Out. So you're alone now," he went on, putting an unlit pipe into his mouth. "So am I. I don't like it. I eat dinner at Hillcrest every night. There's me and my Filipino houseboy and twenty-seven rooms."

"About Stewart," Emma said.

"Are you gonna nag me some more about that?" He shoved the papers around on his desk with an irritable gesture. "He'll get a farewell lunch in the commissary. I'll get the best writers on the lot to write a speech. He'll get a case of Scotch. What do you do when you go home at night? Tell me."

"I eat in front of the television set." She stood. "I have to go back to work."

"What're you looking so sour for? There's no mercy killing in this business. You're in. You're out. Right this minute, I got a Mafia nephew looking down my throat. The beaches are covered with the bleached bones of executives. Nobody's safe. Let's eat lunch together."

"I'm wearing an old suit," Emma said. "I can't go any place fancy."

"I eat lunch at home," he said. "I gotta get away from the agents. They all wear cologne these days — in their armpits, in their crotch. It spoils my appetite. Come on. We'll eat some tuna fish. We'll talk. We'll let down our hair." He got to his feet, groaning aloud, clutching at the small of his back. "Four hundred thousand a year with stock options and I can't touch my goddamn toes. You want to hear something? Some days I'd give my left testicle and this whole goddamn studio to be twenty-five again and with no calcium deposits." He stopped and examined Emma shrewdly. "You don't look so hot yourself."

She was without vanity. "I know. Puffy under the eyes, bad color. When I'm blue, everything goes limp. Even my hair." She shrugged. "You want to change your mind about lunch?"

"I'm going to the bathroom. I'll meet you downstairs." He waved her out of the room peremptorily.

They didn't speak a word in the car, although Emma liked big cars with room to stretch her legs, liked the cut glass vase with a wax rose reminiscent of Irish funerals, liked the back of the chauffeur's neck with its strange squared-off haircut. For a while, she mused on wealth and what she would do with it were it hers. Her mind ran on English chintz and Daumier drawings, on Bois Claires furniture, on tea trays resplendent with Georgian silver, on narcissuses and anemones out of season, on servants, on boiserie, on houses in Siena the color of cinnamon. She despised the way money was spent in this town on initialed handbags and white Rolls-Royces, on dubious paintings and cantilevered tennis courts. Her own extravagances, she knew, would be munificent. A plane-load of friends flown to Salzburg to listen to Mozart, a visit to the Lake District with her mother by her side on long, mist-drenched walks and tea served with cakes of two colors, trust funds that would transform her two sons into Renaissance princelings burnishing to a beautiful golden brown on the sands of the Riviera, a library bound in calf that turned to butter in the hand, wood fires winter and summer, absinthe, pearls, paradise.

The chauffeur ran a stop light and turned an arrogant gaze right and left while a policeman on a motorcycle allowed the transgression and watched a supple girl cross the street.

The house was reached only after a passage through iron gates threatening intruders with attack dogs. Emma worried for the postman, for the casual stroller, for the child in pursuit of a ball, seeing all the mildly curious with their throats torn, a stolen flower still clutched in their hands. Did the dogs chew up discarded lovers, castaway wives, the Avon lady as well? Did they mangle song birds?

When the house came into view, it reminded Emma of an armory. She half expected to see soldiers in exotic uniforms, booted and armed. Stands of fir trees, dry and prickly as wire brushes, dropped needles on the drive. High in the branches a squirrel ran for its life. The fountain before the front door was without water. Emma knew with certainty that its bottom was littered with delicate skeletons bleached almost to powder.

"Pick us up in an hour," Mason said. He got out ahead of Emma, leaving her to fend for herself. There was no answer to his knock. Nor to his foot kicking at the lintel.

"Come on!" His voice was raised. "For Christ's sake, open the door!" He waited with a choleric face, then hauled out a key, let himself in. Emma followed, saw him lope ahead of her across marble floors, his voice echoing back to her.

"Larry, where the hell are you?" She saw him standing in the middle of the huge drawing room, turning around and around as if he expected an assault from behind the curtains.

"Shit!" he said. "He's quit again."

She came into the room, aware of dust curls and dying flowers. She leaned against the doorjamb thinking she would have fired anyone who had let the smell of rot hang in the air like this. She could see the slime in the crystal vases, clotting the stems of dead chrysanthemums.

"Which way is the kitchen?" she said. "I can open a can of tuna."

Mason slumped into a chair. "I don't know where the kitchen is. I never go into the kitchen. I go into the sauna and into bed." He lifted his head and he looked at her darkly. "The wife goes, the son doesn't know I'm alive, the daughter wishes I wasn't, the houseboy takes a powder. Beautiful. Forget lunch.

Let's get drunk." He heaved himself to his feet and made for the bar. "Ice and Scotch or just Scotch? Which?"

"I don't want to drink," Emma said. "I want to eat." She went in search of the kitchen. He picked up a bottle and a glass and followed her.

She whistled when she passed through the swinging doors. The room was cavernous. Instantly she coveted the huge restaurant range, the warming ovens, the chopping block as big as a dance floor.

"You could cook an ox in here," she said and opened the refrigerator, the tip of her tongue protruding in anticipation of white truffles and a pâté crusted with fat. There was a jar of olives and a wizened lemon inside. Her sigh of disappointment was audible. She found a kitchen glass and held it out to him. He tipped the bottle for her.

"There are more calories in this than in a cheeseburger," she said. She sat down on the edge of the table and, feeling cheated, finished off her tot.

Mason eased himself onto a stool. "Well," he said, "so we're both in trouble. We both got the shaft." She saw the pallor, the pleat of flesh beneath the dark eyes, saw the great echoing room as a sepulcher with Mason laid out between a bin of potatoes and the kitchen door. His black suit seemed suddenly funerary, and the sound of a door slammed shut by a gust somewhere in the house was like the rattle and bang of a hearse.

"I don't feel so hot," he said, wrenching at his tie. "There's no air in here." Then slowly, like a leaf detached and floating, he slid down onto the floor.

Emma never remembered exactly the sequence of events that followed. She thought later she had mopped his face with a wet towel or else she had grabbed a bottle of ammonia from under the sink, sloshing it onto his shirt front in an effort to revive him. She remembered shouting before she pinched his nostrils and clamped her mouth to his, wishing she had paid more attention to Charles's demonstration of the proper technique. She remembered thinking frantically that there was more death than Scotch on his breath, but then he opened his eyes and reached for her hand. A tap dripped. A cat appeared in the doorway. The clock hand ticked ahead, and ahead again. No one came. She sat with his head in her lap; she could see up under the kitchen table where someone had written a dirty word. The telephone was across the room.

"The prick's in Las Vegas," he said, breathing heavily. Emma inclined to hear him. "My doctor," he said. "Help me up."

She thought of admonitions and cautions but he clawed at her neck, pulling himself upright. "Get me into bed." Then he fell heavily on her, his weight pinning her.

Emma's knees trembled violently. "Just rest," she said. "Someone will come along."

She heard the front door open and called, but her vocal chords seemed paralyzed and she was sure that she merely croaked. She heard someone enter the hallway, pause, then make a discreet departure.

Mason looked up at her and grimaced. "He's come in and gone out again. He thinks we're upstairs in bed together. He knows me. My bad habits will kill me, Emma."

"Don't talk," she said, and then felt that was unfair. If she were dying, she would want to say something cogent, something sweet, something memorable before she melted like hoarfrost and was gone. What did he repent? What did he regret? What had he refused that he would now embrace as he felt his heart fibrilate and lurch?

"I'll keep Bolen on," he said in a whisper and Emma exulted as she recognized a kindred bartering spirit. "I'll forgive Lew Wasserman," he cried out. Emma felt like a priest drawing out the last act of contrition.

As the slow minutes passed, they began to assume the attitude of picnickers frozen in a pastoral tableau; he the lover with his weight immobilizing her, she staring at the pattern of the green and whte linoleum as if it were a dappled field. Mason lay with his eyes closed for a long while. When he opened them, she was struck by the look of silent triumph in them, as if he had won an enormous corporate victory. With the fine hairs in his nostrils still stirring with breath, he said, "Not yet," to no one in particular and smiled mirthlessly, a grimace that revealed bad teeth, the flash of gold fillings. Emma saw too that there were surgical lines barely visible behind his ears. He had had his face lifted and the sad vanity of it made her look carefully away. She marveled at his choice of fears: he scorned death but must fortify himself for life with the little nips and tucks of the surgeon's knife.

She had already seen the faint tracery around her own eyes, one or two wrinkles looping her throat, but she had shrugged away the sight, unwilling to do battle on that field where one could only retreat before the enmity of time. Anyway, she loathed plastering herself with creams, despised hours spent under the ministering fingers of high-mettled young men who urged diets of lettuce and mineral water on her while they sat and stared at themselves in the mirror before them. Nothing would wean Emma away from pie for breakfast, midnight feasts of chili and leftover pot roast. Nothing would induce her to give up candy, pot, ice cold beer. Charles had forsworn meat and watched her as if she were some kind of strange carnivorous animal when she ate her portion. The more vegetables he downed, the more detached he became; lightened of all grossness, he seemed to rise to some higher plane where she could not follow, mired as she was in pork chops and breakfast bacon.

He had become newly ascetic in other ways, picking a path through their bedroom, as if Emma's clothes thrown over the chairs, her books stacked on the floor, her littered ashtrays, her pseudo–Louis Seize furniture were obstacles barring him from some radiant truth. Some nights he slept out on the porch under a thin army blanket with the gnats circling his head. One autumn day he burned old papers and letters in the back yard, his eyes watery with smoke and tears as he divested himself of memories. It occurred to Emma to ask why he was doing it, but it seemed to invade his privacy, so she only mildly inquired if her letters were among those turning to ashes. He had said no but his face had been as gray as the residue at his feet.

Mason groaned and shifted his weight on Emma's numbed legs.

"They'll kick me upstairs," he said heavily. "They'll make me chairman of the board. Some fucking agent will take over. They'll forget me, Emma. My heart won't kill me. That'll kill me."

Emma, stubborn and without illusion, would not have it. "It won't kill you," she said, refusing him the capitulation she would not make herself. "If you're lucky, you'll die of old age in your bed. If not, it'll be cancer or a boy on a Honda or a plane crash. Read the obituary columns. Nobody dies of replacement." She paused. "I can't just let you lie here. I've got to get some help."

"No," he said, "I want to lie here and talk. Charles walked out on you, didn't he?" he said cruelly. "Left you high and dry."

"No," Emma said, "he left me sadly, as a matter of fact, after much soul-searching and a very nice lunch in a French restaurant. He went over our finances, the life insurance policies and the municipal bonds. He laid in a stock of firewood and cleaned the attic. He had the trees pruned. He phoned my mother. He wrote a beautiful letter to the boys. He hung his house keys on a nail in the kitchen. He kissed me."

She stared at the sunlight beginning to cool into late afternoon, thinking how Charles, walking away from the house, walking away from their marriage, had paused to pick up a garden rake lying across the path, had put it in the garage, worrying that someone would trip over it, that a door-to-door salesman would fracture a tibia or someone coming to console Emma would break an ankle. He would not have comfort impeded by any carelessness on his part.

No, it had not ended in a riot of passion. She had helped Charles pack his bag. They had debated the inclusion of his old woolen sweater, and he had taken a snapshot of her off the dresser and put it among his socks and shorts, looking down into her face with a kind of yearning. That had made her cross because she hated that particular picture. She looked toothy and outsized and hearty, holding up a salmon she had caught in the Rogue River. It was the one and only time she had ever gone fishing. Charles begged her to join him in the early morning forays into the icy water but she had waved him off, pulling the blankets over her head, finishing off some improbable dream in which she flew over rain forests, looking down on Charles in his slicker and waders. She remembered the first hour after his departure, after it was certain that he would not turn around at the bottom of the street and come back, slamming the front door, calling her name. She had cleaned out the medicine cabinet, discarding the bottles prescribed for him. From the number of packets of Gelusil it appeared that Charles's emotions lived in his stomach. His head had ached and his back. He had been afflicted with rashes and disquietude. There were three bottles of Valium. How her own rude health must have affronted him.

"Who's the girl?" Mason asked.

"I hardly know her."

"What was the trouble, Emma? Boredom? Bed?"

"None of your business," she said, thinking that now she must do something. "Maybe I should scream. We can't sit here all day. You need attention and I can't feel anything in my legs anymore."

"Nobody'll hear you. I got two and a half acres around this house. I paid half a million dollars so my wife could swim naked. Somebody peeked and now she's my ex-wife. I'm gonna roll over. You get up and get me some brandy."

Emma assisted him but he cracked his head on the table and swore at her before she was free.

"Are you all right?" Needles of pain stabbed her legs as she rose.

He looked up at her. "I have a hunch about you," he said.

"Yes?"

"You're no featherweight. It would take a tank to knock you over."

"I hope so," Emma said, though she knew he intended no compliment.

"Get me a drink. A big one. Then call Cedars-Sinai. I paid for a whole goddamned wing. I want a little service."

"I'm going to call your doctor," she told him. "No brandy unless he says so."

"I told you. He's out of town. He's shooting craps with the money he ripped off Medicare. His partner fucks his nurse from twelve to two. Call the hospital like I told you." He reared up on his elbow. "Johnny Garfield died in bed with a broad. Make me look good, Emma. Get in bed with me."

Emma saw that he wanted to be delivered and she knelt beside him.

His lips grazed her hand. "I never won any medals for bravery," he said.

"Neither have I," said Emma.

"Two cowards."

She nodded. He closed his eyes and let her go.

Nobody at the hospital knew his name. Emma, after raging into the phone, called the fire department. They came promptly and the two young men who carried him out did so with tenderness, crossing his arms and wrapping him in blankets, making him into an effigy with one tear visible on his cheek.

# Chapter Two

IT WAS CLOSE to seven before Jessup would see her. He took no notice of time, staying long after the studio had emptied out, sitting in the cutting room alone, studying the film that was run for him over and over. He was tireless, yet he had the gray skin and the deep, burned-out eyes of the terminally ill. He was as strong as an ox and it was said of him without admiration that his gut, kidneys and nerves were all steel. His cast and crew hated him without exception. They would work for no one else. He did not know of their hostility, he did not care about their loyalty. His icy terrors were his own. He had been married three times to women who remained silent when questioned about him and who now prudently kept their distance from him. He often denied that his work had any meaning, decried its value. The shape and harmony of what he did now were all that interested him. Though lauded for it, he had never achieved the purity of his own inner vision. He was beyond drink or drugs. He was in fear of God. And he was an old friend of Emma's.

He found her careless and severe at the same time. He was comfortable with extremes. He had been raised by an autocratic half-mad old aunt who lived in Seattle and was by turns bellicose and passionate about him. She had taken him out into the rain-drenched streets to stare at the misty Japanese beauty of the remote mountains and had ordered him to see them as extraordinary. She had walked him along empty beaches exhorting him to notice the woody swirls of sea-tossed bark, the wind-tattered trees, the rocks hampering the sea. She had prodded the shivering jellyfish, looped the acrid seaweed on a stick, thrust it under his nose. She had awakened him late at night, the light stabbing into his eyes, to read to him from books he did not understand. She had set him apart.

Emma found a seat by his side in the darkened projection room. His clothes smelled old and dry; he affected an Irish fisherman's sweater winter and summer, his white hair brushing its collar.

"Who is it?" he commanded in his old monk's voice.

"Emma."

He flipped a button and the images before them flickered and died away. "Yes," he queried. "What is it?"

It was always necessary to re-establish a hold on him. Every meeting began with a stranger.

"William, pay attention," Emma said. "I want to talk to you."

"What time is it?"

"It's seven. William, Harry Mason is in the hospital. I want you to go see him." She lit a cigarette, inhaling it deeply. He snapped his fingers and she held out the pack to him.

"These look as if the mice had been at them."

"Yes, yes," she said impatiently. "William, they're firing Stewart. When Mason collapsed he said something about keeping him on but I think it was just momentary panic. I'm not sure he meant it. You have to do something. You're God around here. Say you won't stand for it. Throw your weight around. Insist." She got up, unable to find room for her legs in the narrow space between the seats.

Jessup appeared not to have heard her. He was often deaf to hard-luck stories, taking a grim pleasure in mischance. He stored away details of operations, accidents, suicides, like a conserving squirrel. He had a diabolical memory for catastrophe.

"Stewart is a relic," he said. "A dry bone. He forgets I won't be called Willie. He called me Willie last week on *two* occasions."

"Why," Emma asked, "is my life full of men who won't allow diminutives? Charles won't be Charlie. William won't be Willie. Are you afraid you'll shrink if somebody shortens your name?"

"Stay and I'll show you this reel," Jessup said. "It has mean things in it. Delicious." He pulled her down beside him with force.

"I don't understand your work any too well and I certainly don't want to see it on an empty stomach. I want you to help Stewart. If you mean to wiggle out of it, don't try. I'm not above reminding you of the night you called me after you cut your wrists. You'd be a dead duck if I hadn't come running."

He regarded her sourly. "I don't remember any such incident. No such incident occurred."

"Oh, it happened," said Emma. "You ruined a brand new pantsuit of mine. Totally ruined it, bleeding all over it." She pointed an accusing finger at him. "Charles and I saved you, lied for you, hid you until you could show your face again."

He rubbed his hands together; it sounded as if parchment were being crumpled. "I was close to some stupefying mystery that night, as close as I've ever come."

"Hogwash," Emma said. "You kept begging me to save you, to save you for art."

"Did I really? You mean I saw myself as an artist at the very last? Isn't that interesting?"

The projectionist opened the door, ducked his head in deferentially. "Mr. Jessup, will you want to see it again tonight?"

"Yes. Now. Mrs. Howard is just leaving."

"She's not," Emma said hotly.

"Start in five minutes." He waved the man from the room and turned to Emma with a vindictive look. "You've destroyed my concentration," he said. "Emma, you used to have more charm. You've become something of a tyrant lately, a scourge. I've seen Charles's new lady. Never mind that she's younger . . . she's softer. I warn you, she's softer by far than you."

Emma got to her feet with lazy deliberation, picked up her coat and draped it around her shoulders.

"If you don't stay too late, stop by the house. I've got some bouillabaisse left over from yesterday."

He grimaced. "You keep fish till it's too high to eat. I got poisoned last time at your house. I shat for days."

"Take it or leave it."

"No, I won't partake of it, thank you. I'll have milk toast at my own place and then go to bed. I advise you to do the same."

Emma paused in the doorway. "Don't forget about Stewart. I'll be on your back until you do something."

He had signaled for the film to begin again. He motioned her from the room and she heard him begin a fretful mutter as the screen racked into focus and a scene began: two people in a close shot reviling each other over a disintegrating marriage.

Emma was fond of her house. It had been built in the nineteen-twenties, when the surrounding hills had been yellow with mimosa and alive with deer. There was still enough brush surrounding it to provide cover for small scaly lizards, and the garden rang with the harsh call of bluejays and the dry rattle of cicadas. The rooms were rather dark and small and damply cool. The tile roof had given way here and there in a wind storm but it cost the world to repair, so she had let it go. Some former tenant, a romantic soul, had built an enormous adobe wall surrounding the property, but the steady scorching of the sun had powdered its surface and ivy had broken through the crevices to run wild across the yard.

The interior was wholly hers. She had lived in this house with a husband and twin sons, but the slightly crazed look of it was all her doing. She had scavenged long before stained-glass windows and odd balustrades and plinths and columns had become fashionable. She had squinted into rubbish piles, retrieving a claw-footed bathtub and a toilet seat of mahogany. She had hauled away ancient porch furniture, an icebox with brass-hinged doors, huge scrolled Victorian beds. There seemed always to be a faint cloud of dust over her possessions, exhumed as they were from other lives, other households long abandoned. No two plates on her table matched, no two glasses. Strange faces, pious and gentle, stared out of old daguerreotypes. Like the rest of her things, they did not belong to her except by right of pillage. Somebody else's aunts, uncles, grandmothers, first cousins came to rest on somebody else's table in Emma's front room.

A psychiatrist friend, on seeing this mangled heap of castoffs, had commiserated in whispers with Charles, saying that Emma must be much in need of love to be so wildly acquisitive. She never had him to the house again.

Neither did she clean, sort or organize, and now that she was left alone with a tortoise-shell cat and two old rheumatic dogs, a kind of charming collapse had taken place. Now all the disparate elements of the house were left to her. The door to the boys' room remained closed. The few traces of Charles had vanished. He had taken with him the severe icon that hung over their bed and his books and a stiff Danish chair he favored for his bad back. His black, English hair brushes were missing from the mess and welter of the dressing table. And his presence. Gone most of all was his presence, that self-doubting, life-betrayed, passionate, vigilant presence.

The dogs sought for it in melancholy snuffling around the legs of the tables and the chairs. The cat, female and moody, instantly transferred its loyalty to Emma, mirroring her sadness in its wide, yellow, unblinking eyes. Emma, who could make no order of anything, struggled to make order out of his departure.

Let's see, she would brood in the dark. In the first place, he is middle-aged, hurtling toward bifocals, tennis elbow, thinned blood, thinned ranks. A second cousin, three years younger than he, dies on the golf course after making a very nice approach to the green; a college friend drowns in his bath. He receives news of strokes, breakdowns, bankruptcy. He tries to recall the last cause of jubilation and finds it was a football score. He yields his anxieties to a psychiatrist, but then it seems a stifling place to be on a sunny afternoon and he walks on the beach instead, where he is overwhelmed by the infinity of sky and sea.

He had questioned Emma endlessly. Had they gotten all they should out of life? Had some cosmic certainty escaped them as they made their way through the supermarkets, visits to the orthodontists, evening bridge parties? Mindful of humble needs, she had said no, she didn't think so. Anyway, she was not certain what he was hankering after. Could he say? He could not. He answered her with excessive kindness and silence.

Later, when he had gone, she thought she had stumbled on the answer. He had packed his old Navy duffle bag, hoisted it over his shoulder and, in much the same way that he had walked the streets of San Diego on shore leave, looking with wonder at palm trees, he had gone to look with wonder at youth, resiliency, naiveté, pliancy, hope. In perfect justice, thought Emma, I might have done the same thing, given half the chance.

That was on reasonable nights, when she had had a good day, a good dinner. When she had heard some superb music, when the fire had drawn properly, when her bath water had been hot and her sheets cool.

On the other nights, enraged, lonely, she consigned him to hell fire, to constipation, impotence, bleeding gums, writer's block, death. Those were the nights of memory. Then she would groan aloud, beat her pillows with her fists, swear, recall. A meeting, far back in time, when she was twenty-five. She remembered herself, not totally accurately, as quite beautiful, wearing a large straw hat, coming out of a hotel in Portofino to meet Charles on a terrace overlooking an ink-dark sea. He had sold his first screenplay and they had gone off to spend every cent of it, to live as if they had printed the money they spent so lavishly. She had tried to hold back, to put them in pensions and guest houses, to save, tucking wads of lire down the front of her blouse, into her rolled-up panties, in the pocket of her bathrobe. He had caught her at it. They had fought like tomcats, then made love, still scratching and biting. He had bought her perfume and hothouse forsythia and two Creil plates and antique earrings. He had shaken his finger under her nose as he told her how much had been denied him as a boy: with two Grant Wood parents on a Grant Wood farm who said prayers over the oatmeal cereal that gagged him, who kept two books on their shelves — the Bible and the almanac — who repudiated the stories he wrote and sent him to clerk in a hardware store. He would be denied nothing now. So there was champagne in tall murky green bottles and train rides to Florence and Verona and Rome. And Emma, staring out of the soot-spotted windows, reflected on his deprivation and took him into her arms and made untenable promises.

Someone was vacuuming. Emma heard it as she parked her car in the driveway. The lights blazed from the windows and the hose was running, soaking into the well around the ficus trees. The dogs came running to her, threatened by the commotion. They were unaccustomed to being turned out, sleeping as they did all day in the middle of Emma's unmade bed.

"All right, all right," she said, pulling their ears. "Whoever it is can't be murderous. They wouldn't be vacuuming, stupid. Get down, Asa. Your paws are wet."

She hurried toward the house, hoping it was not her sister who came every month or so to have coffee and to criticize Emma's housekeeping.

"Zaz, is that you?"

A woman appeared at the top of the stairs, carrying a pail and a dust mop. Her black hair was twisted to the top of her head, her face had smooth, broad planes, half Indian, half Spanish.

"It's a mess up here. You never clean. You'll get sick if you never clean. I've told you that. I've been here all afternoon and I've only made a little path through it, that's all."

"Felicia." Emma blew a kiss up the stairs. "Felicia, I fired you, you know that. I said I couldn't afford you. You said okay. Okay is okay. You're not supposed to be here."

Nevertheless, she was immensely pleased by the woman's reappearance. Felicia embodied the old days when the household had been in a normal state of domesticity, when daily life had been played out in familiar, harmonious scenes: birthday parties, the solemn moments of graduation from grammar school, the boys in new navy T-shirts with new haircuts, Thanksgiving dinners, Charles's speeches of welcome as he ladled out sweet potatoes and divided the pies. The two women had sorted it all out together, regulated by the seasons, cleaning in soap-and-sweat-stained concert in the spring, decorating richly in the winter, lax in the summer heat. Felicia had come to her years ago — she couldn't remember how long, but it had been in the beginning. Emma had been subjected to an intense, probing scrutiny: what are the customs of this house, what are its vanities, what is your temper, your tempo, your style? She had been accepted then; she was accepted still.

"I won't work for nothing." Felicia came down the stairs with her head at an imperious tilt, her eyes already rebuking Emma's untidy dress and hair. "Don't think you can get me for nothing."

"I know, I know." Emma came forward to drape her arms about the woman's shoulders. "But you steal from my kitchen. I ought to take that into account. You've gotten fat."

"Where I worked the family eats meat. The servants, beans."

The two women came into the living room. Emma lit the lamps. They arranged themselves side by side on the couch, old familiars, content in each other's company. Outside, a bird sang blissfully one last time before dark, a cat strolled nattily through the grass seeking the remaining warmth on the garden path, a neighborhood quarrel became audible on a breeze scented with lemon verbena. Emma's stomach growled. Dinner would wait.

What she wanted now was to put her head back against the couch, close her eyes and enjoy that particular pleasure that an hour of exchanged confidences brings.

"Tell me what you've been up to." She popped a cigarette into her mouth, proffered one to Felicia. They smoked in silence for a while.

At last Felicia spoke. "I quit," she said, her mouth drawn tight with displeasure, "without notice. In protest." She exhaled smoke in a long steady stream. "The man pees with the door open. The woman sleeps with the friend of her son. A boy. The old mother in the house has no money. They make her ask for everything. She cries. There's no dignity there."

"There's not too much here," Emma said.

Felicia wagged a disputing hand. "I'm better off here. I've already brought my things, so there's nothing to talk about."

"I'm short of money."

"It won't cost you much. I have money. I run a little business. I bring some girls in from Mexico, find them places. Friends of mine, good friends. There's a little charge. They call me if they get into trouble with men or with immigration." Felicia gave a practical shrug. "In Tijuana they starve, and five or six children starve with them."

Emma ground out her cigarette. "You're in the slave traffic."

"What slave traffic? They call me Madonna." Felicia smiled, showing sharp white teeth. "I'm in no position to choose. Three girls in Hermosillo, two sisters without husbands, a father without teeth. I do what I do."

Emma could always be reached by practicality; she revered common sense. "Yes," she ruminated, "something has to be put in the sock against the day when we're high and dry — no doubt of it. Well then, stay and welcome."

She rose to pour drinks for both of them in oversize water glasses, spurning the cheap, bar bourbon for her best Scotch.

"Have you a man?"

"Two. Three." Felicia's tone was indifferent. "In that way, I'm not particular. With me it's over in a minute and I'm out the door." She hooked her arms behind her head. "If I had had character I would have been a nun. Not an ordinary nun, a prioress. That's not bad, you know — giving orders, having respect shown to you day and night. I don't believe what goes with it. That's the trouble. I've seen too many fat priests and thin children . . . And you? I didn't see any sign of a man — in the bathrooms, in the closets."

Emma finished her drink, warmed her hands in her armpits, shrugged. "You know, in the beginning I was in terrible shape. Did you ever see an earthworm cut in half? The boys used to do it when they were kids being sadistic. Both sides still wiggle toward one another, trying to be whole again. Well, God knows, I wiggled. Bawled all through the night till my pillow was soaked and I had to get up and change the slip. Some mornings my eyes felt glued together. I couldn't look at myself in the mirror. Soaked in brine, I was. Then, all of a sudden, I got calm. I began to sleep in the middle of the bed instead of on my side of it, the way I had for years. Charles always hogged the bed. Now I take up the whole thing."

Felicia nodded her approval.

"And I ate in bed," Emma went on. "Popcorn and pretzels and things that left crumbs. I began to read books again, tomes, Henry Steele Commager and Goethe . . . sometimes till five in the morning. For a while I didn't know what to do about sex, and then I remembered my girlhood and found that nothing much had changed. I could still find my way between my legs, just as I used to."

Both women fell silent, brooding over the narcissism. It seemed less humiliating than other defeats they had suffered. "I said to myself, Emma, Charles doesn't know what he wants but you do. You don't want to be half of an earthworm.' "

She heard an acquiescent groan from Felicia, veteran of the same battles.

"I look forward to the day when I can do without them," Felicia said rancorously.

Emma, softened by the Scotch, was not that intransigent.

"On our own terms," she muttered. "Have them on our own terms." Grandly she formed the manifesto. "If they are bamboozled, then they must live with it. They must accept the perils of age and disillusion and miscalculation. They must know that the worst in them is as visible as the best. They can only be accepted, not venerated. They must replace the cap on the toothpaste." She crunched the last of the ice, licked the last of the drink from the rim of the glass. "I need to eat," she said, getting to her feet, staggering a little. "Let's see what we've got."

They ate hugely, opening cans of tuna fish and anchovies, artichoke hearts and chili peppers. They ate with their fingers, raising glasses of beer to each other while the dogs lashed around the kitchen, anxious to be fed. They took their coffee into the backyard and waved away the swarms of gnats while they sat languidly in the battered garden chairs, Emma loosening the straps on her brassiere, Felicia kicking off her shoes. Peacefully, in harmony, they heard the tree frog, saw a last bird winging west, felt the first stirrings of indigestion.

"I put clean sheets on your bed."

"Yes? Good." Emma yawned.

"There's no washing powder."

"Tomorrow. We'll market tomorrow."

The lights in the house opposite came on and a man stood revealed, scratching the hair on his chest with both hands — a tousled, erect bear, alarmingly masculine.

Felicia snorted. "A beauty," she said.

Emma smiled in the dark. "Yes," she said, "a perfect beauty."

# Chapter Three

It is providential that life makes small demands as well as large ones. The weekend was the treacherous time, when it was possible to be surprised by rue unless the flat, hard hours were somehow completely filled. Emma had grown expert at refining solitude, making certain that it did not resemble abandonment.

She began the day at the market, avoiding Jurgenson's and the overpriced places for a Safeway on the edge of Beverly Hills. With a straw basket over her arm, she marched the aisles, pinching fruit under the black watch of the clerks. She took nothing for granted, lifting the melons to her nose, testing for ripeness, inhaling the perfume with distended nostrils. She was generous with herself, anticipating her evening meal with greed. She was not above popping a grape into her mouth or nibbling a pale green leaf of endive separated from its tight bud. She remembered Charles's spare appetite, so easily satisfied — at least at the table. He had often watched her tuck into her food with a look bordering on astonishment. How many times had his stalky presence across the white cloth made her pause, fork poised, to answer that look.

"I'm hungry."

"So I see."
"You waste food. It's a crime, what you leave on your plate."
"My mother often said that."
"All mothers say that."
"You're gnawing on that bone. You have been for some time."
An upward glance, not discomfited at all. "I love spring lamb."
Silence then, while she peeled a peach, finished her wine.
"I'm going upstairs. I've got a couple hours' work." How tightly he had folded his napkin.
"Charles." She had said his name in the lazy way she had when they were on the edge of a quarrel. "You're like a man with a fishbone caught in his throat. Spit it out, my darling, spit it up. I'm not going anywhere."
He was suspicious, most of all, of tolerance. What a strange man, really. "Everything is easy for you, Emma. Very little is for me." He had shaken his head. "Don't you ever feel the ground shift under your feet? Do you know where you're going every minute? Why? What for? Do you have all the answers, all the time?
She had swirled the wine, gazing into its rose red depths.
"I think I understand. There's too much of me, isn't there? Too tall, too leggy, too much lip — too much of me altogether." She had smiled at him, penitent for what she could not help. "Well," she had said, "I don't know a solution — unless it's to think ahead to when I'm older and vibrate less. That's coming, you know."
He had been contrite then. "It's not you. It's got nothing to do with you."
"Look," Emma said with a calm she did not feel, "don't be afraid to hurt me. You know I don't bruise easily. Be frank. If you're bored, say so. If you feel slighted, tell me. You're a generous man, Charles. Share your mind."
"My mind," he said, "is a drawer full of old socks." He held his hands wide in a gesture of defeat.

Emma, thwarted, brushed crumbs from the table onto the carpet, slumped in her chair, clasped her head with her arms locked behind her head. Impatience prodded her suddenly. "Are we enemies, or what? We're friends. Old, good friends, starting way back when. Maybe I don't say it often enough but I'm a fan of yours, Charles. Your admirer. How many wives of eighteen years say that to their husbands, I ask you?"

His sigh was profound. "Emma, Emma," he said.

"Oh, bloody hell," she said. "Why were you born into that tight-assed family of yours? Why didn't someone tell you it was all right to lose your temper, to weep and wail when something bothered you? I could kick your mother around the block. I *could!* That sweet, good, *dismal* woman!"

She had upset the wine glass. Charles hurried to mop it up. She pushed her chair back, watching him staunch the red tide of wine. How good he was with little messes.

"Put salt on it. No, leave it. I don't care about the cloth. Charles, sit down, will you? Pull your chair up by me. There are three goddamn leaves in this table. You're a mile away down there."

He seemed not to have heard her. He picked up an apple, turned it slowly in his hands, spoke abruptly.

"I'm not happy with myself. I'm not happy with my work."

"That's your old heartache. What's your new one?"

Her persistence brought a wry smile from him. "Just foolishness," he said.

"Then be foolish. Nobody here but us chickens." She knew that he would come to it at his own pace. She waited patiently.

"Emma, Emma, girls pass me on the street and don't see me. I'm unseen, Emma, by the pretty girls who pass me in the street."

"You're wrong," she said. "I've seen them turn."

"I said it was foolish."

"It happens to everyone, Charles. 'I have heard the mermaids singing, each to each. I do not think that they will sing to me.' " She paused a moment. "I know you feel cheated. It all goes so fast. But there's always me and I love you. I love you, I'm dazzled by you, excited by you, pleased and contented by you. I'm glad to have you in the house with me. In my bed. As the father of my children. As a bridge partner."

He remonstrated. "Emma, it's not necessary . . ."

"Don't stop me! I'm just warming up. I think you're splendid, Charles. You're the most honest man I know. You don't hold grudges. You never violate a confidence Parsley grows for you. I don't know why I don't say all this more often. I just assumed you knew that I valued you very highly."

"Yes," he said, "I know that."

"Damn," she cried. "Don't you think I wish *I* were twenty and blooming and able to make your head snap around? But I'm not. You just have to accept my mature adulation, tame though it might seem to you. Think of it as seasoned love and see how that goes down."

He rose, passed by her, paused to let his hand linger on her shoulder.

"I'll be working late tonight. Don't wait up."

"I won't," she said. "I'm dead tired."

He had whistled the dogs to him then and she watched him climb the stairs slowly as if they were too much for him. She wondered what she had left unexplained.

"Lady, that's five cherries you've eaten. Buy 'em or put 'em back."

Emma spat the pit into her hand, found no place to dispose of it, put it into her pocket.

"I intend to buy them. Don't get nervy." She filled a bag. "You've got plenty of rotten ones in there at a dollar eighty-nine a pound!"

"It's not my store, lady. At my salary, I ain't eating any fruit. Okay?"

"Unionize," Emma said, "and you'll eat fruit."

She ambled past him, sauntering down the aisles, leaning over to peer at the labels, announcing to everyone within earshot that there were enough preservatives in the cans before her to kill an army.

"Who wants to live forever, sweetie?"

Emma looked up and saw ahead of her a familiar — blondined, caftaned, rotund and self-assured. The swollen figure visible at the end of the aisle evoked in her a stirring of affection. She had known Millie Asher from her first day at the studio, when she had deferentially asked for a typist from the secretarial pool. In Millie she got more than she bargained for. She remembered her astonishment as she first appeared to her, standing in the door of her office, her huge bulk encased in a poppy-strewn dress salvaged from some ill-lit secondhand shop, her breast a promontory on which rested a nice assortment of amulets and beads. Emma, without malice, thought of piglets, freshly pink and greedy, not without charm. Millie had examined her with eyes that were small, close-set, knowing, and of a very pretty blue. "New girl, right?"

"New girl."

"Okay. Here's the drill. A — don't sleep with Harry Mason. He's got a penis the size of a gherkin, and it won't do you any good career-wise. He likes women who stay home and get pedicured. B — get here early and leave late; Mason thinks he's running a salt mine. C — let the agents take you to lunch. Someday, the way this business is going, they're gonna own this town and, besides, the food in the commissary is dreck. D — any man, repeat, any man in this business would rather close a deal than get laid and that's the bottom line no matter what else you hear. E — be nice to me. I give terrific Christmas presents and I lend money. My name is Millie Asher."

"Emma Howard."

And so they were bonded in friendship, and she watched Millie rise, like a gas-inflated balloon, from typist to private secretary to production assistant to agent, till now, a great dirigible of a woman, she commanded the skies.

Millie Asher embraced her, kissed the air on both sides of her face and linked an arm through hers.

"I've got a cook, right?" she began in her bawling, brawling voice. "A thousand bucks a month, her own color television set, more than six guests and in comes a caterer — and I'm marketing. Why? She has hay fever from my million-dollar landscaping. I go down for breakfast and what's in my deluxe model Kelvinator? Apricot mousse and a bottle of stuffed olives. I've got a butler, right? I ring for him. 'Butler,' I say, 'is there a bagel in this house by any chance?' 'Madame,' he says to me, 'cook is responsible for the kitchen.' Twenty-five thousand dollars a year and he polishes the two pieces of silver I own, a creamer and sugar bowl from my grandmother. You read *Time* magazine last week? You see the job they did on me? 'Millie Asher, agent provocateur' — whatever the hell that is. 'Enthroned in her forty-room, Beverly Hills mansion, feared and fawned upon by the great and the near-great.' You see the picture they ran? I look like I've been eating nonstop for thirty years. I have — but the world doesn't have to know it. Emma, how are you?"

"Splendid, Millie. I'm afraid to ask you. You'll tell me for an hour and a half."

Millie's shrug had ancient origins. "I'm not so hot. And you're not so hot. I see Charles around town with his Tootsie Roll. A matchstick with two eyes. Don't think I didn't say something to him. I did. Fran Stark had a birthday party for Ray. Out by one of the Henry Moores is your husband looking, if I may say so, a little *dahr*. You understand 'dahr?' "

"I have Jewish friends. Pale."

"Beyond pale, believe me. So I go up to him with a big, warm smile on my face and I say, '*Dummkopf*, why did you leave the only *menshy* woman in this town? Stand on one foot and tell me.' He said, 'Millie, behave yourself,' and walked away." She wagged a finger at Emma. "That's *cojones* when you pause to consider that I'm putting together a package with his screenplay and a certain big actor."

"Have you set a deal for him?"

"What do you care? The thin one gets it all from now on.

I'm working on it. You want to hear a funny thing? A certain actor is coming to lunch at my house today. He wants me to tell him the story. He's too busy fucking his brains out to read. Why don't you come back to the house with me and meet him and tell him what the material is? I'll put together a mushroom omelet and we'll sit out by the pool and see what happens. Charles's *nafka* can only go down on him. *You* can make him rich. There are possibilities here." She tweaked Emma's cheek and then patted it.

"No," Emma said. "I don't think so. I think I'll just take my milk home and put it on ice and wash the dogs." She started toward the check-out counter, Millie trundling after her.

"All right, forget it. You don't want to do him a favor. You don't want to do yourself a favor. But I want you to come by the house on your way home. It's a whole other thing. I've had two decorators *potchkeeing* around and so far they've painted everything blue, ripped out two walls and sent me a bill for thirty-five thousand dollars. I'm sleeping on a box spring and mattress, there isn't a chair in the house and I'm having David Picker to dinner next Monday. Come tell me what to do."

They took their places at the end of a long line.

"I do everything Thrift Shop," Emma said. "It wouldn't work for you."

"Oh, no? Where do you think I lived before I got to be Citizen Kane? Fairfax and Mariposa, above the garage. Two director's chairs, Indian batik and a poster welcoming Moshe Dayan to an Israeli rally. Everybody thinks I was born in Freddy Fields' house. Everybody forgets the ten years I made Xerox copies and coffee at Artists' Management. And five years at the May Company before that. And two years selling Tupperware in Burbank before that." She sniffed. "On Fairfax I was warm and fed. Now I've got six dozen rooms, two *faygelehs* in my hair and nothing to eat in the whole goddamn mausoleum. A man wanted to come home with me last week — a man? — an out-of-work actor who knows what to do with his *shlong*. I had no place to put him. We ended up on the floor and now my whole lower back is out." The flow ran on nonstop. "Also, the company pays for the house. I figure you'll throw something together for me for a nickel and the rest I'll put in the cookie jar. The cookie jar," she rambled on. "My little mother used to siphon off from the grocery money and put it in the cookie jar. Nickels and dimes. When she died we found it. That's how she got back at my father. Look who I'm getting back at. A cartel — a movie company and a book company and whore houses in South Philadelphia. Still, in this town, who knows — up today, on your ass tomorrow. I already own a little building down on Western. Fully rented. Two stores on Pico near Olympic, a furrier, a CPA. A nice ring or two. A few municipal bonds. All for when I'm sitting on the front porch of the Motion Picture Relief Home, waiting for my sister's kids to visit me on Sunday." She ran her pudgy fingers through her unruly hair and grinned at Emma.

"I'll stop by," Emma said.

"Turn right off Saint Cloud Road. The sign says SENTRY DOGS but forget it. That's from the former owners. Just blow in the squawk box and I'll let you in." She glared at a woman who tried to push in ahead of her. "Take your turn, will you please? People are waiting here." She turned back to Emma. "*Chutzpa*," she said. Emma merely smiled.

He was parked at the gate, dark glasses shoved up into his hair, his face upturned to the sun. He appeared older than on the screen; there were streaks of gray and lines and a rumpled carelessness about him, as if he had selected his clothes with his eyes shut, stuck shut with grainy edges from a hard night. His car was an old convertible with the top cut away. Both tail lights were smashed and there was a tattered bumper sticker with MCGOVERN barely visible.

Emma drew up behind him in her rented car, waited, finally blew her horn.

He turned to look at her with a mild, unfocused smile. "I'm in your way."

Emma thrust her head out the window, studying the car slued before her. "I once failed a driving test for parking like that," she said. "The driving instructor said if it were up to him, I'd never get behind the wheel of a car. Are you a beginner?"

The man shook his head. "Been driving for years. Safe as houses. I'm not myself right now. I think I've been up all night. That's it. I've been up all night." He made a face as if he tasted some foul chemical in his mouth.

"A celebration, perhaps?" Emma suggested. "A happy event, I trust." She leaned her elbow on the window ledge and cupped her chin in her hand. She saw that it would take some time before she could make any headway with this recalcitrant fellow.

"Sorry to hold you up. The thing is, I'm not feeling much below my knees. First time *that's* ever happened. Damndest thing. Right from the knees on down. They say the legs go first. That's what they say."

"Yes," Emma said, amused. "I've heard that. What were you drinking?"

"I don't rightly know. Isn't that something? I think we started off with a little white wine. I recall a little white wine for openers. You could give it to a baby. The French do."

"Well," Emma said, "do you think you could manage to back up and let me through? I'm a bit late already."

"I apologize for any inconvenience. I sincerely do."

"Not at all. We all have our off days, don't we?"

"Now, I don't know about that," the man said. "Some people just sail right along, steady as they go. I have a brother who strictly eschews all drink. Lives on Orange Julius and chocolate milk."

He seemed fairly launched on a family reminiscence while Emma sat tapping her fingers on her steering wheel. "As for me, 'a little wine for your stomach's sake.' And my father before me. A good trencherman, a good man with a glass, my father. Died last year at eighty-seven. I attribute his longevity to the malt in his liquor." He paused and looked at her for confirmation.

Emma murmured appreciatively, "Eighty-seven. A fine long life."

He nodded emphatically. Then he eased himself gingerly out of the car, hitched up his chino pants and walked with great care toward her.

"Come to visit Millie?" he asked, bending down to look at her.

"Yes," she said patiently, "come to visit Millie." She opened the door, took her purse and keys, and got out of her car.

His bright blue eyes swept over her. "Do you know who I am?" he asked suddenly.

"Yes," Emma said. "Alan Hammer. I've seen all your movies. I liked some of them."

"Which?" he demanded.

"The detective thing you did. The cowboy picture."

He licked his lips. "I'm a helluva cowboy," he said and laughed. "I went to Yale. My father was a pediatrician. Threw me out." He looked her over. "You're a very tall woman. You look like the whole goddamn back forty. You're as tall as the Jolly Green Giant. God, I'd have to stand on a box to lay *you.*" He grinned, showing very white teeth.

"If such a thing were to come about," Emma said, "yes, you would."

He rubbed his nose. "I've been consorting with low company of late. I would ask your indulgence if I've been offensive. I'm not at my best in the morning. I'm not much at noon, either, come to think of it. The thing is, I can't handle success, or at least that's what my Jungian head man tells me. I made forty-five motorcycle movies and slept in my Volkswagen van before the prince, my current producer, came and kissed me. I used a lot of booze and rose hips and other goodies on the way up, thus addling my brain." He stopped and shook his head. "Damned if you aren't taller than my brother. I will say that waking up to see you in all your full grown glory would be quite a sight. Generally a man finds himself on a curb with his head between his knees, regarding old chewing gum wrappers and other debris.

Would you came and make love with me under the Santa Monica pier?"

"Not just this minute," Emma said.

"How about Wednesday? I like you."

"I see that you do."

"Wait, wait," he said. "You think this is old Barleycorn talking here, don't you?"

Emma smiled.

He stopped in his tracks, his face dismayed. "See, that's the trouble. That's the goddamn trouble. You don't know me so you got no way to sort this out." He pulled his nose and pondered. "You couldn't wait till I've sobered up, could you? Millie up there might let me take a shave and a shower and get some coffee into me and that would give me a chance to show you what's under the stubble here."

"Saturday's my busy day," Emma said, beginning to feel that she had dawdled long enough. "Clothes to the cleaners. Getting my cat spayed."

"Don't do that."

"Don't do what?"

"Leave the cat alone. You don't want to be responsible for doing a thing like that to a little kitty." He spread his arms wide in a kind of benediction. "Don't meddle with nature," he intoned, "let the mountain streams purl, let the meadow grass grow and let us regroup and stay close to one another."

"That seems sensible. Now I really think we ought to go see Millie."

He bowed, then put his mouth to the squawk box and hallooed into it. "Millie, the hordes are at the gate. Open up. Let us in."

The gate swung wide upon the command. "I love technology," he said. "Now, lady, let me see you up the garden path. Maybe some breeze will blow through my head while we stroll."

He tucked her arm through his and they began the steep ascent. Halfway up he paused. "I'd like to make a statement."

"Another?"

He smiled on her, found her delicious. His eyes remained fixed on her face with impudent insistence. "I'm a mind reader," he began. "This is what you're thinking. Here's a dumb, drunken, unshaved, horny actor making a dumb, horny move at me. Wrong. Judgmental and wrong." He straightened his tie, which had slid askew. "I play the violin," he proclaimed. "Not like Itzhak Perlman but I can play. I was an English major. You think Kris Kristofferson was a Rhodes scholar? I was cum laude in English. You want me to quote Yeats?"

"No," Emma said.

"Well, I can. Yards of him." He leaned forward and peered at her. "Patrician," he said to her. "Fucking elegant. Well might the topless towers of Ilium burn for you. I burn for you."

"Yes. Well," said Emma.

"Dante saw Beatrice on a bridge and that was it. You know that, don't you?"

"So they say."

"You'll hear from me again. Are you married?"

"That's a long story," Emma said. "For another time."

"It's no secret that I have affairs with married ladies," he told her cheerfully.

"Mr. Hammer," she said, "there isn't a man in God's green world I'd embark on a love affair with at this point in my life. Understand, I'm as fond as the next woman of the flattery and the hanky-panky and the hormonal improvement that goes with it, but the time is out of joint, Mr. Hammer. I have other objectives at this juncture." She patted his shoulder. "But you've made me laugh and I've enjoyed talking to you, and for that, much thanks."

Millie appeared on the terrace above them, caftan billowing like a balloon sailing the breeze. "Come up, come up," she called. "The coffee's cold."

The women moved slowly through the house, commenting on the abused condition of the mansion, the fallen plaster and rain-stained floors, seeing themselves reflected in mirrors that swept up walls and continued onto the ceilings. Someone's ego had been endlessly placated, room after room, by refracted images seen from every possible angle. None of the glass shone, however; none of it had been washed in twenty years.

In a sauna off the master suite, Alan Hammer, eyes shut and mouth agape, naked and sprawling, his stomach muscles slack, lay steaming. Millie disdained the sight.

"All my life," she said, "I've had someone sound asleep in my house. My brother's friends, leftovers from a party, boys who threw up and couldn't make it home. I'm like a fire hydrant — every dog can lift his leg on me. Well, listen, I bring it on myself."

She pulled a hairpin from the knot on top of her head and scratched her scalp inelegantly. There was as yet no furniture in the room besides the bed, which had pride of place, heaped with dozens of small pillows; nervous clients with lots of time on their hands had embroidered them with homilies: "Every day in every way I'm getting better and better." "Never explain, never complain."

Wearied by the long ramble through the house, the two women settled onto a window seat and looked into the garden, where the heat shimmered over the white rock paths and a marble faun spilled water from a marble penis into the pool. There was scarcely any breeze. Perspiration stippled Millie's face, giving her a high and hectic color. Emma felt a lazy inclination to lay her head on her arm and listen to the familiar sounds rising toward them like a sustained note drawn from bow and strings. The day seemed to belong to bees and butterflies restless over the heads of roses.

On such an afternoon in her girlhood, Emma would have rolled down her stockings and sat in close concert with a friend, eating plums and exchanging confidences, innocent of embarrassment, bonded by the same display of tight little breasts and baby fat as they unbuttoned their blouses against the heat.

Suddenly, unaccountably, Emma wished herself back in that free and unfettered time ringed by trust and certainty and simplicity. She wanted to put her face against moss, to taste the spicy nasturtium leaf, to feel her skin shrink against the assault of the Saturday night scrub in the bath, to lie awake, hair plaited in long ropes, in perfect ease of mind, in a past when she was not wife or mother or indebted in any way to life.

Millie abhorred silence. She broke it by a little grunt, shifting from one buttock to the other until finally she could contain herself no longer.

"I have to tell you. Kill me. I have to tell you." She put a much be-ringed hand on Emma's knee. "That's what I really got you here about. The house? I don't care about the house. Emma, are we friends?"

"Yes, of course we are. If you have something to say, Millie, say it."

"No, wait. We are friends. When I had hepatitis, you were at the hospital every day. Some other people I could mention, clients for a hundred years, they didn't come. I got flowers. I got Hallmark cards. *You* came. You brought ice cream. You sat, you stayed. In my book, that's friendship."

Emma subdued an impulse to shake her. "You can be so damned annoying," she said shortly. "Stop backing and filling. What is it?"

"Do you *dump* bad news on people? First things first. First I want you to understand I'm not telling you this to make myself some kind of a big shot. You can't have two loyalties. When marriages break up in this town, you're either a friend of the wife's or you're a friend of the husband's. I'm a friend of the wife's."

Emma got to her feet. "What's Charles been up to?"

"Your husband borrowed five thousand dollars from me last month." Millie wiped her face with her wide sleeve. "He came into the office, asked my girl to leave the room. I thought he'd raped somebody from the way he looked."

"Five thousand dollars?" Emma was disbelieving.

"That's what he took from me. He's been to Jessup. He's been to Mason. He's in hock in eleven places I know of. I'm the only one not charging interest."

Emma felt a peculiar chill in her bones at the thought of Charles, principled, despairing Charles, lying in the dark, his eyes wide, his worries harassing him, his stomach uneasy.

He would, she knew, make meticulous promises of repayment, all the while thinking wildly of night jobs as a desk clerk or a waiter or a used car salesman. He would return the money before the first leaf fell, before the first snow flew. He would give up smoking and wine and secondhand bookstores and all his indulgences. He would labor like Sisyphus, eschewing holidays, sleep, all the occasions of felicity.

Emma wished suddenly they could sit down together as of old, chewing on the ends of pencils to see if they could really go to Majorca with the children or buy flagstones to lay a terrace. Poor Charles, born and bred in the stern virtues, wrestling now with profligacy and ruin. And for what? What demands were being made to keep this new love alive? Oh, thought Emma woefully, what must his love give in return to have so unsettled him. She must reward beyond all imagining.

"You have to do something," Millie commanded. "You're the one with sense."

Yes, thought Emma without bitterness, it's true, I am. She was familiar with these moments. That pragmatic tack of hers. It was Emma, squinting against the smoke of her cigarettes, to whom he came with his work. Yes, the script about the fruit pickers in Fresno was very moving, but the one about two cowboys who rode with Custer was the one that would sell. Yes, she loved his poetry, but could he wait a little, could he do it on the side, could the left hand be the dreamer, till they had paid for Adam's four wisdom teeth and the car insurance? Sometimes Emma noted his pale smile and wondered what it portended. Still, Charles did as advised. He also moved a cot into his study. In her own room Emma protested the injustice of it. Had she brought a winging bird to earth, shooting him down with stopped-up toilets and broken shower heads? Half in remorse and half to justify herself, Emma came across the hall on nights when she felt like it and told him to move over. Once she fell out of the narrow bed and bruised her tail bone. Sometimes they laughed. Sometimes they didn't.

Now, it was Charles in love . . .

"Millie," she said patiently, "Charles has a new lady. It breaks my heart but there it is."

"It's so nice," Millie said crossly, "it's so polite, it's so understanding, it's so tolerant — I don't understand you! He's wrecking himself for this big amour. A Jewish wife would scream and cry and call her father!" Millie's sigh was exasperated. "I'm trying to do you some good. I'm trying to do myself some good. Talk to Charles about his script. He hasn't so many more chances in this town. Every morning another baby writer puts the paper into the typewriter. I've got two of 'em at Fox right now — twenty-two and twenty-three, with big black cigars in their mouths and big fat contracts in their blue jeans. You want to hear something? A director I know and you know flew to Rio last week to get his face lifted and the liver spots taken off his hands. A brilliant director, worried about liver spots and a little flab under the jaw. Charles had his hair styled, Emma. He went to Vidal Sassoon's and sat under a hair dryer, for Christ's sake. Help him."

Emma pulled her nose and looked forlorn. "I'll have lunch with him," she said. "We'll talk about his script."

"Smart," Millie said. "Now you're being smart."

Emma quarreled with that view. Her mood was not one of benevolence. She had gone to great pains to separate herself from her old allegiance. She foresaw the peril. He would be charming, cajoling, grateful. They would be at some distance from their past, easily swept into gaiety. They would traverse familiar ground, make common cause, end up in bed, sufficiently strangers to make it worthwhile. She had never been ungenerous there, and how cross *was* she with him when all was said and done? She smiled. Certainly she would lunch with Charles — lunch, dinner and breakfast if it fell out that way. She resolved to buy new underwear. She could use it in any event.

# Chapter Four

MOSES AND ADAM were exactly alike except that Adam had a notch in his ear and a yellow fleck in one of his blue eyes, and Moses had a small birthmark like a drop of coffee just below his navel. It was in their temperament that they differed. Moses was the victim of moods, strongly affirmative one moment, all tumult and dark foreboding the next. He resembled his grandfather who had to the day he died remained unreconciled to his station in life — agent for the Northwestern Life Insurance Company — who had deeply loved a red-headed, buxom neighbor to whom he wrote impassioned letters and on whose doorstep he left wild lupine and overblown poppies which she swept off her porch with a vigorous broom.

Moses spent all his allowance the day he got it. He could foretell rain and imminent death. He kissed his mother on the mouth and cried openly over hurts of all kinds, were they psychic or sprained ankles and fractured fibulas. He was troubled by his appearance. He sniffed his armpits for offending odor, he brushed his teeth after every meal, he showered morning and night, standing absently under the torrent for fully half an hour at a time. He was ceremonious about occasions, commemorating birthdays and anniversaries into the farthest reaches of the family. Distant cousins often puzzled over cards and letters sent air mail from California. He never expected replies. He cared for his father but in a painful way, feeling sad and inept in his presence, seeing him as greatly gifted and unacknowledged; he felt it unjust. He went pale with emotion and broke out when he ate tomatoes or strawberries. He was desperate to lose his virginity and did so with a silent little girl in his Elizabethan poetry course who had dreadful head colds and who finally moved to Phoenix for her health. He adored his twin but would on no account lend him money, books or his hat, an Australian allagash with a sweat-stained leather strap and a curled feather in its band.

Secretly, he thought himself the more intelligent of the two. Adam did not rejoice in Dylan Thomas, did not care a fig for Marlowe. He did not rise early to gaze into the blue light of morning, he did not feel unreasonable anxiety.

No, Adam was another sort altogether. He ran on cinder tracks. He wrote letters to his congressman and enclosed stamped envelopes to insure answers. He took up with older women in a swaggering, unflustered way, finally bedding one with great style in a downtown hotel in Santa Barbara. He saw both sides of any issue and took his own position based on facts scrupulously examined. He followed Moses' mystical forays into religion merely to keep him company. He saw equity as the only morality, fairness the only credo. He loved Groucho Marx and low humor of any sort. He made a sixteen-millimeter film of himself standing in the backyard, telling awful jokes with immense energy. He fell off his chair every time he ran it through the old projector onto a bed sheet, although no one else in the family considered it particularly funny. He thought himself handsome, but in a dispassionate way. He was not vain. He redressed wrongs wherever he found them; he made himself available — many a girl had asked him to accompany her while she got an abortion or told her family she was leaving home. He was always a reasonable presence, forestalling anger and recrimination. He loved Mexican food and beer and little children. He was always late. He considered Moses an amplification of himself. It went far beyond love.

They arrived home with a bundle of dirty laundry, a crate of melons they had purchased along the way and one pale girl between them. The dogs had gone wild and Felicia, hearing their yapping, appeared and was swept into embraces, kisses raining on her head and the side of her neck, on her nose, on her eyebrows.

"Felicia, Felicia. A little pound here or there but gorgeous, gorgeous." Adam hung around her neck and gazed deeply into her eyes. "Bella signora," he growled and nipped her with his teeth.

"Hello, Felicia, it's nice to see you back," Moses said.

"Your mother's not at home. You should call before you come. We have two lamb chops in the house. Introduce this girl. Show some manners."

"This young lady is Cleo," Adam said. "She irons her hair. She is a vegetarian. She is very shy."

Felicia sniffed. Moses said, "She had no place to go for summer vacation. We said she'd be welcome in our house."

Cleo looked around her. She had large, innocent eyes, a gentle, unsettled air. She attracted light; she seemed to have a nimbus, an aureole. "I love the Tiffany lamps," she said, "and that Spanish shawl on the piano. I could sleep in the garden."

The boys vied gallantly. She could have Adam's bed. She could have Moses' bed. She could have the best the house had to offer. She lifted her long fall of greeny gold hair from her neck and sighed in the heat — from the long journey, from some inconsolable hurt they knew not of — and she asked if they could all go swimming. They pounded up the stairs then, carrying her between them. They showed her into the bathroom, bright with pink tile and stately swans; they offered her privacy and an old swimming suit of Emma's which she would find under the sink, under the enema bag if they remembered correctly.

They shucked their own clothes, leaving them on the floor.

They looked critically at themselves in the glass, Adam sucking in his gut until his ribs stood out and Moses wondering if that was truly hair on his chest or only the dye from his T-shirt. There was a callous on his toe he knew to be unsightly. He was still dizzy from the ride home with Cleo between them on the front seat of the car, pressed like a faded violet in a book, colorless, sweet, faintly fragrant. He had had an ache in his balls from the Ventura County line all the way to their front door. He had it now. He wished fervently that Cleo would forego his mother's latex bikini, that she would float naked and seraphic on the surface of the pool while he, from its depths, gazed upward at the two round halves that made the glorious whole of her beautiful bottom.

"Getting a little pot," said Adam, pinching his middle. "Too many tacos. Too many burritos."

"You eat junk food," Moses said. "The body is a holy temple. I keep telling you that."

Adam hummed, shadowboxed his image. "Let's go," he sang. "Let's go see all ninety pounds of her. Let's see the little raisins that are her nipples."

"I think I'll shave," Moses said.

"You shaved yesterday. What're you going to shave for? There's nothing there. Two hairs coming out of your mole."

"I have no mole," Moses agonized. He put an anxious hand to his chin.

"She's waiting," Adam said. "She's out there with her two bony knees pressed together, waiting for us."

"I'll come in a minute."

Adam paused in the doorway. He discerned. It had always been that he was first up the tree, hauling Moses after him, first into the wave to beckon him on, first into a woman's bed to describe later the intricacies and satisfactions of it all.

"I've got to take a leak," Adam said. "You go on down and get started."

Moses raised his head, smiled his slow and grateful smile.

"Well, okay. I won't show her any terrific dives until you get there."

All the long afternoon they churned through the water, heads down, legs flailing, splattering the windows, drowning the poolside plants. Moses, thrashing into a turn at the end of the pool, peering upward with chlorine-reddened eyes, was ever aware of Cleo, ripening like an apricot under the sun. He saw there would be a heat rash, foresaw himself slicking her skin with Mentholatum, ministering, attending. Moses was easily moved to love. Sometimes it took no more than the sight of a blue-veined wrist with its small quaking pulse to gaff him. It could be a hooded eyelid, a pigeon-toed walk, the suggestion of a lisp. Once he had been dazed with passion for a week at the sight of a blueberry-stained mouth. He marveled at his own susceptibility. There had been the waitress at the Rexall Drug Store with her downy arms and her hot black eyes; there had been the meter maid with her aggressive thighs and booted legs; there had been a lecturer in Greek; a paddle tennis champion acrid with sweat; an usherette, invisible in the dark but scented with musk and gardenia. His nerve ends bristled, reaching out to touch and be touched.

His one and only time in the bed of his docile classmate seemed a heartbreaking sham. He had been so anxious, so hasty. She had, he was sure, been watching the television screen over his shoulder. He had wept on her underdeveloped breast. She had crunched Vick's cough drops and had answered the telephone by the bed on its first ring.

He had fastened his hopes on Cleo. He felt he could cast his net of passion over her and haul in a rare bird, fluttering, pulsating, merciful. He burned to have her, laying elaborate plans as to where and when and how. He wondered if they could possibly shower together, steam-shrouded, merged. He wondered if he could descend the stairs this very night and end up with her on the kitchen table, the light from the open refrigerator shining on their two naked bodies wrestling among the remains of a baloney sandwich and half-eaten apple. He thought of his clothes closet, dark and private and cedar lined. He thought of Asa's kennel, odorous and flea infested. He thought of the tree house, rotten with termites, hazardous with splinters, open to the stars.

Then he saw her rise and come forward to the pool's edge, holding a towel for Adam. He saw her hands pat, pat, pat down to the trunk line and below it, saw the sky darken, heard a roaring in his ears, felt the bash of jealousy like a roof beam falling on his back. He went to the bottom of the pool, held his breath, rocked in the green water, wishing it were the restless fluid of the womb, coughed, choked, rose gasping to the surface, spewing.

"Are you all right?"

He saw the delicate triangle of Cleo's face bending toward him. "Sure."

He hauled himself onto the coping with one hand, exhibiting, he thought, both poise and muscular control. She did not drape *him* in his Cannon towel, her hands did not adore *him*. He flopped face down, gulping chagrin and the last of the water burning his throat. Cleo sat on her heels.

"I hope," she said in her light, shivery voice, "I hope I can stay." She drew her long hair around her in a protective mantle. "My mother's on the verge of getting married for the third time and she's gotten this huge trousseau together and we live in a one-room apartment. She bought twenty-seven pairs of shoes and they're all over the place, in their boxes. As well as in all the suitcases. She's been dividing things up for months. I get half the Dickens set, half the Creuset ware . . . and the hand mixer, not the electric beater. She gets the hair dryer. I'm supposed to keep the dog. We're going to throw out all the old magazines. The plants are mine. The hooked rug is hers. I guess we'll flush the goldfish down the toilet."

The boys looked at each other. Cleo had not spoken above ten words in the seventy-five miles they had driven together. They encouraged her with their total absorption.

"I may not stay after she moves out. I may get my own place. I'm tired of living with smokers and drinkers. My mother grinds out her butts in the cereal dish. I don't want any more plastic. I want natural fibers all around me, sisal and cotton. I want the windows wide open at night. I don't want any pills in the medicine cabinet. Or a telephone. I won't cook anything in water from the tap. I won't have meat on the premises in any form, or eggs, or dead fish. No cut flowers either. They feel pain and I won't be responsible for pain. My mother has crying jags and menstruates irregularly and is generally inharmonious. After the wedding, I won't see her anymore. You're the children of divorce, aren't you?"

Moses was silent. Adam spoke for the family. "My folks are just separated." Dignity kept him from saying more.

"Once scattered, ever scattered," Cleo said. "I've said good-by to two fathers. Winter love never lasts. My mother is forty."

Moses ventured an observation. "I guess you'll be lonely. Being on your own."

Cleo's blue stare was as cold as lake water. "There is transcendental love," she said. "God is a living presence. Nature is our first mother. We are the family of Man. I'm surprised you're not aware of all that."

"I am, I am," Moses said hastily. "I was only thinking of you on Christmas morning and stuff. On your own. All by yourself."

He thought of himself in that dreadful time when his mother had sent him to one summer camp, Adam to another, to see if they were as indivisible as she feared. He had sat in Crafts, blindly weaving his Indian blanket upside down. He had wet his bed and thrown up the macaroni and cheese dinners every single night for a week. He had stuck it out to arrive home seven pounds underweight, with a persistent low fever and a newly acquired nervous giggle.

"I'm gregarious," he said. "I mean . . . I love people." He meant her, of course.

*

The routine was unvarying, habitual, comforting. While the streets still glared with late afternoon sunshine, the false and persisting light of daylight-saving time, Emma drove to Jessup's house to fetch him home with her to Saturday night dinner. They were usually meals hastily assembled: tuna fish salads with lettuce beginning to brown at the edge or something with creamed peas in it or pizza, soggy in a box delivered by a boy with dirty fingernails. Talk was the main dish, the necessary dish. Even when Charles had been part of the household, Jessup had come for these desultory suppers, sitting out on the veranda, watching the slick movement of the garter snake in the grass, prodigiously full of himself.

Charles, his own ego hampered by Jessup's, would excuse himself after the first long monologue, the first barbed and embittered recollection, leaving Jessup to fold his long white hands in his lap while Emma smoked and slapped the mosquitoes and listened. She was fully aware that she was being studied, she and Charles, and every nuance of their uneasy, lurching marriage. She knew she would come upon herself again, barely once removed, barely disguised in his handwritten screenplays: "*Emma (or Neda or Mildred) seen in her garden: impatience just below the surface, rue almost visible. She does not allow illusions. He cannot exist without them. She calls dreams lies. He meets reality with long silences. They rely on manners. Betrayal will only make her indifferent. He is the one who will weaken. She knows what can take the place of love. He is helpless. Note that his dress has changed. His shirts are expensive. He has bought new glasses. She has allowed a strand of gray at the temples.*"

It both exasperated and amused Emma. She threatened to sue him.

"You will be played by a younger, prettier woman. You will fight, strive, break apart. You will have all the complication only I can provide. You will have interesting neuroses and a lover. You should pay me."

After Charles had departed, Jessup's interest waned. He had

harvested the hard kernels of their life and was finished. He was like a vulture, winging away from a picked cadaver.

"You're late, you're late." Jessup came down the weedy path that led from his house to the street below.

Emma shifted the groceries into the back seat, deaf to his grumbling. He climbed in beside her, showing her his beaked profile, the loose fold of flesh under his chin.

"Are we having any sort of a decent dinner? I am very tired. I would like some fruit. None of those bruised and battered leavings you pick up off trucks in vacant lots . . . some succculent fruit. On a clean plate."

"Felicia is back. The plates are clean again."

"Good. Order restored. High time." He leaned back, closed his eyes. Exposed to air and sunlight, he seemed to decline into old age. Under the hot lights on the sound stage, he was infused with color; no one could match his pace, keep his hours, survive his meticulous, punishing attention. At the end of the day, he was old.

"Are you feeling well?" Emma made this anxious comment every Saturday and was answered the same way.

"I will die this year."

"Nonsense."

"I am considering religions."

"Scared, are you?"

He was brusque. "You don't understand. I want the best death has to offer. I'm shopping around. Nirvana. Purgatory. Eternal life. I want them to trot out their wares . . . the priests, the rabbis, the ministers. Let's see what they've got."

"I don't think," Emma said, "the choice is open."

"I had a nervous breakdown once," Jessup said with some satisfaction, "when I was twenty-two, tubercular, in Paris. Virginia Woolf said she heard the birds speaking Greek. I saw the face of God. He is made in my image. I was so anguished at the pettiness of that face, I fled back to sanity."

"That is open to question." Emma honked at the car in front of her. She wanted to get home, wash her face and water the roses before dark. She intended to leave death for another time.

"Tell me something cheerful," she said to him. "I've had a tiresome day."

With charming promptness, he changed moods. "I am in love. She is eighteen. Very small bones. Her feet are dirty. I've only seen her once. She ran past me on the beach. She leaves very even tracks on the sand."

"Lord, Lord," Emma said. "What next?"

"Between death and love, nothing. At my age, it must be one or the other."

"William," Emma said, "I think you're liverish. Death, love. Let's just have a chess game and not talk."

He grunted. "You are inherently unsociable," he said.

They heard the shouts and the laughter as they turned into the drive, voices of exactly the same timbre, exactly the same pitch.

"My darlings," Emma cried, waving her hand in greeting, "hello, my darlings."

They charged the car then, belting across the lawn, shaking water from their hair, shoving each other, suddenly childishly determined to have the first kiss.

"Hey, mom, hey!"

"Mom, hey, mom!"

She was clutched, inundated, smothered, each of them at her through the open window on either side of the car. A cold wet cheek pressed against hers, a wet hand left a mark on her dress.

"Yes, yes, yes," she said, pulled at, mauled. "Easy, whoa, whew. Enough!"

They fell back then, allowing her to open the door, sweeping her into yet another embrace as she stood up.

"My God," she said, "you can't have gotten taller?" She pushed them from her. "You have."

Moses remembered his manners. "Hello, Mr. Jessup. Nice to see you. You're looking fine."

Jessup was looking past him to where Cleo sat, knees to chin on the grass, watching. He seemed rewarded at the sight.

"Moses," he answered absently. "Good evening."

Moses followed the gaze, walked gravely away, pulled Cleo to her feet and led her back across the lawn. "This is Cleo," he said. "My mother and Mr. Jessup."

Cleo stared at Jessup. She was in the presence of a sacred flame of genius, of incandescent talent.

"What a woebegone visage," Jessup said. "A true waif."

"I'm the child of a third son," Cleo said. "My father drowned." He had actually fallen off a ladder that he had climbed to replace a burned-out light bulb on the front porch. Cleo told it that he had been swept away in the wide reaches of the Columbia, the Rio Grande, the Sacramento, the Susquehanna, depending on her mood. She kept relics of him: a bow tie, his Exxon credit card, a ticket to the S.C.–U.C.L.A. football game, and a copper bracelet he was convinced would ward off arthritis. She had long since forgotten what he looked like.

"You're a Blessed Damozel," Jessup said to Cleo. " 'The bar she leaned on warm, and the lillies lay as if asleep, along her bended arm.' Do you see it, Emma?"

"She's very pretty," Emma said. "Let's all go in and have a glass of wine before dinner. If you kids are through swimming, pick up your bath towels. Has anybody fed the dogs?"

Emma strode toward the house, the boys in her wake. Cleo moved closer to Jessup. "Is she a jealous woman?" she inquired of him.

"I shouldn't think so."

"I planned to stay a week but only if I'm welcome."

"Doesn't all the world welcome you?" Jessup took her hand. "Sit by me at dinner. I'll feed you bits of orange."

It was almost eleven o'clock when they finished eating. Asa fell asleep under the table, his head on Moses' tennis shoe. Felicia mopped the kitchen floor. A light wind came up and caused the curtains to drift inward. A branch of eucalyptus rattled and fell to the ground. The boys talked and talked and Emma yawned and wondered, as she looked from one to the other, which she loved best.

She saw changes, pondered their source. At Christmas, Adam had made callow jokes. He had left the books he loved, for hours hunched before the television set. He had worn the same socks day after day and had never spoken his father's name. He had slept till noon and smiled mysteriously when she wanted his attention. Now he smoked a pipe. He pulled his nose before expressing an opinion, a habit of his grandfather's, whom he had begun to resemble. He spoke slowly, judiciously. She felt he had already come to conclusions he would hold all his life. She wondered what tutelage had altered him, from whose bed he had risen a man. It began to look as if he had hopscotched two squares ahead of Moses.

Moses of the bitten fingernails, Moses of the squint and scowl. He had fumbled somewhere. She was sure of it. He had drawn the sheets up over his head, had turned his skinny buttocks to a girl already sitting up in bed, already adjusting a bobby pin. Try again, darling, she urged silently over the melting vanilla ice cream and the cooling coffee. Give it another shot. Doubtless he would, too. She surmised from the intensity of his stare across the table at Cleo that it might be this very night. She wondered if he had clean pajamas. A Trojan. She cursed his departed father. It was only fitting and proper that there should be a father to send him on his way to a blue-veined breast, girded with optimism, to pass the night without jeopardy, to welcome the morning.

"I propose," Jessup suddenly said from the head of the table, "to put two of these three beautiful young people into my motion picture. A week's work. One scene. To be written on the spot. Possibly improvised. I need these faces. Just these faces. I'll test all three. One boy must drop out. But you're used to giving way to each other. You did it in the womb. Emma? What do you say?"

"Actors? I don't think so."

"A week's work. This week."

"You must let them," Cleo spoke breathlessly. "Oh, you must."

Emma held out her wine glass to Adam to be filled. She drank it down in two gulps.

"William," she said, "this isn't Central Casting. This is my home."

"I played Ophelia," Cleo said. "In high school."

"Everyone has," Jessup said. "Emma. Give permission."

"No," she said. "What happens to the one who loses out? I'll have a suicide on my hands."

"There's no contest," Adam said. "I'll get the part. Moses talks through his nose."

"I don't," Moses said nasally.

"There. You see?"

Cleo's eyes snapped, brightened. "'Oh," she said, "I'll die if this doesn't happen. There's so much excitement already."

Cleo wept in the night. Put to bed on the couch, under Emma's dusty patchwork quilt, cradled there among Emma's yellowing Victorian pillows, Cleo wept.

Emma rose to the sound. With an ear attuned to childhood's fretful cough and fearful call, Emma slipped into an old robe of Charles's and came downstairs. She passed the open door to the boys' room, took in the familiar tableau, Adam with a foot thrust out on the side of his bed, Moses with a foot out the other, their hands relaxed and fingers touching, two goslings downy with sleep — and, in the room below, a dove, weeping.

Emma descended the stairway swiftly, cautious where the old Oriental rug was torn, knowing the peril on each step. She was still clouded with sleep, still occupied with the remains of a dream. She had been on a bright strand of beach, staring into a vivid sea. Charles emerged from the water, bearing a girl on his shoulders. The boys, young again, ran from her toward the other two, and all together they made a tableau, happy, distant, united. As she approached them, they vanished. Disconnected, disturbed, she had pulled herself awake — to the sound of tears. It was as if someone else suffered in her place.

She was beside Cleo now, hiking her up close. One hand felt

for fever, the other swept a handkerchief from her pocket, mopped, blotted.

"There," she said. "What's all this? Tummy ache? Bad dreams? Shhhh," Emma soothed. "Nothing to worry about. Too much wine, maybe. Too many stuffed green peppers."

Cleo clutched at her, "Oh, let me stay," she sobbed. "Let me stay. I don't want to go and live in one room. I want someone to scold me, someone to ask why I'm late getting home. I love this house. I love your silver pattern and your tablecloth with a hole in it. I love the way you hold Moses under the chin. The way you give Adam food off your plate." Tears tangled her beautiful eyelashes; she flung herself into Emma's lap. "I went to sleep thinking of you," she said. "You're so regal. And the boys worship you. Yes, they do. I've never seen a boy stand up when his mother comes into a room. I've never seen a boy pull out his mother's chair. And you have dogs. And roses. And you don't lock the front door."

"Well," Emma said stroking her bent head, "you've taken in quite a lot, haven't you?"

Cleo sat up, the storm quieting. "I've been everywhere looking for someplace to light. I have a second cousin in Chula Vista but I couldn't live with him. There's no movie house there. I have an aunt in Corvallis but she lives on a farm and is as deaf as a stone. And that's all there is in my dying-out family. No one else anywhere. I wouldn't be any trouble," she said. "I'll do your gardening. I mulch. I don't use pesticides. I plant garlic everywhere and that does the trick. I'm better than any Japanese gardener." She gulped for breath. "I bake wonderful whole wheat bread. I can crochet. And iron. I can make corn relish and grape jelly, the kind you squeeze through a bag. And I'll be a sister to the boys. A loving sister."

In the dark, Emma smiled. She thought of the third child she had wanted, a daughter, and of the special and cheerful communion there would be between them. She saw herself sitting on the front porch on a summer afternoon by her own mother's side. A bowl of peas in their laps. The smell of soap and clean laundry in the air. The loving design of it, one ameliorating the lot of the other, passing old truths one to the other while the pods fell at their feet. She heard herself lauded, in her mother's low dry voice, as perfect, perfection itself. Yes, she was untidy. A minor blemish. Her mother would straighten her drawers for her, hang her dresses in neat rows, pick up the fallen books. But see how witty she was. How pretty she was. See her style.

"Emma," her mother had said of her. "My sunshine." How she had profited by that unreasoning approval. How she longed for it now. It was her legacy. Her only inheritance.

"*I think there's another woman, mama.*"

"*Foolish, foolish man. Don't cry, Emma. You can lose everything but your dignity. You can't live without that.*"

"*But I want to be loved.*"

"*You are. I love you. And you must love yourself. And eat well and walk a mile every day.*"

"*I'm sorry for myself. I am, I admit it. I'm forty. Alone. I'm angry. I'm miserable.*"

"*I forbid you to be miserable.*"

"I forbid you to be miserable," Emma said to Cleo. "Now blow your nose. Blow hard."

Cleo obeyed.

"This room is as cold as death," Emma said. "Come in the kitchen. We'll light the oven and have cocoa."

Cleo flung back her hair, turned an imploring look on Emma. Her eyes were pooled with tears, like a child's, abruptly finished with disconsolation and now ready to laugh.

"I love cocoa," she said, "made with milk."

"Always with milk," Emma said.

It had grown light without their noticing it. Exuberance succeeded gloom. Now Cleo bustled around the kitchen, setting the table nicely with cups and spoons, arranging the sugar bowl, setting the chairs straight at the table.

"Could we have French toast? And jam?"

"Who eats that at five-thirty in the morning?"

"I slice the bread an inch thick. And use two egg yolks. And vanilla. And tons of butter."

"Make it," Emma said. "I'm salivating."

Out came the pots, out came the pans. A clatter ensued.

"Just sit down. I'll wait on you. Just sit and wait till it's golden brown." She snapped the napkin open and laid it across Emma's lap. Then she caught sight of herself in the kitchen glass, swept her hair on top of her head, skewered it with a hairpin. "I hate it when people drop hair into the food they're cooking. I ate Chinese food last week and there, nested in the noodles, was a *long, black* hair." Her voice rose with disdain.

"Imagine that," Emma said. "But we have to be quiet. Felicia is asleep right next door. She gets very sore if you wake her up. She'll curse you in Spanish."

"Can I stay?" Cleo said suddenly, stopping in her tracks. "Can I?"

Emma was tempted. She was charmed by motherhood, sensuously pleased, inattentive to its details. She forgot to change diapers. She refused schedules. The boys often slept in the day, were awake in the night, lying across her belly while she smoked and listened to chamber music. She was obstinate about her priorities. It was more important that they should feel the curled waves at the beach than be toilet trained. She wanted them to be familiar with the tree toad, the blue jay, the dog and the cat. She fed them strangely — the black beads of caviar, the firm flesh of a nectarine, little sips of watered wine. She spoke to them cordially, existing side by side with them as if they were something more than pink and shriveled innocence. She dropped ashes into their cribs, swore profanely in their hearing. She was lavish with her time. She could wait all day for a comprehending smile, an alert response. She was jealous. She was inclined to see only herself in their faces, feeling she had marked them utterly for her own. She did not try to get her figure back for months after they were born. She remained complacently overweight, unbuttoned, swinging in a hammock under the trees.

When she emerged from this cocoon of maternity, she felt resplendent, imperturbable. Perhaps at this point Charles turned away. No. Impossible. She would not admit the possibility. She was at her best at this time.

Across the table from her, Cleo waited, an insistent, revering presence.

If I take you in, Emma thought, it will be because I am charmed by your pinched and repudiated face.

"You'll have to make your own bed," she said, "and wash the tub after yourself. Don't get pregnant. Don't get arrested. Don't tell lies. And don't expect too much from me. I'm in a stew these days."

The zeal of Cleo's grateful kiss broke Emma's brand-new, eighty-three dollar glasses. It was an inauspicious beginning.

Moses said later that, while his bowels had turned to water when he stepped out under the lights, he had experienced, at the same time, a singular exultation. He vibrated with brilliance. He felt certain he must be giving off visible currents of energy. When he was asked to turn his profile, right and then left, he felt he was showing a fighter's firm jaw, a young man at the peak of his power.

He had arrived at the studio with Adam early in the morning. They had been shepherded into separate cubicles. A young dandy with a softly drooping mustache and a large opal on a chain around his neck had combed his hair in a new and becoming way. Someone else had pancaked his skin to a glorious brown shade, covering the spatter of freckles he loathed along the bridge of his nose.

He had been handed beautiful blue jeans, warm from the steam iron, and a body shirt he knew for a fact cost sixty dollars. He had been careful to use a deodorant. Now the sweat seemed to have been diverted to the inside of his thighs and the backs of his knees. A girl with lovely high breasts and a faint Italian accent had gone over the lines he would say, gently reminding him when his memory left him and he sat open-mouthed and distraught while the words refused to come. Then suddenly he could have recited all of *Ulysses* in one breath.

Next door he heard Adam making a laborious job of it. He pitied his lame-brained and uninspired twin. Earthbound Adam, uh-uh-uhing his way while he, Moses, soared, high on the elixir of exhibitionism. God, he was an actor. There was no doubt of it. He hoped old Jessup would give him his head. He was miles beyond the narrow confines of the scene. He had the character's whole history in his mind; he was flushed through and through with that history. He waited with his palms on his sweated knees. A muscle jumped in his cheek. He willed it to continue. He wanted to use it; a mark of passion, evidence of tension.

"Tell us your name," said a disembodied voice behind the blaze of light. "Your name and where you go to school and something about yourself."

Giddy with the heat and the attention, Moses took a deep breath and sallied forth on the story of his life.

"Moses Howard," he said, his voice resonating in the lowest register he could manage. "Moses Dayton Howard. I'm a freshman at U.C. Santa Barbara. I am a student," he paused for a significant beat, "not only of books, but of life." He smiled widely, trying to see faces in the white glare in front of him. "I make it a point, on Saturdays, after I've washed my socks and my shirt, to walk the city streets. I do this religiously. I make a regular visit to the Mission for Christ, where I am pretty well known by now. I talk to the winos and others who come to eat breakfast there. Their faith is pretty well tested by the life they lead and I'm curious to see if it holds up in the long run. There are quite a few Mexican prostitutes walking around, but I haven't made any headway there because I think they know I'm a student and not too well off financially. Their time is valuable, and anyhow my Spanish isn't too great. So that's how I spend my leisure time. On Sundays I play a little volleyball with my brother on the beach just to stay in shape. I have been approached to join the Communist Party by quite a nice girl in my Zoology section but I don't think I'm that political.

"I'm a twin. I think my brother's out there getting fixed up to take this test next. I think I should say something about being a twin because it's kind of unique in a way. I think my brother is a terrific person. He has a very fine mind and is in control of himself about ninety percent of the time. He says I'm thin-skinned and sensitive, but I don't agree with that. I would say that he has more on the ball than I do. For instance, last year he got us our job in the shoe store. They only wanted one salesman but he did a big number on them and they took us both. He said they were getting four hands and two brains — I think they thought they were hiring an octopus. Actually, I did all the work. He's pretty lazy. I would say he shows more poise than I do in almost any situation. With girls particularly. He has a good self-image. Too good, sometimes, but he gets all he can handle." Moses shaded his eyes and tried to penetrate the lights. "If there are any ladies out there I don't mean to sound crude. I believe in absolute equality for women. I get that from my mother."

He shifted his weight from one foot to another. He was beginning to feel tired.

"It isn't easy to show every side of your character in just a few minutes. I'd like to be a poet, although I know I'll have to earn my living some other way. Maybe I'll be an actor." He laughed loudly. "Doesn't seem to be much to it." He swallowed vigorously.

Somebody from behind the bank of lights laughed. Moses lifted his head like a skittish foal.

"Was that what you wanted?"

"Thank you, Mr. Howard. That was just fine. This test is just to see what you look like on film and hear your voice. You can take a chair now."

Moses lingered. "This has been very enjoyable for me. I'm usually pretty knotted up but I feel very relaxed up here. It's like somebody else is standing here. I think I could do this all day long. Look out, Steve McQueen." He laughed again.

"Right. Thank you, son. Just take that chair."

"Will I get to see myself on film?"

"You'll have to check with Mr. Jessup."

"I nicked myself shaving this morning. Hope it doesn't show. I was pretty nervous."

"Uh-huh. Well, we just wanted a look at you."

"This is your shirt and pants. Where will I leave them?"

"Wardrobe, Mr. Howard. Just give them to wardrobe."

"It's a great shirt."

"We're a little short of time . . ."

Moses smiled. "I guess you need a hook to haul me off. This is the first time I've ever done anything like this."

Someone emerged from the dark and walked toward him. It was Jessup. He came up and put his arm over Moses' shoulder. "We have to look at Adam now," he said. "We have to be fair."

"Well, sure. Would it be okay if I watched?"

Jessup nodded. "Go sit in the back. Out of his eyeline."

"His what?"

"Where he can't see you."

Moses shook his head. "I felt very peculiar up there, Mr. Jessup. It was like when I took gas at the dentist to have a molar pulled. I felt like I'd shed my skin, like everything had just sloughed off. What a feeling. What a *great* feeling."

"You were charming," said Jessup. He beckoned to an assistant. "Give our young friend here a cup of coffee. I don't think he ate his breakfast this morning."

"No, sir, I didn't. But I don't drink coffee or anything with caffeine in it."

"Milk, then."

"I drink a lot of milk."

"Moses," said Jessup, "you understand about this little scene I proposed. It's just a moment. Nothing important. I sometimes need atmosphere to give texture. Very often it's a kind of background, a counterpoint to another melody. You understand?"

"I never even thought about acting until today. I'm sure thinking about it now."

Jessup nodded. "You're an unusual boy. A fine boy. I would enjoy seeing your poetry. Maybe you'll send it to me."

"I'd be honored."

Adam got the part. Moses rose to his feet and came forward manfully. He managed to hug him, pound him on the back, offer congratulations. He said he would wait for Adam in the car. He wanted, he said, to hear Archibald MacLeish on the radio. He stopped to get a drink from the water fountain on the way out. The water was warm and rank.

He was weeping bitterly in the front seat of his old De Soto when Millie found him.

She had an appointment on the lot but the mother-fucker could just wait. She climbed in beside him, her caftan catching in the door, her Egyptian jewelry clanking metallically. Without a word, she took him in her arms. An hour later, they were in bed.

What Moses could not offer in virtuosity, he made up in homage. Where others had rampaged, he feasted, marveling at the fleshy and abundant femininity under his hand. All chilling uncertainty left him in that wide and yielding bed. Energy and pride set him buoyantly on his course. Never had he seen such plentitude; all was velvet, plushed, fluffed and fleeced.

Inexplicably composed, he murmured lovely things into her ear, boldly lifting her hair away so that no word was lost. When at last he fell asleep, it was with his head on her belly, his arms clasping her ample waist.

He came back to consciousness slowly, wanting to protract the languorous depletion, the delicious exhaustion, already feeling the pressure of fresh demand. He had new wisdom to display, new curiosity to satisfy. He chose possibilities like a connoisseur. He threw his bare leg over her great thigh and smiled up at her.

"Don't tell your mother," she said. "She'd kill me and she'd be right."

Moses stroked and reasoned. He felt fully in command. "This," he said calmly, "is between us."

Millie groped for a cigarette, snapped a match along the bedpost. "Jesus," she said, exhaling smoke in a steady stream. "What got into me?"

Moses reared up beside her, presenting his lipstick besmeared face and firm resolve.

"May I call you Millie?" he began politely.

"Are you kidding?"

"I suppose," he said, "you're a little embarrassed." He reached for her hand, laced it through his. "There's nothing to be embarrassed about. I'm very happy right now. I feel very happy."

Millie made a funny face. "Me too," she said. "How about that?"

Moses hitched the blankets around them. Her bulk required the larger share but he did not mind about that. He wanted to offer her every comfort at his command. He thought of the mean-spirited girls who had come before and he bent and kissed Millie's knee. How richly available she had been.

"I'm only thirty-two," she said suddenly, "and that's the *emmis*. I'll show you my birth certificate."

"You have a beautiful complexion," he said.

"Thirty-two last month. Oh, hell," she said. "So what! Nobody got killed." She kissed him boisterously on the mouth. "I'm a cuddler, so kill me. I'm a hugger and kisser. Can you see a kid crying his heart out and not do something?" She ground out her cigarette, unwrapped a toffee from the dish by the bed and tossed it into her mouth. "I blew a two-hundred-thousand-dollar deal for this. Today was the deadline — it was a preemptive bid — and that prick wouldn't give me an extra twenty-four hours if I had rabies." She sighed. "My heart rules my head, *shmuck* that I am. I wonder if I should put in a call?" She glanced at her watch, shrugged, heaved herself down in bed.

"I remember my first time," she said, arching her arm above her head. Moses was so dazzled by the golden fuzz he saw in her armpit he refrained from correcting her. It was not, in fact, his first time, but no matter.

"He was a dentist. Harry Niemuller, or Henry Niemuller. No, Harry. He had offices in Westwood. My aunt sent me to get my teeth capped. I weighed two hundred pounds but she thought if my teeth were capped the whole world would propose to me. We did it in the dental chair. All the time the water kept swishing around in the basin and the goddamn Muzak played selections from *The Merry Widow*. Good old Harry. He even kept on that little headband with the mirror on it. Afterwards he sent me a bill. And the caps went yellow. I had to have it done over. My *mazel*."

Moses could not contain himself. He had to stir the hornet's nest. He had to know how far the line stretched as he took up his position at the end of it.

"You're very beautiful. I guess a lot of others have said that."

Millie wagged a finger under his nose. "You're not a talker," she said. "I'm not a talker."

"Yes, but . . ." Moses felt the sharp teeth of sudden jealousy.

"No buts." She pulled him to her until he rested against the great shelf of her breasts. "Never open closed doors," she said. "You won't like what you see. My God," she went on, "what a skinny. Nobody fed you cheese knishes, I can see that."

His mouth was full of her. Unshyly, he fed. He moved off into a dream under halcyon skies, he groaned his pleasure.

"I've got a screening tonight," she said over his head, and then, "The hell with it." She slid down to meet his mouth.

When he awoke again he was alone in bed. He smelled onions frying and heard someone singing in the kitchen below. He wondered if he should phone and say he would be late for dinner and then hated himself for his childish adherence to old rules: Phone if you're not coming for dinner. Let someone know where you are. Why bake six potatoes if only five people are going to be home?

How removed he was from all that now. He thought briefly

of himself in a Chinese dressing gown. He wondered if red roses would cost more than ten dollars. He had only sent flowers once and they had been to his mother on her birthday.

He rose from the disordered sheets and padded into the bathroom. He saw a damp towel on the floor, lifted it to his face. She had bathed. He had slept away the opportunity of frolicking in the water with her, showering her with bath powder, drying her toes. He wanted to call her back to the chaos of love. But the onions smelled good. He loved fried onions.

He washed his face and hands. He determined as he looked at himself in the mirror that he would grow a mustache. There were other resolutions as well. He would perceive himself differently — matured. He would contain whatever pain he felt so that he was never an object of pity. Tears were behind him forever. He would be a sumptuous, tender and dedicated lover. He would bridge the years between himself and Millie so that all her misgivings would be baseless. He would write a poem. Already it had formed itself. He wrote the first words with her eyebrow pencil on a piece of toilet paper.

# Chapter Five

ONE BLOW ALWAYS follows another. Emma's mother had repeated it all through Emma's childhood, following the statement with a strange resolute smile that seemed to say: "No matter what the problem, I will do battle with it." And it had been so. When money thinned out — which it did frequently, as Emma's father was an indifferent provider — her mother had put on her old felt hat, pinned a mosaic brooch to the front of her dress and had sold the ladies of the neighborhood cosmetics and perfumes that smelled nastily of synthetic rose and lilac and lipsticks of a poisonously dark color that made them all look haggish and near death.

She had wanted an independent and unfettered old age. She had wanted to learn to play the piano. To speak French. She had wanted to read all of Balzac. She yearned to travel. Not to distant places. To San Francisco's Chinatown. To Calexico. To the banks of the Willamette River in its full spring flow. She had thought of turning Catholic. She loved the sonorous Latin chants and the acolytes and the swinging censers, although she was sceptical of everything else.

She would have liked to see Emma every day. That was the

true grief, the secret abiding sorrow; she wanted her daughter where she could see for herself how matters stood with her. Besides, she liked Charles. He came from a hardy family and he had good looks. She liked men with brown hair and gray eyes. Also there was a dark side to him, a Weltschmerz, that she found appealing. He had once pointed out the planet Venus to her and talked to her about her girlhood and gave her maps and an atlas for Christmas.

Emma's uncle called her at the studio and said she ought to come down and see what could be done about Aggie. She wasn't herself and he couldn't get her to say exactly what was wrong. Emma listened with a sense of foreboding. She drove there like a madwoman.

On the journey to her mother's side, Emma examined her allegiance to her. Her turn of mind came from her mother, that quirky and rather fractious way Emma had of looking at the world, for one thing. Her hardihood for another.

She was blunt and Emma was blunt after her. She used the word *wicked*. Lies were wicked. Greed was wicked. Soaking too long in the bathtub was wicked, as was gossip about your neighbors, failing to flush the toilet, family bickering, grudges, cheating in any way, large or small.

Emma thought as she drove past orange groves withering in drought that she would be inconsolable without her. She mistrusted herself without that presence somewhere in the background of her life. She would grow ferocious without that calming hand, that zealous scrutiny. Who would be vigilant for her? Who would be so laudatory of her, available, acclaiming?

When she arrived at the house, her mother was seated in a straight-backed chair near the window. Emma marveled at the beauty of her profile, so pure of line, so exactly formed.

"I'm all packed," her mother said, looking at Emma. "I suppose two house dresses and a sweater will be enough. I doubt if they dress to the nines where I'm going."

"There are seventeen boxes here," Emma began mildly.

"I made my selection. What's left isn't worth preserving.

How come you're here? Did they give you a day off? In my day we gave a good day's work for a good day's wages. You probably lied and said you weren't feeling well."

"I said nothing of the kind." Emma took out a cigarette, held it unlit in her hand. "Now what's all this with you? You seem perfectly bright to me. You had enough sense to put all this together, I see."

The mother knew the child; she would not have matters glossed over, evaded. Emma must understand how treacherous her mind had become, that corners were dim, with strange shapes looming there.

"I'm old," she said querulously. "It's not much fun but there it is. I want you to put me somewhere where there are nurses and doctors. I'd prefer it if it didn't smell of urine. And I don't want to have to eat with a spoon. I'm absent-minded, not crazy. I want it understood that I can button my own sweater. I don't want anyone calling me by my first name unless I expressly give permission. I don't want to be called 'dearie,' either. I'm taking my geranium plant with me wherever I go, let's get that straight. I don't like leaning on you, but false pride is useless."

Emma opened the window and put her hand out into the warm air. She wanted to rage, to swear vilely. Instead, she lit her cigarette, made an agonized grimace her mother could not see and remained perfectly herself.

"Well," she said, "I don't know as anybody would have you. You're a handful. You'll do this, you won't do that. I think you'd better come and stay with me. You can have the sewing room but I don't want you gabbing all day long with Felicia. She won't get any work done. As there's no man in residence at the moment we can stay up all night and talk and drink and carouse. It ought to suit you."

Her mother hardened her voice. "It doesn't," she said, "and I won't come."

Emma kept herself to an easy tone. "No? Why not? We get along when you're not too bossy."

She was answered stridently, harshly. "Don't pretend you

don't understand what's going on here. Every day is less, a new infirmity, a new renunciation. I don't want to have to put on a brave face. I will endure what I must but I'll do it in the company of those in the same leaky boat. I don't want to groan alone in the night. I want a chorus of groans, on all sides of me. I want another shaking hand to hold mine. The bed in your sewing room is terrible. You'll tell me your troubles. I have my own."

"Mother . . ."

"Yes, what is it?"

"Don't be so miserly with yourself. I need you."

Her answer was cross. "You've had me. For a good part of your life. Show some imagination, Emma. If there's any final harmony, I have to find it. I'll write you postcards."

"What am I to do with you?" Emma cried.

"Do what I say. Put me in a home. But no bridge players. No finger painting. I intend to read *War and Peace*."

# Chapter Six

THE FIRST VIEW Emma ever had of Bartolome was a distillation of all that followed. His head was thrown back, his bellow volcanic, the room shook with his outcries and pronouncements. Though ever after she could hardly credit it, he had spat on the floor. Spoon in hand, glaring like a prodded beast, he had spewed a mouthful of soup, spraying an unfortunate nurse and the cook standing perilously near him. Eyes fierce with malice, he rounded on them.

"Slop. Utter slop. Pig slop. Saltless, flavorless, nutritionless slop." He advanced to the counter where the food steamed in unappetizing mounds, snatched off covers, flung them aside and, finally, with a sweep of his heavy arm, he cleared the whole into a mess of broken crockery and scattered vegetables. That done, he stormed to the tables where old people watched, one or two with delighted smiles, the rest with the anticipation of children viewing an antic clown.

"Minkus," he growled, bending toward one of them, "what would you like to eat? Tell me, Minkus. Tell me in a loud voice. What would delight you? What would make the saliva flow, eh, Minkus?"

"A nice brisket," said Minkus promptly, "with potato *kugel*. A glass of beer. Strudel with sour cream. Coffee. A cigar."

"Ah-ha!" trumpeted Bartolome. "Good. Fine."

He moved down the line. "Mrs. Peterson? Mrs. Peterson, the table is set with white linen. The candles are lit. The house is clean. What is on the table, Mrs. Peterson?"

The woman shrugged thin shoulders, hid her pleasure behind her liver-spotted hand. "Anything?" she inquired timidly. "Can it be anything?"

"Anything! Command it. Conjure it. Name it!"

"Roast pork with apples and prunes, then red cabbage with poppy seeds — although with dentures I cannot eat them. An almond tart with little flowers made of the dough on top. Real cream in the coffee."

"Of course real cream," he shouted and moved on. "Mr. Horowitz? Speak out, Mr. Horowitz. What sugar plums dance through your head? What forbidden delights?"

Mr. Horowitz cupped an ear. "I've forgotten what I like," he said.

"You have not forgotten," Bartolome cried, "you have suppressed. You have given up! Think, Horowitz. You took a young lady to dinner. You looked into her eyes, her wonderful velvet eyes. You unfolded a menu as big as a door. You put your hand on your gold watch chain and you said, 'Anything you like, Esther. Anything at all!' "

"Caviar," said Mr. Horowitz in a dreamy way, "a spoonful on a piece of dry toast. A glass of wine. Two glasses. Only there was no Esther."

"Esther, Miriam, Persephone — it's all the same, Mr. Horowitz, all the same."

"It was a big bill," said Mr. Horowitz. "I still remember that."

Bartolome stood before them all. "Everyone," he said, "everyone at once. Call out. Sing out."

There was a babble, a joyous chorus. "Ice cream from Rumpelmayer's." "My mother's white cake." "The first strawberries." "My Aunt Hilda's fudge at Christmas." The voices soared, swelled, until he held up his hands and lunged again toward the hapless staff, grabbing a plate from the table to thrust under their noses.

"Dog's dinner," he said. "Meat of indeterminate origin cut into nasty little bites. You clods have put this food before a judge of the superior court. You have asked a man of sagacity and brilliance to appease the little appetite he has with *dog's* dinner. You have put before these ladies of quality this sludge, this muck. How dare you?" He slammed the plate on the floor. Peas scattered like hard little pellets in all directions. He was not finished with them.

"And when does this travesty take place?" he inquired harshly. "At four-thirty in the afternoon. With the sun still high in the sky, you drag these abused persons into this dingy hall and feed them at your trough. Four-thirty in the afternoon, the middle of the day, storm troopers, is a time for tea served in a fine bone china cup with a slice of lemon and a delectable cookie. It is a time to converse, to listen to Schumann, to recollect in tranquility, to anticipate, to meditate."

He turned back to his flock. "Everybody," he shouted, "everybody on his feet and into the garden. There will be a poetry reading in fifteen minutes. Bring sweaters, it's getting cold. Leave the food. These good people have repented. They're going to make us all a nice omelet with fried onions and little potatoes boiled in their jackets. They're going to make a good pot of coffee and a piece of warm gingerbread with chocolate sauce poured over it. They're going to have it on the table at seven o'clock so we can have time for a nice shower and a little lie down and a back rub — before we come to the table like ladies and gentlemen. They're going to do that or I'm going to have their asses!"

Emma and Aggie, standing in the doorway, laughed aloud in concert. He looked toward them, lifting his massive head. Emma saw then that he was handsome, knotty, vibrant, embattled. His hair sprang from his forehead in black and white streaks, he had an air of impatience, a scornful mouth, a scar slanting across one eyebrow. He had amused eyes.

"The storm has blown out to sea," he said to them. "Come in. I'm Dr. Benjamin Bartolome and, if you're new here, don't be frightened. I'm as meek as a lamb until provoked."

Emma's mother spoke first. She seemed curiously freshened by the hullabaloo — alert, interested.

"I'm Mrs. Agatha Plimpton and this is my daughter, Emma Howard. She's come to look this place over before she unpacks my suitcase. You cut quite a dramatic figure, doctor. A shade actorish."

He was mild as milk now. "I enjoy showing off," he said. Then he looked at Emma, a slow, full look. "You'll want to talk to me. Come into my office." His attention returned to her mother; he inclined toward her, he was benign. "Mrs. Plimpton," he said, "we are reading Conrad Aiken in the garden. 'This is the shape of the leaf, and this of the flower, and this is the pale bole of the tree.' "

"Yes, yes," Agatha said impatiently. "I know the work. I don't like being recited at."

"Maybe you'll read to us. You have a fine speaking voice. Reminds me of a silver dinner bell."

She sniffed. "Indeed."

"That's what it sounds like to me."

"You have a dull ear," Agatha said. "Which way should I go?"

"Out those doors. To the left. You'll smell the roses. We have good healthy roses here."

Emma's mother paused to caution Emma. "Don't be too fussy. Any corner will do me fine. I'd like to be near the bathroom. I get up at night. And I won't take my teeth out. I can't bear the sight of them floating in a water glass by my bed. That's all you have to tell him. He'll discover me a little at a time." Her glance rested on Bartolome. "That's the kind of man you are," she said and she walked slowly out to the roses.

"I will be fussy," Emma said. "Very fussy."

"Don't begin on a quarrelsome note," he told her.

Emma made instant decisions. Her life with Charles had begun like that. She had met him feeding sea gulls on the beach one raw March morning and she had thought she liked the ungainly match of man and birds. She like the deliberate, coaxing manner he had with them, the way he ran and flapped his arms when he had used up all the bread. She had loved a boy in her youth because he had a boxer's broken nose and a hearty laugh. She had always begun with inconsequential things, letting herself be led by the first element that charmed her. It was a risky business, following hunches and intuitions. It did not really signify if a smile reached the eyes. It was no evidence of character if a shock of hair grew this way or that. She'd got into more than one fix on impulse.

She liked the way Bartolome stroked his cat. He sat on his spotted and disreputable couch and made a cradle of his knees. He dabbled behind the cat's ear, softly pulled its tail. He spoke not a word at first, waving her into an uncomfortable chair and addressing himself entirely to the animal.

"Puss, puss," he said without the slightest trace of self-consciousness, "Puss-in-Boots." The cat purred and humped and rubbed against him, well suited by his foolishness. Finally he dumped it onto the floor, turning it out.

"What was your first name again?"

"Emma."

"Emma," he echoed. "Jane Austen wrote of an Emma. Willful girl. Beautiful, but a meddler."

"Just so. About my mother."

He wandered across the room, sat, pushed an untidy pile of papers away to make room for his legs and swung them atop the desk. Elegant haunches, Emma thought.

"Well, this isn't the Ritz, is it?"

"No," she said. "Not even close."

"Most of them are dumped in here," he told her in a wintry tone. "Their worldly possessions are stuffed into old suitcases closed with leather straps, and they come with shameful old toothbrushes and snapshots in silver frames. They put the sheets over their heads the first night and hide. They don't eat the first night — or the second. On Sunday, the kids call from Palm Springs or Las Vegas and speak to the head nurse. 'Tell Papa to be a good boy.' 'Tell Mama to be a good girl.' Sometimes I take those calls." His smile was ferocious. "Indeed I do."

Then he swung around in his chair, opened the window, waved to someone passing. Emma waited.

"Tell me about your mother," he said. "Tell me what you know about her. Let's see how smart you are."

"That's not hard," Emma said. "We're alike."

"Wrong," he interrupted. "She petitions for every single day. You're in your prime. She weighs every pain. You ignore yours. Sex is a memory. Come, come, you know all that."

"She approves of me. I approve of her."

"In short, you love her," he said.

"Any fool could see that," Emma said. She buried her face in her hands.

He was not kind. He was not comforting.

"I've no time for self-pity. If you're going to weep, go down the hall to the ladies' toilet."

Emma lifted her head. "I'm not crying," she said hotly. "I'm nervous and frazzled and you're not helping any."

"Why isn't your husband with you?" he demanded abruptly.

"I don't have to have my hand held," she said.

"I'm not a mean man," he told her. "I'm a burdened one. If you still smoke there's a box on my desk. Help yourself. There's some licorice in that dish. Help yourself. Do you like licorice?"

"No," Emma said.

He shrugged. "One of my patients died this morning. A darling man. Damon O'Casey. I'm very angry about it. He'd been here five years. He was a socialist and a zealot. He insisted on involvement. Mine, his, anyone he could collar. He was always presenting me with petitions and pamphlets. He was a gabby fellow, a windbag, but a great talker, florid, extravagant.

He called me 'dear' and 'son of my bosom' and gave me cheap cigars and rotten bananas when I looked in on him. I don't think he ever washed his feet or his private parts. Wouldn't let the nurses near him. He never complained. He weighed ninety pounds at the end." He got up and began to stride back and forth, his hands jammed into his pockets. Emma felt the weight of his mood.

"I called his son in New York to tell him. He asked me if I could handle it at this end. I said, 'Listen to me, pricko, if you mean can I wash his body and put him in a blue suit and ask a priest to mumble a little Latin over the cheapest coffin I can find, yes, I can do that, you son of a bitch. Can I marshal a few mourners to come and blow their noses at the graveside, yes, I can do that too. Can I say he was cherished and valued when his only son can't get off his fat ass to fly out here? No, I cannot." He picked up a heavy book and slammed it down on his desk.

"Do you take them all this hard?" Emma asked.

"I liked his cheap cigars."

The cat leaped on the desk. He picked it up, draped it like a fur collar around his neck. "The masses are asses," he said. He popped some licorice into his mouth. "Penny candy is good — only now it costs fifty cents. What are you doing about dinner?"

"I haven't decided."

"I'm supposed to take a carton of yogurt. Will you take a carton of yogurt with me? And maybe a little drive, with the windows down and some music on."

"Yes, I'll do that."

"I gained ten pounds this year. I go to a Jewish doctor who is insane on the subject of weight. We could go to an Italian restaurant. I'm Italian and I know good food."

"Listen to your doctor," Emma said. "Let's stay with the yogurt."

He picked up a sweater from the general tangle behind his desk. "Old people are my business. Your mother will be all right."

"I'll hold you responsible if she isn't," Emma said.

"I won't bother to answer that," he said. He walked out of the office ahead of her. Emma and the cat followed.

Emma heard her mother's voice carry on the still, warm air. Bartolome strode into the garden toward the sound, pausing as he came on the tableau. The old people were settled in their chairs, their faces lifted and expectant as they listened. Here and there a head nodded as they followed the cadenced verse, each pursuing a separate dream, recollecting the things they loved best.

"*Sing the pure phrase, sweet phrase, clear phrase in the twilight,*
*To fill the blue bell of the world;*
*And we, who on music so leaflike have drifted together,*
*Leaflike apart shall be whirled. . .*"

One woman raised a fragile hand as if the words had blown toward her and she was gathering them in. "Yes," she said aloud. No one admonished her. They were composed, provided for beyond their everyday needs.

Emma, standing at a distance, was as infatuated as the rest. Her mother seemed a luminous stranger to her, her cheeks flushed scarlet, her white hair a silky nimbus. She was intoxicated, inspired, as she spoke the shaped and chosen words:

"*Into what but the beauty of silence, silence forever? . . .*"
*. . . This is the shape of the tree,*
*And the flower and the leaf . . .*

Her voice trailed off. An old man bobbed up and clapped vigorously. The others sighed and stirred and looked into one another's faces.

Bartolome thanked her gravely. "If I weren't ashamed in front of all of them," he said, "I would cry openly." As it was, he took out a handkerchief and blew his nose.

"Maybe we won't eat dinner," he said to Emma. "Maybe we'll just sit out here until dark and get drunk on words. 'Like dancers,' " he quoted, " 'who wait in a pause of the music, for music the exquisite silence to fill.' "

"You know it by heart," Agatha said.

He nodded. "A verse or two."

Someone spoke querulously. "I want my dinner."

"Yes, the sun is down."

Another voice quavered. "I'm tired."

Slowly they drifted and fluttered toward the door, those ahead pausing to let the laggards catch up, wanting to move in concert, embraced by the same feelings.

Her mother paused at Emma's side. "Run along now," she said. "I'm going to like it here. I'll queen it over them all."

"No doubt," Emma said. "Shall I see you to your room?"

"I'm not a baby to be tucked in."

"Will you give me a kiss, then?"

She received a peckish one. "Now don't be silly, Emma. I hate tears."

"So do I."

"Well, then, off with you."

"I'm just going."

"You're not. You're standing there gawking at me."

Emma did not trust herself to argue. Bartolome rescued her by bearing down on them.

"This is not a final leave-taking," he commanded. "Say good night to your mother and wait for me in my car. It's the dirty Chevrolet parked in front. Go on."

Emma did as she was told. From across the yard she turned, but Bartolome had offered her mother his arm and they were walking away, heads inclined to each other like old familiars.

His car smelled of dog and stale pipe tobacco. There were stacks of books on the seat and candy bar wrappers and a pair of rakish dark glasses hanging from the mirror. There was an Indian blanket of scratchy wool folded over the bulging springs of the torn upholstery. There was a curved and beautiful seashell resting on the dashboard and, beside it, a boy's pocket-knife, a resplendent knife with a corkscrew and a can opener with a file attached to it. There was one shoe with a missing heel.

Emma sank into the disorder with a sigh of pleasure. She thought without guilt of her own untidied desk, of her unfinished work. She thought of calling home and then decided against it. She needed to be cosseted, if only for an hour or two, and she meant to be good to herself. There was something salty and tonic about the doctor; better he than a solitary drink and fitful thrashing through the night. In a moment of honesty, Emma admitted a further truth. She liked the ferocious downward curve of his mouth. She liked his extravagant, operatic air. He *had* been close to tears at her mother's reading. She marveled at emotion so quickly summoned, so full, so charged. Charles lived deep within himself. Life with him had been like fishing, with numb hands, through a hole in the ice. How often she had come up empty-handed from those forays. But was she ready to emerge from her cocoon of lazy solitude, of greedy self-indulgence? Was she willing to give up those long meditative hours that belonged only to her; was she prepared to adapt, to welcome, to accommodate? She was, she decided, prepared to eat a carton of yogurt in the company of this slightly imperious and undeniably romantic fellow.

He got into the car beside her, wind-blown and impatient. "I have to be back in half an hour," he said. "Mr. Galliston has indigestion. He wants to resort to an enema, and he'll take it himself if I don't get back in time to stop him. No music, no ride to the beach. I am underpaid for the life I live."

The car would not start. He pumped gas until the engine flooded, he jiggled the key in the ignition, he put his face in his hands. "Nothing works," he said. "Last night the smoke from my fireplace came back into the room and blackened the walls. A Makonde tribal fetish fell from the bookcase and was totally destroyed. The water heater went cold. I have not been in a good humor all week. I have had bouts of most unpleasant melancholy. I feel an absence of rationality in my life. It's from living alone, I would say. Do you know that you can die of a broken heart?" He nodded his head. "Yes, of a broken heart. It's literally true. People living alone pine and fade and grow ill. They die on the stalk."

"Then why do you?" Emma asked.

"I'm a widower," he told her, "and have been for five years."

"I'm sorry."

"Yes," he said. "It's made me irascible and unpleasant. That mustn't happen. My work with old people requires profound calm and tolerance. I burn the toast every morning. It's a bad start to the day."

"How long were you married?"

"Fifteen years. Blissfully." He glanced at her. "There's a price for everything," he said. "And you? Are you married? Divorced? Living celibately? Living wickedly?"

"In limbo," Emma said. "I don't talk about it."

"No? Why not?"

"Because it's a boring, familiar story. Because I can't entirely exonerate myself." Even as she spoke, she made a firm resolve not to grumble or whine. She wondered if she could come upon her old manner, her old methods. She had been told on occasion that she was capable of witchery when she tried. Quite suddenly, she wanted to appear at her best with him. She did not want to chronicle woes. She wanted to trot out her wares. She used to have quite a good mind, she thought, and quick humor and a direct and guiltless lust. She could lay claim to some small accomplishments: she could speak two languages and shoot pool, she could whistle and stand on her head, she was fearless, she was never tired, she was rarely jealous. She did not entirely lack dignity.

"Well," he said, "I don't care about your past, when you come right down to it. And mine is a closed book." He frowned and looked rather severe. "I wasn't disposed to ask you

out, you know. I did it deliberately to see if I could manage it."
She was disbelieving. "You're not shy," she said.
"No," he said, "I'm still in love with my wife."

The waitresses knew him and pampered him. They kept bringing little dishes of odorous pickles and limp, gray sauerkraut to the table.

Emma reached into her pocket for a cigarette. Bartolome glared at her.

"Don't smoke. I object to smoking where food is served."

Emma said, "You're cantankerous, aren't you?" She put the pack away, leaned her elbows on the table. "I don't know," she began dryly. "All my life I've been surrounded by touchy men. My father was full of crotchets. We were not allowed to drink water with meals. We could not read in bed. He frowned on high heels, as he was convinced they threw a woman's pelvis out of line. My uncle Ned has claustrophobia and believes in astrology. He won't speak to you on certain ill-augured days. Except to my mother, he does not give birthday or Christmas presents on a principle he has never explained. My husband would not make love on Wednesdays. He would not wear green. He was afraid of lightning. He buttoned his shirt from the bottom up." She paused and pulled reflectively on her ear lobe. "I'm not sure I can stand any more eccentrics."

Bartolome regarded her. It was an appraisal. "You're one yourself."

"No," Emma refuted, "I'm no such thing."

"I can't give you particulars. I merely sense it. One of my oddities is a touch of clairvoyance."

"Oh, my God," Emma said. "I think you may be the worst of the lot."

Bartolome picked up his tea. It was in a glass, at his particular request, with a napkin wrapped around it. He drank deeply, letting her wait for him.

"You're an interesting woman," he said almost reproachfully. "You appear to be concerned, emotional, rather slapdash, tart, arousing. You stir up a breeze in your wake. Maybe a hurricane; I don't know yet. I'm not sure I want to go any further with you."

Emma raised an eyebrow but she was far from indignant. She liked encounters on this plane, rather high-handed and aggressive, combative.

"You're like the Mad Hatter," she said, "asking for more when you haven't had any."

"See here," he said sharply, "I'm not inclined to go through the usual foolish rigmarole, the courting dance, the mating dance. I've no time for it. I do important work. I'm tired. My temper is short."

"Yes," she said. "You're on a short fuse, I can see that."

"Damn," he said hotly. "I hate all this mucking around that has to go on before there's a connection. I had a wife who was used to me. Who understood me." He ran his fingers through his hair, gazed wrathfully around him. "I can't live like a monk. That's not my nature. I tried it. For a long time I wanted nothing but quiet and peace, but now it's all coming back, all the old feelings. My health is suffering. I suppose you're like the rest. Avid for flattery. I suppose you want petting and pampering, avowals — all that nonsense!"

"What," Emma asked coolly, "are you offering instead?"

"Nothing. This is madness. Absolute madness. You're a stranger. I've no business with you. None at all." He picked up his napkin, slammed it down again. The people at the next table glanced furtively at them, arrested, forks in hand, anticipating a crisis, a fracas, a scene. Bartolome rounded on them.

"Back to your bread pudding," he said. "There will be no more ruckus. Eat up."

Emma laughed. "How did your wife put up with you at all?"

"Tessa," he said darkly, "was a divinity, no mere woman."

"She would have had to be, I fear."

"My dear lady," he said haughtily. "I have, when I wish to resort to it, considerable charm. Understand that I had an Italian father with a barrel chest and bedroom eyes. A father from

Genoa who could quote three thousand lines of Dante and who maintained an erection, or so he claimed, for five consecutive hours. A father whose wife kissed his hand with gratitude at the breakfast table. My mother was an artist, impassioned and beautiful. I am the child of uxoriousness. Do you want something more to eat or are you finished?" He beckoned the waitress with a snap of his fingers.

"Bartolome . . ." Emma said.

"If you are speaking to me," he told her, "I have a first name. Benjamin."

"Very well, Benjamin. Dare I call you Ben?"

"Why not?"

"Some men object to diminutives."

"Ben, Benjy, Beniamino . . . I answer to all of them."

He turned in his chair, called for the check with choleric insistence. "I haven't got all night over here!"

Emma waited. He turned back to her.

"You were saying?" His attention was scant, he was looking at the clock on the wall, checking it against the one on his wrist.

"I was about to ask," Emma said, "if we could possibly begin calmly."

A long look passed between them. For a moment Emma saw with immense pleasure the two of them grappling, close, disheveled. She saw herself performing with marvelous agility, a veritable acrobat, poised on his chest, his flanks, his supporting arms. She saw herself striking attitudes, experimenting, submitting at last to authority. She almost laughed aloud.

Then she saw that his eyes were cool, his glance obstinate and inaccessible. "No," he said, denying her. "Not calmly. I'm in an agitated state. In a rash mood."

"And I," Emma said, "am in a wary one."

If only he could see her history spread before him. Look where imprudence had led her. My God, the men accepted on whim, in haste, on trust, the airy arrivals and departures of her life.

"Listen to me," she said. "I am forty years old. My husband

is off gallivanting and sporting with a woman half my age. I have two very tall young sons to dig worms for as they sit in the nest with their craws open, demanding to be fed. In some area of my life, it's time I showed good sense. I can't just go throwing my hat over garden walls. I have responsibilities. People are pulling at my coattails. I would like an affair. More, I would dearly love one. But I have enough disorder in my life, enough gall and wormwood. I want to lie on my back and yawn and scratch. I don't want to be mauled and reprimanded. My God, I believe you'd leave your thumb print on my windpipe, the way you carry on. I really do."

He hurled past her prudence, he would have none of it. With a threatening finger thrust under her nose he launched into a harangue. He was a doctor, a psychiatrist, these matters were his daily study. Let her take heed, let her be warned that the complaint he heard most often uttered from old people was regret for missed opportunities, for moments of indulgence, foolishness, lighthearted, wildhearted abandon they had never dared sample. Why hadn't they run off with the Russian fiddle player instead of settling for the gentle dentist? Why had they weeded their gardens when they might better have entwined their hair with vine leaves? Why had they ministered and tended, saved and scrupled, when they might have nibbled the crisp, cold, forbidden apple and felt the dry coil of the snake embracing their bare legs?

"No," he said violently. "I don't think you and I would get along. I'll look elsewhere."

He scraped back his chair and rose. He did not help her into her coat.

"Well, damn you," Emma cried. But he did not hear. He was already halfway to the door.

# Chapter Seven

THE TWINS SANG in the bathroom above Cleo's head, one alto, one tenor. She imagined them in clouds of bath powder, hard buttocks bunching as they anointed and scented and dried beneath their scrotums. She found their exuberance altogether too much for her. She wished they would be quiet so she could hear the two notes of the blue jay calling over and over from the red hibiscus bush. She preferred the hum of the telephone wires, the barely audible sound of the bubbles rising in her goldfish tank. It sat on the bedside table with two puny fish bumping blindly into the gravel in search of food. Cleo admired that patient rooting. It was akin to what she did, ever searching, ever seeking, turning every stone. She overfed them regularly. Two had died on her already. She knew she was too anxious about them. She wondered if she kept them only to study the pitilessness of death.

She had taken over the sewing room and made it hers. She had put the sewing machine out of sight. She had set out a jar of sunflower seeds, a small plaster Buddha with a foolish smile on its plaster face, two tins of tea, one chamomile for health and one scented with jasmine for use when she felt a black mood coming on. And come on they did. She had hung necklaces on the bed post and had lined up her ballet slippers in a neat row along one wall. She had asked for a key to the room, obtained it, hung it around her neck on a yellow cord. She had nothing to conceal but *terra incognita* was a way of life with her.

Her sleep on the narrow bed was troubled. She was not certain she was at home in this house. The wind tossed the trees at night and Felicia spoke on the telephone at all hours, exhorting her lover in Spanish to go to the immigration office and to the bank and to the grocery store. Cleo felt the man must be at his wits' end with the constant stream of directives. There was never an endearment. Generally the conversations ended with Felicia slamming the phone down on its cradle. Cleo, ear to the wall, was like a lizard transfixed in the sun. She could not move away from the malediction, the violence. She half-expected the man to come to the house and kill Felicia. She rather hoped for it.

One night, when she was sure she was unobserved, she opened the door and slipped into the hall, picking the phone up by its long cord, dragging it back into the room with her. She sat cross-legged on her bed and thought for a moment. Then she dialed. Her head ached slightly, the muscles in her neck were stiff, there was a rapid excited pulse in her throat.

"Mr. Jessup, please." She was routed through an irate cook, a Filipino houseboy. She waited. At last he came on the line.

"Mr. Jessup? This is Cleo . . . *Cleo.* Do you mean to say you don't remember me when you've asked me to appear in your film? . . . Well, don't tease. I'm not noted for my sense of humor. If you keep on laughing, I will not be able to give you my message . . . What? I don't understand what efficacious means . . . Laughter is efficacious? Oh. Well, Mr. Jessup, what I wanted to say was that, per your request, Adam and I are coming to your house to rehearse. If you wish me to remain afterward, after Adam leaves, I'm willing to do so. I come and go as I please . . . Yes, I know how old you are. It doesn't matter . . . Well, Mr. Jessup, if it comes to that, there are many impressive old things — redwoods for one . . . Why are you laughing again? . . . Stay the whole night? I can't say yes or no to that at this time. My moods alter. I never decide in advance." She hung up abruptly, holding the phone in her lap. She felt a strange shiver that was not cold nor heat. She was pleased with herself.

Emma went back to the studio for her briefcase and a stack of manuscripts. The corridors were empty. She passed Stewart Bolen's office and saw that the name plate had been removed. It had been done overnight. There remained only two small holes on the door; it looked as though it had been peppered mischievously with a BB gun. She went in, stood in the middle of the room. It was as if a pernicious wind had scattered the ashes of a dead man. She thought furiously of Mason's promise when he thought his own death loomed before him. He had recovered — Bolen was gone. Nothing remained behind but a cheap glass ashtray and a hooded typewriter. Gone were the pictures of his wife in a becoming leghorn hat, his white poodle, his ancestral home in Virginia. Gone, his Waterman pen, his French paperweight. She prowled uneasily, lifted a window, hoping to dispel the sour, exhausted air. They had left not a shred of him. There was no residue of the twenty years he had spent in this room.

She sat down in his chair, musing on the other indignities he faced. There would be the explanations to friends: Early retirement. Yes, he had elected early retirement to grow artichokes and read Cicero. There would be the harrowing leisure to fill. A walk in the park in the morning, the pretext of papers to be put in order in the afternoon, no subterfuge for the evening at all. It would be passed in the dark, silently, with his hand resting on his dog's head, his breath coming slowly, his heartbeat coming slowly, his mind dying slowly.

"Emma?"

Emma looked up. Mason watched her from the doorway. It seemed to her that his face had altered, that some force had undone the surgeon's work, that he had been punished for vanity with extra shadows and folds. He was no longer natty, his eyes were full of mute appeal.

"I'm not supposed to be here," he said. "The doctors want me to stay in bed. Who can stay in the hospital? Who can use a bedpan? The goddamn nurses stand outside your room all night talking about getting laid. How are you, Emma?" He squinted at her. "Your mouth's like a prune. What's the matter?"

She indicated the empty office. "So much for deathbed promises," she said flatly.

Mason made an irritable gesture, advanced, dropped wearily on the sofa. "Am I God?" he said, looking at her. "What do you want from me? I was in the hospital. I was hooked up to a machine. I had a tube up my nose, in my penis. I had other worries. Someone fucked up. They let him go. Kill me."

"I'd like to," Emma said.

Mason took a cigar from his packet, stuck it, unlit, into his mouth. "I can't even have a smoke. No steak. No liquor. No women. I'm supposed to take walks. Wonderful. If the Board gets a look at my medical records, I'll take a walk all right. Out of here! Goddamn vultures. Wait till it's their turn." He chewed the end of the cigar into wet pulp. "I've been thinking about you, Emma," he said.

She accepted that with no show of interest whatsoever.

"I'm gonna put you in Bolen's job. We've got to move a woman up, so it might as well be you. You're the only woman around here who doesn't think with her cunt."

"Charming," Emma said coldly.

"It's not a favor. I don't do favors. I want this department brought into line, sharpened up. We've missed a couple of hot properties. Agents come to us last. I want 'em here first. The exhibitors are crying. They've got nothing to sell but popcorn. They're showing reruns in empty theaters. We're going to take some chances from now on. When I don't see a story, make me see it. When I say no, make sure I'm right. Stay on me. You'll be looking at scripts. If they need work, send 'em back, get rewrites. Don't let some kid director *tell* you what he's got in mind — see it on the page. Bring your beefs to me. Scare 'em downstairs with that. You'll have an expense account. Don't remodel your kitchen on it. I check it myself. You get it all, Emma, and you don't even have to sleep with me."

He waited for Emma's response. She took her time.

"A dead man's shoes," she said. "You're putting me in a dead man's shoes."

"If they fit you, wear 'em."

"Stewart was a friend."

Mason undid his collar, wrenched his tie loose. "You wanna hear something?" he said. "My father was a rabbi. A scholar. A gentleman. For twenty years he served a congregation. He married 'em, he buried 'em. He listened to their troubles. He sat up with 'em when they were sick. He closed their eyes. You know what he got for it? Fired. They wanted somebody younger, a nice-looking rabbi with charm. A new face. They'd heard my father's sermons. They wanted something new. A little est, maybe, a little dianetics . . . something to keep up with the times." He smiled wolfishly. "Religious people, I'm talking about. Not movie makers. My father took sleeping pills. He washed them down with sacramental wine. Nice touch, huh? The new rabbi buried him. Take the job, Emma. It's the world we live in."

They sat in silence for a moment. A cleaning woman appeared with mop and pail and looked blankly at them, then moved on. Mason rose, threw his cigar out the window, stared into the night.

"Who's your agent?" he asked.

"Millie Asher."

"I know her. She'll drive nails right through my heart."

"Probably."

"Well, what do you say, Emma? I could use one friend on the premises." He coughed heavily, clutching his chest. "Nobody came to the hospital. In two weeks. Not even you."

"They told me, 'No visitors.' "

He nodded, placated. "I sleep with the light on," he said absently. "Like a little kid. A fifty-year-old man."

"Enough," Emma said. "I'll take the job."

"Smart," he said.

She half-expected him to spit on his hands. His forebears had, but she had no way of knowing that.

Felicia fed the kids in the kitchen — tacos, burritos, chili beans. The boys wolfed their food, Cleo ate a lettuce leaf, a thin slice of tomato. She was fearful that the smell of frying meat had already permeated her newly washed hair. She felt as if her life were about to take a new turn and she wanted to come to it in the utmost purity, with an empty stomach, shampooed tresses, garbed in a blouse with white butterfly sleeves.

It was plain that Felicia had been smoking the cannabis leaf. She slammed the plates on the table, kissed Adam fiercely on the forehead, laughed uproariously at every sally. She took a carton of ice cream from the freezer and sat spooning it into her mouth as if there were an empty sack just below her gullet.

Judicious Adam was concerned. "Felicia," he said, "grass is a very dumb move for you. You're going out on the town tonight and some cop will cruise by and see you at the bus stop and, the state you're in, you'll whack him on the butt. Next thing you'll end up in the pokey."

Moses stopped him. "Let her alone. Is something worrying you, Felicia?"

"My life worries me." She waved a spoon at them. "My children of three different fathers worry me. Your mother worries me. You worry me most of all." She threw the empty carton in the direction of the sink, chucking it backward over her head. It missed. Ice cream oozed across the floor.

Moses hitched his chair close to her. "It's Hermanos, isn't it? He hasn't been around here lately."

"Hermanos," she made a dismissive gesture. "Without me around, he cannot wipe his ass. Also if he fornicates with fifteen-year-old girls, they will cut off his balls and deport him."

She seemed to grow cheerful at the thought. "He will not be able to watch the Angels play baseball. It will kill him." She seemed to become aware of Cleo.

"I can see through your shirt," she said sternly. "I can see the two little peaches in there. If my fruit was that green, I would not put it out on a plate. Who is this child?"

"That's Cleo," said Moses. "You already know that, Felicia. She's a friend of ours."

"I don't think so."

Cleo brushed her hair back with her hands. "Shouldn't we be going? I don't think we should be late."

Adam glanced uneasily at Moses. "What's on for you tonight?"

"I've got something fixed up."

"Yeah? What?"

"Something. You go ahead."

Adam stirred uncomfortably in his chair. He was not accustomed to Moses edging away from him; he was not used to his air of stealth, of carefully preserved privacy. Besides, Moses had made special ablutions. He had cut his toenails and trimmed a wayward hair from his nostril. Moreover, he appeared to have forsworn Cleo, taking a new brotherly air with her, as if he had never longed for her favors or burned for her touch. It was strange, strange. Some line had been snapped between them, some connection severed. And there was the matter of his having aced Moses out for the picture. Ordinarily Moses was a bad loser, sulky, stormy, an asshole in fact, when nosed out. Now his attitude was insouciant, his smile close to lewd.

"Who is she?" Adam asked, feeling rivalry in his bones.

"Tut," said Moses. "Tut, tut." He beamed brightly.

"What's that supposed to mean? Okay. So you've got something going. Fine. Wonderful. Who gets the car? I need wheels."

"I'll walk." Moses was affable. "I don't mind walking. If I get tired, I'll put my thumb up."

Adam cocked his head. "There's something cooking here."

Moses swaggered a little. "You two go act. Act up a storm. And when the time comes I'll buy a ticket, sit in the front row and clap my hands. I'll be your biggest fan."

"Maybe I'll come with you," Adam said, suddenly wanting to.

Cleo cried out in protest. "I can't say my lines without you. You're committed to this evening. You can't run off with him."

"I always have," Adam said. "Rick and rack, tick and tack, isn't that right, Mo?"

"To date," Moses said, "that's the way it's been."

"Who is she?" Adam asked again. "I'll tail you. I'll track you down. You know that, Mo."

"I'm going to the bowling alley," Moses said, "where I'll rack up an enormous score. Then I'll have a beer, tell a joke or two and come on home. I'll laugh myself sick at an old Buster Keaton movie, drink some milk, eat some cookies, and retire for the night."

"The next thing you know," Adam said, "you'll be joining up with the CIA and have a microphone wired to your ass." He shook his head. His brother was bothering him.

"You have to know everything, is that it?" Moses' voice rose, as it did when he felt prodded. "Have to be in on everything."

Cleo rose to her feet, held out her arms. In her wide-sleeved blouse, she looked like a young priestess imploring peace.

"Stop it. I can't stand fighting. I can't endure dissension. Don't you know you're David and Jonathan, Damon and Pythias, two halves of one seed?"

Adam cooled, grinned. "Hey, Mo, you're half a seed."

"Fuck you," Moses said. His blood was up.

Felicia rose and collared them both, bringing their heads within an inch of each other, then thrusting them back into their chairs again.

"Now I'll speak," she said.

"No," Emma said from the doorway, "I will." Even in her wrath, the boys doted on her. They sensed her purpose, admired her fiber, knew her virtues. They had witnessed her briarish hold on life, had felt the spit and hiss of her anger, knew her for flesh and blood. They loved what was raw and demanding in her, what was bawdy and high-kicking. They endured her reproaches for the acceptance that invariably followed hard on its heels.

"Now," Emma said, "what exactly is going on here? I heard you clear out in the driveway. So did our neighbors. What's the fuss? And talk one at a time."

"Nothing," they said in unison.

"Nothing, huh? 'Fuck you' is nothing?"

Adam tipped back in his chair, in charge of things. "Well, this pup here was trying to get off the leash. I was merely checking on him. It's common knowledge that in this twosome I'm the one that's got the horse sense. If he wants to rear up and resent it, there's nothing I can do about it."

Emma turned to Moses. "Stop biting your lip and tell me what's eating you. Briefly."

"If you'll excuse me," Moses said on his dignity, "I have an engagement."

Emma threw her bag and the car keys on the table. "Listen," she said with ire, "both of you. I've had a hard day. I've put my mother in a home, my head aches and I'm in no mood for your growing pains. I'm the one to be considered around here tonight. Is that clear?"

"Yes, ma'am," Adam said.

"I'm sorry," Moses said. "How is Grandma?" He came to Emma's side, put his arms around her. She smelled bay rum.

"Grandma." Emma sounded weary. "Grandma's old. And it's a lousy prospect any way you look at it." She pushed the debris on the table away from her, sank into a chair, closed her eyes.

"All of you," Felicia said, coming to life, "all of you, out. And don't make any noise when you come back. Your mama and I will be asleep."

She dug into her apron pocket, came up with a brown cigarette, held it out to Emma. "It's very good stuff," she said. "I have it growing in your back yard."

Emma roused herself, looked at her. "What did you do with the parsley?" she asked.

"What good is parsley?"

Emma took the cigarette, lit it, dragged the smoke deep into her lungs, passed it to Felicia who followed suit.

"Well," Adam said. "I guess we'll be going."

"Good night, Mom," Moses said at the door.

"A good night is on its way," said Emma. "And not a moment too soon."

"Once again," Jessup said, "and this time without making faces, young woman. You and this boy are about to run away from your home, your families. Hell will break loose over your heads. You are trying to take comfort from him. He's going to be your mother and your father from now on. There's not much sex in it."

"We've done it twenty times," said Cleo. "Why are you so finicky? We know all the lines."

"Forget the lines. I'm not concerned about the lines. Have you ever missed someone? Been homesick? It doesn't have to be a person: a dog, a doll, a room, a time in your life. Yes... think of a room, your own room, with a pink seersucker bedspread on the bed and a little vase of wild flowers on the table. You've dropped your dress on the floor, the afternoon is quiet. You've half fallen asleep over a book. There's a little sweat on your upper lip. It's a hot day. No one disturbs you. Look around. There you are — the essence of you — your brushes on the dresser, a note from a boy which you have read twelve times, a powder puff — not a clean one — a hair ribbon. You've awakened every morning of your life to the same light on the wallpaper, the same shadow from the same tree. Now all that's finished. There will be a room overlooking a neon sign. There will be a dirty bathroom with one melting cake of soap. There will be the smell of other people, strangers, on the sheets, on the pillows. Someone has burned the covers with a cigarette. Perhaps someone has jumped from the window. That's where this boy is taking you, and the hand he holds out to you is none too clean. What about that? You shrink from that too." He paused, waiting for a response. She looked at him blankly. "Nothing, eh?" He sprang up with electric energy. "We'll try once more."

"I'm tired," Cleo wailed.

He balanced lightly on his feet, did a capering little dance of a step or two. He pursed his mouth. "You have made an agreement with me. If I had bought a horse from you or a pig, I would expect you to deliver me a horse or a pig."

"I think she's pretty pooped, sir," Adam said politely.

"Then go home," he ordered peremptorily. "I am kind to my actors."

"It's three in the morning, sir."

"I do not wear a watch. Finished. Done. Good night."

He walked across the large, empty living room, his footsteps echoing on the Spanish tile.

Cleo looked at Adam. "You run along," she said. "I want to clear something up. I'll take a taxi."

Adam intervened in a mild tone. "You'd better come back with me," he said, "because what you're after you're not likely to get. Honey, this man is pretty close to seventy. He's going to put some liniment on his back and get himself some sleep now."

"Please don't interfere with me," Cleo said. "I'm accustomed to deciding for myself."

"You aren't showing much sense." He took her by the hand. "We're being shown the door."

Jessup agreed from his position near it. "You're wrong about the liniment. I'm remarkably agile and free from all pain, but you're right about my going to bed. As you can see, I'm on my way."

Cleo tugged free of Adam, gave him a mean little shove. "I want a word with you in private," she said to Jessup. "And, anyway, I need to use the bathroom. Which way is it, please?"

"You'll find it through those doors," Jessup said.

Cleo marched away. Jessup beckoned Adam to his side.

"Are you in love with this girl?" he asked.

"No, sir. I'm just here for the ride."

"And how old are you?"

"Seventeen. Eighteen in July."

"Old enough. My dear boy," Jessup said. "I have nightmares — angels and demons locked in combat, with my poor self as the prize. I have tried everything. Psychoanalysis, warm milk, barbiturates, marriage. I find the only remedy that is at all helpful is a young woman. Yes. There seems to be something about those thin arms locked around one, that sweet and milky breath, that is remarkably comforting. King David resorted to them, if you know your Bible. I have never been in love. Three former wives will testify to the truth of that. I am indifferent to everything but my work and my death. Can you find your way down the path? I've shut off the lights to conserve energy."

"If you liked women," Adam said slowly, "I'd feel better about walking out of here."

Jessup let out a cry and clasped Adam to his bosom. "Delicious! Chivalrous! So much like your mother." He urged Adam to the door, opened it. Together they stepped out into the soft night air. "My dear good child," he went on, "you'd do better to worry about me. Good night, Adam."

Wordlessly, Adam made for the stairs. Jessup called after him: "There's a broken flagstone near the bottom — mind where you go."

When he returned to the living room, Cleo stood before him, entirely naked, entirely willing to play his game.

Moses approached Millie's house with two bunches of daisies in his hand. He had bought them off a sly-looking boy who was selling them on Sunset Boulevard, boldly setting up his stand on a private lawn. The boy had finagled him into buying two bunches, telling him that they had been picked fresh that morning and he was only giving him the two for a dollar because he had to meet a girl and he was already late. When Moses protested that the flowers had seen better days, the enterprising lad picked off the drooping leaves, dunked them into a bucket of water, shook them vigorously and pronounced them perfect.

Moses felt slightly foolish wandering around Beverly Hills with daisies in his hand, but he had been brought up to be thoughtful and the flowers seemed like a properly sentimental gesture. There were lovely things growing in the gardens he passed and he was more than tempted to add to the bouquet, but he had also been brought up to be scrupulously honest, so he let well enough alone, except for sniffing a fine bud here and there as he walked along.

There was some anxiety in his state of mind as well. He thought his initial success with Millie had been compounded of an odd mix. The more he mulled it over, the more he saw how it had come about. There had been something maternal in it on her part and something slightly babyish on his. He wanted to put all that aside now and sail boldly on like the man he felt himself to be.

He considered himself in some ways older and wiser than Millie, even though she ran a hot-shot agency, saw her name appear in the newspapers and called a major Eastern potentate by his first name. Take the extra weight she packed, for instance. Hunger pains and other pains had something to do with each other. He perceived that she was lessening some old affront, some painful slight, when she gobbled the peanuts she left on her bedside table or the huge sandwiches she had brought to their bed. He found nothing gross in that — she made very good sandwiches — but it was Moses' way to get to the center of things, and he thought that any lady who did away with two candy bars and a quart of milk before she turned out the light had something on her mind. It wasn't that he wanted to pry. He wanted, if possible, to offer some kind of comfort if he could find a way that wasn't rude or discommoding. He liked Millie enormously. He liked her bellicosity, the sharp jab of her gestures, the peal, swell and alarum of her voice. He admired the way she could talk on the phone with one hand while she cupped his balls with the other. He loved looking up at her pensile breasts. He marveled at her peppery way with the language, oath following upon rotund oath. He wanted to tell her his troubles and have her annul his miseries. He wanted to be friends.

There were others before him. Moses saw a hundred cars lining the street below her house and on the driveway leading to it. He saw half-a-dozen prompt young men in red uniforms snapping doors open and helping ladies alight, calling out, "Watch your step," and, "Have a nice evening," as they palmed five-dollar bills or slid them into their skintight jeans.

He approached warily.

"You on foot, bub?" This last was spoken in a spirit of utter contempt by one of the jumping jacks.

"My brother took the Rolls tonight," he said. "It was his turn."

"Where's your invitation, friend? This is an invitation-only party."

He held out his flowers. "Florist delivery," he said.

"Are you kidding?"

"No," Moses said mildly, "some people believe in simplicity, is all."

A Jaguar roared up beside them, diverting attention from Moses. He walked on, unaccosted by anyone until he reached the door and rang the bell.

"Good evening, sir." The black man who stood before him was seven feet tall with an Atlas spread of shoulders.

"Hello," said Moses. "How are you?"

"Just fine, sir." The man blocked the doorway. He could have blocked a standing army.

"I wonder," said Moses, "if you could put these in water while I go in and catch up with everybody."

The butler examined Moses' tennis shoes and the section of jeans he had sewn together earlier that very evening.

"I see you're looking at my clothes," he said. "These are my good clothes. My everyday clothes are pretty cruddy, but I figured since this was a party..." He looked brightly beyond the man. "Is that a fountain I hear?"

"Yes, sir. A wine fountain. Recirculating. You know what I think, sir?"

"No, I don't," Moses said.

"I think you've come to the wrong house."

Moses nodded. "I can see where you'd get that idea. I guess I look like I should be at a dog fight or something similar. I've got a cashmere sweater at home but it's a warm night so I didn't put it on. Would you have let me in if I was wearing a double-ply cashmere sweater? The reason I ask is I think it's a shame how we go by appearances. For instance, you look like a killer and I'll bet you're a deacon in your church."

"I'm both," the man at the door said.

At that moment Millie sailed by in a mirrored caftan. She had a red flower behind one ear. She had removed her shoes and was carrying them in one hand. Her face looked as if her feet hurt, and they did.

"Moses," she cried, spotting him. "What the hell are you doing here?"

"Visiting," he told her.

She hurried toward him, breathing fire and gardenia eau de toilette. "Shit," she said, "this is no place for you. I've got a goddamn party going here. I've got studio heads. I've got clients. I've got *tsuris*. Come in." She grabbed him and kissed him moistly on the mouth. He felt a sudden, delicious faintness.

"My nephew," she said to the doorman. She linked an arm through Moses'. "Are the flowers for me?"

He nodded, looking around at the trees bedecked with gardenias, the hothouse tulips, the forced hyacinths.

"If you paid more than four bits for 'em you were had." She laughed. "David Jones socks me two grand for all this and what do I love? I love those *farfoilt* daisies. Do you want to stay?" She moistened a finger tip and smoothed his hair back from his face. "It's a fucking baboon cage but there are a lot of pretty girls."

"It looks like a pretty good party. I'll stay and help you clean up afterwards."

She cocked her head and looked at him. "You walked over to see me, huh?"

"I called you this afternoon," he said, "but nobody answered."

"I cut off the phones," she said. "Come. Look. You'll see why." She pulled him along, past the blazing candelabra, across the slickly polished floor. In the next room Moses could see couples dancing. In the library men sat around and watched the Dodgers play the Giants, hunched over in their chairs, grunting at a good play while they dropped cigar ashes onto the carpet.

Then they were in the dining room. Moses gasped aloud. The tables stretched from wall to wall. It was an Aladdin's cave of food and flowers and crystal and silver and napery. Swans fashioned of ice cradled plovers' eggs in their depths. Chafing dishes blazed as though an arsonist had been turned loose. There were mounds of sour cream like freshly fallen snow and quenelles. There was herring and chopped liver and Russian salad. There were grape leaves glistening with olive oil and vegetables in cold, curried mayonnaise. There was puff pastry and chocolate gateaux and strawberries and raspberries and purple figs and grapes of the palest green. There was cheesecake and pound cake and tarts and petits fours.

"I'd like to stay here," Moses said, "till early tomorrow morning."

"Fill a plate," Millie said. "Nobody in there will touch this stuff. They're too goddamn busy putting coke up their noses and bourbon down their throats. The liver is gorgeous. Taste the liver."

Moses complied. "It's very good," he said, licking his fingers.

"Of course it's good. That's not calf's liver. That's chicken liver, with chicken fat and chopped eggs and onions. Put some on a cracker for me."

He did as he was bidden. She leaned forward and nipped it from his fingers. They stood alone in the vast room, nibbling this and that.

Stuffed celery in hand, Millie sighed. "I've got to go circulate. I've got my biggest, craziest client sitting in a corner with her dancing teacher. She sits at home till ten o'clock and when nobody offers to bring her she calls her dancing teacher. He wears an earring. In one ear. He's got more curls than a *yeshiva bucher* and a little gold earring. She makes a million dollars a year and she had to go out with a tap dancer. Listen." Millie leaned against the buffet. "I'm not going to say a word. She used to call *me* at two, three, four in the morning with her craziness: 'I can't sleep. I'm hyperventilating. There's a burglar in my garden. My mother hates me.' Now she calls him. And he tap dances over." Her shoulders suddenly drooped and she regarded Moses with a strange woebegone look. "And I have you," she said, "a seventeen-year-old kid." She dragged a handkerchief from between her breasts and wiped it across her face like an exhausted prize fighter. "Who am I to talk!"

"We're friends," Moses said, feeling a wave of tenderness and a lump of strudel caught in his throat.

Millie sampled a cookie, fed the rest to Moses. He nearly choked on its sweetness. "I'm nobody's friend," she said. "Ask around — they'll be glad to tell you. This is not Friendship City. If I died tomorrow, you know who would come to my funeral? My tax man and my cleaning lady. Possibly my Uncle Herman if he didn't have a golf game. I'll leave it in my will: 'Bury me after one o'clock so my Uncle Herman can make it.' " Millie pulled a sour face. "They hate me in this town and it's mutual. You want to hear something?"

Moses felt he had heard quite a bit but he nodded gamely.

"I wanted to be a doctor. A surgeon. I had the grades too. You can check the records at Fairfax High School . . . top of the class. You know who went to medical school? My brother, David. You know who went to work at the May Company selling pantyhose? You're looking at her. My brother," she snorted, "a dermatologist in Redwood City. A *yold.*" She took a deep breath, let it out in a gusty sigh. "So, if it wasn't going to be 'my daughter the surgeon,' it was going to be 'my daughter Mr. Irving Lazar.' Typing, shorthand, throat-cutting. I took all the courses. I poached so many clients, half the agents in town had to close their doors. Now they're heading studios. And coming to my house. What's the moral? I'll tell you. I'm not a nice lady. You're not in bed with a nice lady, kiddo."

Moses was unperturbed. "What I usually do about people," he said, "is make up my own mind. I don't believe in polls or random sampling or what four out of five doctors recommend or anything like that. When somebody tells me six million people use Colgate and I ought to use Colgate, I quit brushing my teeth. So, if you don't mind, I'll wait around tonight till everybody goes home." He smiled peacefully at her.

"A fan," she said dryly.

"Yes, Millie," he said, "a fan."

She was silent at that. She who was rarely silent.

"I think I'll go see who's here," he said cheerfully. "Check you later."

Moses took one last brownie to show her he appreciated her culinary gifts, and he started for the door. When he saw his father, tall and pale, his enthralled, misguided, much-loved father, in the company of a young girl, coming through the front door, his tolerance and insouciance deserted him utterly. "Oh, Christ," he said. "Oh, hopping Jesus Christ."

Millie moved with remarkable swiftness. She crossed the room and slammed the dining room door and turned to face a shaken Moses. "All right," she said tartly, "now let's get our shit together. That's your daddy out there with his friend. He was invited. I didn't expect him to come. I didn't expect *you* to come. You're *all* here. So let's not panic. Let's keep our heads." She tottered to a chair and sat down, her legs splayed in front of her. "I needed this."

Moses stood transfixed before her. "Man of the world," she said to him, "are you going to handle this or aren't you?"

Moses groaned. "She's so much younger than my mother. She looks like she's younger than I am."

"She's almost thirty, so relax. They can't get him for child molestation. I know it's a shock seeing them together, but, sweetie, I've got an actor out there who's in love with his twelve-year-old daughter. Takes her everywhere. She's out there right now with a dress cut to her belly button, drinking Manhattans with him at the bar. They register as man and wife at motels. Upstairs, two married ladies with kids in the Peace Corps are making it in my bedroom. Down the hall a famous director is trying on my caftans in front of a seven-foot basketball star, and they're both loving it. Where've you been living, under a lettuce leaf?"

Millie rose, took hold of Moses and steered him to a chair. She put a piece of pound cake into his hand.

"Try the pound cake," she said. "It's all butter."

"I could go out the back door," he said.

"No, you can't!" Millie cried. "Not if you ever want to come through the front one again. He saw you. Now blow your nose and go out there and say good evening. To both of them. Like a *mensh*."

It was all very well for Millie, armored by years of mounting attacks on enemies real and imagined, to send him forth to confront his father. She had, at her command, every conceivable weapon: a tongue of brass, a honeyed smile, a shark's heart. Not so Moses. His armpits were awash with sweat and his heart spasmed in his chest. He would have given ten years of his life to have Adam at his side. Adam would have struck the right note, conciliatory but independent, lenient but not wholly forgiving. Adam would not have carried the awful burden of love that was Moses'. He was not as admiring of their father, did not see himself in his image. For Moses, his father embodied the perfect pattern of manhood. It was the mold he wished to be cast in himself. He was even pleased that his eyes were the same slate color and that he toed out when he walked in exactly the same way. They were often taken for one another on the phone.

They both hated salad and loved Mozart. He was sure his father feared the dark as he did, although it had never been admitted between them. They both revered a cordial God who directed their fate and pardoned their transgressions. One summer he and his father had walked past a Unitarian church, entered it, been charmed, embraced its faith. They had lapsed at the same time as well, but they still walked together many a Sunday morning, discoursing on how the hardness of life could be propitiated by good will. How could he see such a man grown lewd and deceitful? How could he say "good evening" without shattering? He would vouchsafe nothing beyond a curt nod and a greeting, nothing at all.

The doorknob was slippery in his hand. He threw back the doors and stepped out. His father was gone.

A waiter passed with a tray of drinks. Moses beckoned him.

"Could I have one of these, please?"

He took a glass from the tray, downed it in one gulp. He neither choked nor sputtered. He held out his hand for another. He had a sullen purpose in mind: let him drink till the well was dry.

Moses moved blindly toward the sound of voices. The party oscillated around him. It seemed as if people were square dancing on an endless stretch of terrace. Some had obviously been felled by heat and exhaustion. They floated, belly up, on the surface of the pool. Fireflies danced in the air.

Somewhere, two or three or four miles from him, his father leaned against a column, stars cold above him, an unseated Zeus, pipe in hand. He saw the handsome set of the head, the wolf-lean body. He even knew the Harris tweed jacket. He had intended to inherit it one day. He lurched forward, full of feelings and folly. He wished he had a horse between his wobbly legs, a staff of knotted wood in his hand. He wished he had the speech of Savonarola, the scalding gaze of a priest or a prophet. He wished his stomach would stop growling.

"Father," he croaked, "I want a word with you!"

He marched forward, the music of a discordant band sounding

inside his head, martial music of unpleasant brassiness. Then he stopped, forestalling any embrace, keeping the length of a yard-stick between them.

"Well, Moses," his father said, "I'm surprised to see you here."

"Yes," Moses said, hating the absurd quaver in his voice, "I guess you are surprised." He took a deep breath to fortify himself and to feed oxygen to his brain. "So. I'm fine, and you look all right, so we don't have to waste any time going into that. I've got something on my chest and I'm tired of carrying it around."

His father nodded. It was typical of him that nothing showed on his face. Moses recalled the utter calm his father displayed in crises large and small. He had admired it in the past, often trying for that stoic visage himself.

"Let's take a little walk," his father said and, lo, he was beside him, linking his arm through Moses'. At once he felt the familiar code of closeness and warmth surge through him. He clenched himself against it.

"Had a little wine, have you?" His father's inquiry was mild.

"Gin. I've been drinking gin."

"It was grape juice not so long ago. When did you take to drink?"

Violently, Moses pulled away. "I don't think you'd better try to be paternal," he said hotly.

They were crossing a smooth green lawn, thick as a carpet. The air seemed uncommonly rich with the scent of Havana cigars and orange blossoms. Moses, balky and stubborn, halted beneath a tree whose fruit hung in rich festoons over his head. He was not soothed by the tender night. A hatred of inconstancy coursed in his blood. He would have his say.

"When I was little," he began, "and I did something you didn't like, you had a word you used. You'd say, 'Moses, that is inappropriate.' I remember getting the kids on the block into a poker game up in our attic. I played like a demon, never lost a hand all afternoon, and took fifty bucks off them in dimes and quarters and fifty-cent pieces. One of the kids started to cry because I had his allowance for a whole month. You came up the stairs and you stood there looking at me. 'Moses,' you said, 'this is inappropriate.' The next time I heard it was when I took Gussie Harper's underpants off in the back seat of your Oldsmobile. You came out to wash the car and found us there. 'Moses,' you said, 'this is inappropriate.' God, how I *hated* that word. It was so *cool.* I used to wish you'd whip off your belt and whale me, like all the other fathers on the block did with their kids. But not you. 'Gentlemen,' you'd say to me and Adam, 'this is inappropriate behavior.' In-fucking-appropriate. Well, father, I think that just about pegs you and that lady you dumped my mother for. Yes, sir. I think that just about puts it in a good old nutshell. What we have going here is an inappropriate situation."

He hiccuped loudly and hooked his fingers through his belt. He rocked lightly on his feet as if awaiting the counter-punch of an adversary.

He saw that he had been wrong about his father. The man could be bloodied. Melancholy had descended on Charles like a black cloak and, for a moment, he seemed without recourse. Then he fumbled for his cold pipe, stared into its bowl, pushed it absently back into his jacket pocket.

"Let this cup pass away," he said to no one in particular. Then he leaned against the tree trunk and, to Moses' eyes, he seemed part of its whorled and punished bark.

"Mo," he said, "I'm a failure. Noted and recorded in your mother's all-seeing eye." He sat down on the wet grass and Moses, not being able to lord it over him, stumbled and sat beside him.

"I think you're a very good writer," he blurted out.

"I am not a very good anything. Not husband, not father, not even lover. Moses, I want you to understand about all this because I like you so very much. You'll notice I didn't say love. We take that for granted, I hope. I like you. You're implacable and good and unusually modest for a young man your age. Sometimes you're a little humorless. Not often, but sometimes when it's important not to be. On the whole you're a great credit to your mother and myself. Mostly to your mother because she's really shaped you. I haven't left your mother so much as I've wandered away in search of myself. A new version. A more spirited one with some hope, some sense of anticipation. An egocentric quest, if you will, but better than suicide or something equally ill-advised. Your mother's a splendid woman. I needn't tell you that. An admirable woman. Beautiful, witty, tough as hell. And she has my number, Moses. It's hardly fair to expect such a woman to cheer on a man whose every weakness has been displayed over a long marriage. She knows I'm lazy. She knows I procrastinate. She knows I envy my peers in a hundred petty ways. She knows my pretenses and my shams. She knows all my jokes as well. She sees the slumped shoulders, a thin spot on the top of the head. I'm no longer a surprising lover. She's heard every turn of phrase at my command. I'm an old commodity, Moses, no bargain."

Moses gulped. "You don't have to run yourself down," he said.

"No, I needn't do that. What I have to do is make you see how this all came about. Look at this tree. See here, there's a forked stick holding up the branch. Someone reasoned that while the tree would live it would bend and bow and possibly break. So it is with your poor old dad, Mo. I needed holding up, a prop, a brace. I've found it. If the excuse is a poor one, it's all I have to offer."

Moses, in his youth, in his severity, in his wrath, was unappeased. "Damn it," he cried out, "Mom knows how to make you feel good. You just got tired of her, that's all. Look at you! You've got a twenty-dollar hair cut. You're wearing a dumb gold chain around your neck. You're running around with a girl young enough to be your daughter. You're too *old* to be a cocksman, can't you see that? You just look *foolish*, that's all. And you're right about being a failure. You're right about that, all right. You're only thinking about yourself. I didn't hear one goddamned word about Mom's life and what's going to happen to her. You think it's easy for a woman to start all over again when she's forty years old with two big kids on her hands? You know what she does? She stays home reading Isak Dinesen. She smokes pot. She worries about bills. And what's wrong with showing your true nature to a woman you love? You think you look any better to that girl you're living with? You don't look good to her and you don't look good to me, either. I think," he said, scrambling to his feet and weaving unsteadily when he had attained them, "that you're a prick." And with that pronouncement, his heart fell into his shoes.

"Let's get you some coffee," his father said, rising also.

"I don't want any coffee. Caffeine is poison."

"Then let's drive you home."

He approached Moses and put out a hand to steady him. Moses relived the moment that followed for the rest of his life. He knotted his fist and slammed it in the direction of his father's jaw, seen only dimly through a haze of tears. He connected. In a flash, Moses was all over him, swinging wildly, bawling, pounding, smashing, digging divots from the lawn with his feet, sobbing, snot and tears raining down his face. Finally he was grappled against his father's chest, against his scraped and bloodied chin.

"Enough, enough!" Charles fought free of him.

"It's not enough!" Moses spun back into the fray, his arms windmilling, flailing, thrashing. Then he was grasped from behind by a man he had never seen before and swung clear off the ground.

"Even if this is a family affair, it's gone on long enough," said Dr. Bartolome. "Let cooler heads prevail."

Moses was never quite certain what followed. He dimly remembered his father moving off in the solicitous embrace of a girl with long hair who seemed to have appeared like a summoned wraith. For himself, he was propelled back toward the house in the muscular clutch of the stranger who seemed unabashed at hauling a drunken and despairing boy past the circling dancers, the musicians, the revelry.

Moses was still in the grip of terror at his act. He had repudiated his father. He had struck his father. He had unseated him where he had reigned supreme — in Moses' deepest love. He groaned aloud. The man who had him in charge steered him to the nearest lavatory and slapped him with a wet towel.

"How's the young souse now?" he inquired.

The front of Moses' shirt was wet through. The knuckles of his right hand were skinned and raw. He felt his soul to be in jeopardy.

"Terrible. I feel terrible."

He opened his eyes and saw that he was being regarded with impatience by his rescuer. Instantly Moses wanted to put matters straight. The events of the evening must not be seen as a loutish scuffle. He flung the towel away from him and struggled to focus his gaze.

"You don't understand!" he cried. "That was my father."

"So I gathered. Well, you're not the first to butt heads with your daddy. I knocked mine down a flight of stairs once. I don't recall the cause. In the main, we had a very high regard for each other. When he was gone, I was inconsolable. Why? I could have found other people to pit myself against, plenty of them. But I needed to try myself against him." He prodded Moses with the toe of his shoe. "All right," he said, "where do you live? I'll run you home."

Moses shook his head in bewilderment. "I can't just walk out of here."

"Why not? You've thrown your best punch."

"I don't want to leave it at that." Moses wiped his nose with the back of his hand. He did not want to reveal his family's scandal to a stranger. He did not want anyone to see his father as unworthy or with honor stained. Indeed, he wanted to take the blame on himself.

"I have a very hot temper," he said. "It was my fault."

"Probably," the man said. "Most young people are a pain in the ass. My name's Bartolome, Dr. Benjamin Bartolome, and I would like to get you off my hands as soon as possible, since I have a long drive and a hard day tomorrow. I appreciate the need to purge yourself, but I'm getting sleepy. I hate these bloody parties. I'm here under protest in the first place, so get on your feet and let's call it a night."

"I should say good-by to Miss Asher."

The man snorted. "Millie's out among the hyenas, making deals right and left. We won't be missed. Come on, sonny, let's not dawdle."

Docilely, Moses followed Bartolome out past the weary butler, past a young lady asleep under a potted palm, past a couple oblivious in an ardent embrace, the man's hand hefting the woman's dainty breast as if to test its weight.

Then he was shoved onto a car seat whose exposed spring bit into his buttock.

"Turn right. Five blocks to the signal and up the hill," Moses said. "And this is very kind of you."

The man grumbled ungraciously. "I had tickets to a concert. Bartók and Stravinsky. Then that woman got me on the phone. She knew my wife. Ever since she died, Millie's been trying to matchmake, to solace, to interfere. Drives me crazy. 'Come to breakfast.' 'Come to lunch.' 'Come to dinner.' She's a goodhearted soul but my liver's inflamed."

"How long have you known Miss Asher?"

The man tromped heavily on the brake, narrowly missing the car ahead of him. He rolled down the window and called loudly to the driver to signal when he wanted to turn. "Let me live — I love life!" he shouted at him.

"Millie?" he asked as he resumed driving. "I knew her brother, David. A total innocent. No brains, but a lovely man. We played checkers. Millie made fudge. A hundred years ago. I don't see any house. Where's your house?"

"You have to go up this hill. It's a little bit narrow. If anyone's coming down we're in trouble."

Dr. Bartolome seemed at the end of his tether. "I'm always sucked in," he said. "Always volunteering. When I went through my analysis, my analyst said, 'Benjamin, you'll go to any length to be liked. It's a compulsion with you. It's too accepting, it's too passive. You can say no once in a while.' " He guffawed loudly. "My analyst. Tells me to learn to say no. He gets married five times." He guffawed again. "They're all crazy."

"What kind of a doctor are you?" Moses inquired politely.

"What else? An analyst."

He swung the car up the driveway. It stalled halfway up, began to roll backwards. The doctor wrestled with the wheel. "Damn thing's like me — getting old." Then he started it again, clashed the gears and they labored upward. They came to a stop in front of the house.

"Advice," Bartolome said, "given without charge. Go in and go directly to bed. Don't talk about tonight. Don't think about it. Don't trouble your sleep. You can offer your *mea culpas* in the morning. Your father will always love you. You can find out that he has feet of clay and it's all right. Real caring doesn't evaporate with a harsh word — or even a blow. A couple of other points, although now I'm on golden hours and this would ordinarily cost you a mint. Men need coddling and affection. Men yearn to stay young, although they deny it. Men are afraid of being alone. Men go through a kind of menopause. It knocks them for a loop and they don't handle it nearly as well as women. A lot of men hate themselves. When they fail to reach their ideals, they buckle. There's a lot more I could illuminate for you, but I've got serious problems to face in the morning and I want some sleep. There are some good books on this subject. Go to the library and check them out and you won't have to hit your father at social gatherings anymore. Good night." He reached across and opened the door. "If you're going to thank me, do it quickly. The hour grows late."

"Thank you," Moses said.

"You're welcome."

The door opened and Emma stood framed there in her nightgown. She had on old bedroom slippers and her hair stood on end.

Perhaps she was at her best, rumpled, half-asleep, half-stoned, brown feet bare on the floor, because Bartolome did not hurry away into the night. He apprised himself of the facts. She was the mother of this tall, intoxicated boy. There was another, a twin to this one, asleep in the house. She did not marvel at having her son delivered by a relative stranger, she did not question, did not upbraid.

Together they led Moses upstairs to his room, peeled him out of his clothes, laid him down among his lumpy pillows. They might have been fond parents gazing down at him as he plummeted into sleep. Bartolome drew the blanket up around Moses' shoulders, Emma hung his pants and shirt on a chair. Adam muttered a word or two from the other bed, turned and thrashed, was soothed and slept again. Bartolome raised the window high. He believed in fresh air. They both lingered a moment, enjoying the absolute repose the young could so easily command. Then Emma led the way down the stairs and into the living room. She picked up an afghan and wrapped herself in it. She made herself comfortable on the sofa. Bartolome was left to fend for himself. He sat down in a chair that rocked unsteadily beneath him.

"You appear and reappear in my life in the course of one day," he began. "I hardly know what to make of it."

Emma yawned. She was beyond considering it. Fate had often dished up surprises, rather like a mess sergeant dumping food on a plate. She was not prepared to produce either an explanation or an apology. Still, she was not unpleased by his reappearance. She had given him the better part of an hour's thought before she had fallen asleep. She was coming, she knew, to a certain point in her life. She was tired of the old bruises left by an old love. She was bored with suffering, weary of examining failure. The air around her had, for too long, been filled with complaint. She was ripe for merriment, for unruffled friendship. Let camaraderie take the place of love, let there be a new man, let there be a new ease between herself and that man.

"How would you like an egg sandwich?" Emma began on firm ground. She knew Bartolome liked to eat.

"Do you have brown bread? I don't touch white bread."

Emma rose and stretched, the blanket falling away from her. "Yes, yes," she said. "Brown bread. Come along into the kitchen."

He went directly to the refrigerator as if he had lived in her house all his life. He brought out the eggs while Emma rummaged for a pan and butter. He washed his hands and gave her a stern look until she joined him at the sink.

"I'm clean," she said. "Not to worry."

Nonetheless, he handed her the soap, held out a towel. Emma washed obediently. Outside a horned owl began to court a quail he mistook for his mate. Bartolome found plates and paper napkins. He set the table neatly, lining the salt and pepper shakers with precision. Finally he sat down, tilting his chair back, examining the clutter Emma piled onto the drainboard and counter.

"You're not very neat," he said.

"Not very." Emma broke the eggs with one hand, turned to let him see how deft she was.

"I'm about to offer an apology," he said, "but don't equate it with self-effacement. I was boorish on our first meeting. I was going to call and tell you so. Please don't salt that egg. I don't use salt."

Emma went about making the sandwich. There was already salt on the egg. She didn't intend to do anything about it.

"I'm not easily put off," she said. "Say no more about it. I thought we got along famously up to the last few minutes. You're a little outlandish. So am I." She put his plate in front of him, took a huge bite of her own sandwich, the egg spurting onto her chin. He handed her a napkin. Emma grinned. She saw at once that he would be forever tidying her, adjusting her collar, brushing away ashes, bending in the street to tie her shoelaces.

"This is very good." He used his knife and fork, making small neat morsels on his plate.

Emma finished five minutes ahead of him and was smoking. "How did you happen across my son? Where did you find him?"

"At Millie Asher's."

"Are you a friend of Millie's?"

"Of long standing."

"I wonder what Moses was doing there."

"I've already told him not to talk about the evening. In deference to him, I won't either. He'll either tell you or he won't. He's a handsome boy. He looks like you."

"Well, he was obviously in some kind of a state. He never drinks. If you extricated him, I thank you."

He took the cigarette out of her hand and stubbed it into an ashtray. "I'll want you to give up smoking. In fact, I'll insist on it."

Emma shrugged. "I don't bicker over small matters."

"Here's where I stand," he said. "I'm lonely. I intend to do something about it because I am on the edge of depression. I have very little to give any woman at this point. But I like what I see of you. I particularly like you in this unbuttoned, unseductive pose of yours. I like the maternal aspect, though I'm not looking for mothering. I would like to spend some time with you. I'm not one of your narrow medical mechanics. I know music very well indeed. And books. I play a very competitive game of tennis and I'm as good a cook as you will find outside of Provence. I will take you to concerts and to the beach and I will prepare *vitello tonnato* for you. I don't know how much optimism you may entertain about sex. I have long, passionate dreams of my wife and have had every night for five years. If it were possible, I would go and pipe her back as frantically as

Orpheus, but that is romantic and hysterical and will pass. I think we might become excellent friends. I will think about your welfare. I sense that you will think about mine. You may say something if you wish."

"Come to dinner tomorrow night," Emma said, "and the next night if you feel like it."

# Chapter Eight

EMMA ROSE EARLY from her bed. She was always in advance of her household, anxious to be out in the yard with the dogs, hungry for the first breath of the day's untainted air. She could not abide late-risers, dawdlers. The day was meant to be seized. She loved the morning hours, she loved rigorously private time, when her thoughts could tug and roam at will. She went about her tasks with gusto, watering the dozens of plants that stood on every tabletop and ledge, idly dusting the piano keys, often singing at the top of her voice, inconsiderate of her neighbors but jolly.

Bartolome was, in some way she had not yet divined, responsible for an extra surge of energy. It had been a long time since a man, or even the idea of one, had stirred an itch in her. She would be far better off with some such disturbance in her life, something ripening and juicy and delicious. She wanted to smell a man again. To taste him. She wanted the benefits derived from sexual fiddle-faddle. She very much liked the flush and the fury of it; it braced her. He could say what he wanted about being out of her reach, frozen with grief. In due time he would heat up. Already she felt toned and lively; at another time in her life she would have said she was *con amore*.

She arrived at her office with her blood up and a run in her stocking. A custodian was screwing a brass plate into her door, her named engraved on it in elegant script.

She paused and whistled.

"Who told you to do that?" she inquired.

"Mr. Mason. You've got a new couch, too, and a leather chair. He's inside, waiting for you."

Mason sat behind Emma's desk, a pair of heavy spectacles riding the bridge of his nose. A script was open in his lap, and as he turned the pages he paused to stare out the window as if he heard a voice calling to him, a honeyed Lorelei from some other time. He looked up at her through heavy eyes. "I've been here all night," he said. "I slept a little on your couch. I ate an apple I found in your desk. I'll replace it."

He removed his glasses, tucked them into his pocket. "This is a nice office, Emma. Like a home. Plants. Books. Mess."

She saw the remains of a sandwich and a piece of cheese that she had left two days ago and that by now must be as high as a kite.

"One of these days, I'm going to clean up in here."

"Leave it, leave it. It's like you. With a run in your stocking."

She glanced down to confirm it. Mason had a disordered look of his own. Emma marked his socks lapping over his elegent shoes, his rumpled jacket.

"Did you say you were here all night?"

"It's not the first time," he said, "and I wasn't alone. No, no, there was no girl," he added sourly, "only producers who didn't want to go home. Everybody thinks: Hollywood, casting couches, people going down on each other in offices. You know Abe Keller?"

"Yes," Emma said. "I know him."

"He was here. Eating his soup alone in the commissary. You know Tom Schiller?"

Emma nodded.

"Here too. Pouring his heart out to the janitor. I walked by his office, the janitor was leaning on his broom, a big cigar in his mouth. Tom was telling him about his son being a fairy and how he cries when he thinks he'll never be a grandfather. Next door, Mario Picelli . . . the big writer. What's he doing? Not writing. Putting powder in his nose. It wasn't snuff. Somebody was even taking a shower. Saturday night in the fraternity house. I ought to charge rent for these offices. A hundred thousand a year they get. Two hundred thousand a year. Nobody wants to go home. Joyce Haber. Rona Barrett. They think this town is one big erection. They should stay late here. All right. Enough of that." He held a script aloft. "You know whose script this is?"

Emma recognized the cover of robin's egg blue. Charles liked that color. Emma always thought he chose it in some kind of homage to his boyhood rambles, which brought him to fallen nests and to eggs of that particular hue.

"Yes," she said. "I know whose it is. It was going to be sent to me. How did you get it?"

"Never mind. I got it. I think it's wonderful. I'd like to buy it if you agree with me."

She started to speak, but he held up a silencing hand. "Only if you agree with me. Only if you say it's good. Maybe if he makes a big sale you and Charles will get together. Maybe I'm cupid. I like Charles, Emma. He's a nice man. Once he gave back money to this company because we didn't like his script. You remember that."

"Yes," Emma said. "We were going to buy a new stove with it. And take a trip. I told him to keep the money, not to be so noble."

Mason rubbed his jaw, rubbed the morning bristle. "You know how I started out in business? In a fish store in Toronto. The Warner brothers started in the meat packing business. We all came from humble beginnings." He paused. "We had every kind of fish you could mention in that store. Halibut, cod, snapper, whitefish, sea bass. I haven't eaten fish like that in years." He pursed his lips, as if tasting the iodine tang anew. "I had a partner," he went on. "David Cooperman. If he took a piece of herring out of the jar, he put a nickel in the drawer. Also if he made a personal telephone call. An honest man . . . like your husband. You want to give up a man like that, Emma?"

She explained it once again, patiently. "Harry, Charles has somebody else. He's dancing around the Maypole."

"I know. You told me. I know all about it."

Emma fished in the ashtray for a butt, lit it, expelled the smoke in a steady stream. "I don't know if I want to do him a favor," she said. "I'm not a saint. I'm angry. I'm hurt."

Even as she spoke, she wondered what gratitude might bring, what it might mend. She saw herself interposed between Charles and havoc, saw him rejoice in good fortune. He would buy himself a first edition of A. E. Housman. He would send the boys extravagant cashmere jackets. He would write a check for the Y.M.C.A. and another to a poor aunt in Pacoima who doted on him. He would be atypically boisterous. He would buss the cleaning lady. His spiritual winter would end.

With a little ripple of pleasure, she thought of Charles calling her to celebrate. She could hear his voice cracking into two notes as it did when he was pleased. She saw him butting open the door, carrying a clutch of daisies, wearing a huge face-splitting grin. Why deny him? Why deny herself? She wanted to be taken to lunch in their own haunts; she wanted to peel shrimp and taste garlic and drink wine, looking at him with approval.

Emma glanced at Mason. "If I hadn't been with you when it quit on you," she said, "I'd never have guessed that you had a heart."

He disdained the compliment. "This could be a big picture. There are parts in it. They can be cast. No locations. I blew my nose three times while I read it. But you don't tell him any of that. Tell him it's a nice little story. Get it cheap."

He moved toward the door. "Incidentally, you left the lights burning here all night. Take a minute and turn 'em out before you leave. It only takes a minute to turn 'em out." He was gone without another word.

She sat at her desk, the script before her. She reached toward it, and then, with a gesture of cowardice, swept it into a drawer. Slowly she leaned her face on her hands to think and reason and rationalize. She did not do a lick of work all morning.

Moses slept on and on, so it was Adam who answered the call. He was instantly taken by the sound of her voice, which carried in its burnished tones reminders of good schools and country clubs and the smoke of autumn leaves burning. Adam had long had in mind a girl without coyness. He did not want an eager girl, keyed to disappointment, who would first be gullible and then furious. He hoped for a practiced girl who would put the finishing touches to his capabilities and leave him, if it turned out that way, with an ironic smile flung over her perfect shoulder.

He saw his future without confusion. He would go to law school, espouse those denied mercy, rise to eminence, purchase a foreign car and father two children with a woman of stunning beauty. It was his firm intention to be happy. He had seen where misreckoning and self-doubt had led his father; he had even, on one dreadful morning, heard him weeping in the bathroom, the shaving soap drying on his face unnoticed. He had been touched to the quick but unable to do anything beyond inviting Charles to play paddle tennis with him, a game his father loathed. He had thought of suggesting a psychiatrist, he knew a very ebullient and clever one at school, but his sense of propriety stopped him. He couldn't bring himself to suggest remedies for a hurt his father so carefully concealed, so he went into Beverly Hills and bought him a handsome silk tie instead. Unlike Moses, whose emotions were as visible as the shirt tail hanging over his pants, Adam moved carefully around pain and joy. Though he had not confessed it to anyone, he was jealous of the way in which Moses, racked with love, would sit on the toilet seat while his father bathed, talking volubly about every coil and knot in his psyche. How often he had heard his father, clearing his throat as a beginning, launch into counsel on how Moses might best survive and prosper. Waiting his own turn, with a towel wrapped around his loins, he had eavesdropped on his father at his very best. How tranquil and sure of himself did his father appear then. Moses must not pursue money in a depleting or demeaning way. It would be fine if he could hark back to the times Charles remembered of his own life on the farm. Adam knew very well that nothing his father recalled was totally true, but it was lovely to hear him evoke snowy woods and hours on an icy pond with his skates whistling under him, ice chips spattering, and the dark round eyes of a beaver watching from the bank. Then he would put on his shirt and his jacket and his sad wintry smile and go to the studio to write movie scripts in an office that hummed with air conditioning and was lit by a fluorescent tube.

It was part of Adam's scheme to buy an acre of land and give it to Charles so that he could plant and sow and reap, in a small way, if the housing developments did not devour the open country before he could make his pile.

The girl on the phone was his father's lover. Adam felt as if her warm breath were filling his ear. He had to make an effort to concentrate on what she was saying. He had speculated on their life together, wondering what form it took. Once he had driven past the house they occupied and had been charmed by its weedy and overgrown air. He wondered if the lacy curtains blowing out the window were in their bedroom, if they slept locked together in a narrow bed, feet entwined, arms entwined, breaths mingling. He had even imagined he had seen her indistinct and shadowy silhouette, but then the mailman had come along the street and Adam had gone home, feeling in some brutish way he had assaulted her. Lately, when he thought of them, she was on all fours and his father bestrode her and all was debauchery and gross and unnatural behavior.

Her clean and liquid voice spoke his name.

"Are you Adam?"

"Yes, ma'am."

"This is Carla."

Adam made insouciant inquiries about her health. Was there anything he could do for her? Any old thing at all. He would be happy to.

"This is very difficult," she said. "I really hate what I'm doing."

Adam had no response. He had no idea what was on her mind. But he was predisposed to support her in any trial.

"I want to talk about your father to someone in his family. Not your mother, of course. Could someone come and see me? Could you?"

Could he? Wasn't the Hellespont spanned, Everest conquered?

"No problem," he said. "Where and when?"

"Well, I suppose here. I mean, at my house. Do you know where it is?"

He knew. The lace curtain blew through his mind.

"He'll be gone all day. I could give you lunch if you like. A peanut butter sandwich or something . . ."

"I'm a peanut butter man," he said jauntily. She thanked him and hung up.

He wondered if his shirt should be changed and if he would have time for a haircut. And then, because a part of him had grown up, he wondered if he was being disloyal to his mother and if he should disassociate himself from her rival, who was so much younger and, God help him, in fuller bloom than she. He would, he knew, be ennobled by refusal, but he was mired in a desire to see her up close, to venture where there was peril. He was already a victim of the warm summer day, of some vague excitement that might have come from red meat or fifty pushups or simply from the delight of being alive. He had to see if her skin was as white as his dreams of it and if her appearance matched her matchless voice.

Above him, on a peg, hung Emma's gardening hat. It was battered, stained, unraveling around the brim. But she had put a Mexican paper rose in the band and suddenly she appeared in Adam's mind as a resplendent and decretory figure, a kind of oracle warning him not to stray where his father had strayed before him.

"Hell," he said aloud, "I'll just mooch over and see what she wants. That's all."

The dryness in his mouth gave it the lie. He knew he wouid polish his shoes and take a bath and chew cloves, rub on some Mitchum's antiperspirant, that he would heed nothing but his feckless heart.

Felicia came into the hallway, her arms full of wash, her glance shrewd and penetrating his very backbone.

"Who was that?"

"Wrong number."

"I heard you talking for five minutes."

"You're crazy." He smiled and smiled at her, then walked over and kissed her on the cheek.

"I had a bad dream," she said. "Stay home today."

"*Ojo mágico*," Adam said, mocking her. Much later he would wonder how he had let the warning go unheeded.

It was exactly twelve o'clock when Adam reached the house where his father lived his new life. There was a firm latch on the gate and Adam knew that it was the work of his father's hand. He was sure he had given all of one Sunday morning to it, going to the hardware store, chatting pleasantly and at length with the clerk, finally buying one that was neither the most expensive nor the cheapest. He would have lingered afterward, walking up and down the aisles, admiring the hammers and nails, wrenches, ratchets, galvanized buckets and the screw drivers, none the tools of his present trade but those that conferred upon him a kind of peace, that recalled to him that once his work had been simple and unconfining and wholesome.

What was first in his father's dogma was that work came before pleasure. How often had Adam been called from the handball court or the swimming pool to stack firewood or to replace tiles on the high and windswept roof.

He wondered how his father managed as a writer, if he assembled all the words, the emotions, the beginnings and the endings, and joined them as he did the linoleum squares on the bathroom floor — cutting, fitting, pausing to wipe the sweat from his forehead, feeling pain in his knees and his back. He had seen a look of bewilderment on his father's face as he came out of his study, as if the parts were all wrong, as if the joints were not plumb, as if the task belonged to someone better endowed for it.

It occurred to Adam that this love affair might have had roots in the same desire to simplify, to put away the demands and complications and rituals of family life and live on impulse and rapture out of his old Gladstone suitcase. Yes, Ariel had replaced Eve. Adam knew it as he heard the jangling of wind chimes strung across the front porch, sounding on the air like faraway Japanese music. There was a neat strip of tape across the doorbell and a neatly lettered sign informing that the bell was out of order and to please knock. No doubt his father would attend to that in due time.

Adam peered through the stained-glass panel into the room beyond, before he made his presence known. He wanted to establish the nature of the terrain, to see what he could make of things. He was astonished at the cool and chaste appearance of what he saw. It might have been a Buddhist cell with its straw mat, a low cushion or two, a vase holding one white begonia. There were no afternoon papers strewn on the floor. There were no ashtrays, no dogfood bowls, no beaded pillows, no mold-speckled prints, none of the things he was accustomed to in his mother's house — only delectable emptiness. Love in such a room would be stately, slow, a pavan divested of all inhibition. Adam, who had sex on top of record albums, in beds acrackle with potato chips, with girls too lazy to wash, was utterly charmed.

A girl moved toward him through the filtered sunlight, bare legged and in some sort of thin white dress, and Adam saw, with a rush of tenderness, that she was slightly and endearingly knock-kneed. She opened the door and waved him in with one gesture, and he felt as if he were being beckoned into the curling waves of the sea by a Siren, albeit one with rather dirty feet.

"Come out back," she said. "I've left the hose running on the tomato plants."

He followed her through a kitchen that smelled of spice and herbs, that was scrupulously clean, with glasses turned upside down to drain on a spotless linen towel. There was a big bowl of washed and polished apples on the table and another of some kind of seeds and raisins. She paused to hand him one and to offer the bowl of seeds and he realized with a startled and hungry pang that this was lunch in its entirety. He wondered if he would be invited to drink brackish water from the tap outside. Very likely.

The garden flourished so that Adam felt there must be six of every growing thing in the world climbing up stakes and walls and along the deeply turned and richly dark furrows. He wondered if she rose in the night to trample snails, to pick squash of phallic size and shape, to stand in her nightdress like Persephone entwined with pea blossoms and sorrel. He felt she must taste of greenery, of endive and escarole and arugala. To lie down with her would be to lie in meadow grass, in clover, in fern. In his mind's eye, how he laid himself down in green pastures!

"Sit on the steps," she said. "Look out for splinters first."

He sat down, apple in hand, feeling the warm wood beneath him. She turned the hose off, flopped it away, sloshed through the puddles to retrieve a hoe and a rake. He felt pleased that he alone was privy to this athletic and sensuous bending and stretching as she hung the implements on nails driven into the wall, wiping them first with a handful of leaves, just so. He remembered his mother's bamboo rake left to rot apart in the sun and how his father chided about it. Did neatness in mind and spirit bind people together, then?

She came back to him, sat on the step just beneath him so that he looked into her golden hair. She turned, gave him one brief glance and hugged herself as if the day had suddenly grown cold.

"You're taller than your father." The way she said it conferred nothing upon Adam. "I used to hate it when people started that business with me. How tall you are. How you've grown. Like it was the only thing I knew how to do. I suppose it's an icebreaker. God knows I'm looking for one."

Adam was perfectly at home with uneasy girls. His history was strewn with them.

"Look," he said, "just plunge on in. I've got all the time in the world." He bit into his apple. "This sure is a good apple."

He carefully averted his glance so that she could speak her piece in peace. A direct gaze, he had found, jarred some girls, and panicked others. He wondered if she could still be called a girl, because there were fine lines visible on her forehead and around her mouth, but her back was straight and her breasts peerless.

For a long time Carla said nothing at all, spoke not a word. They sat on the steps under the spectacular sun, breathing in the air that smelled of rich manure.

Silence was no problem for Adam. Not that he did not like to talk. He was by far the gabbiest member of his family, said by them to be nosy, inquisitive and brash. It was Adam who was the first to know his father had thought of adultery, the first to know he had committed it. Nor was that knowledge, or any other he was privy to, a burden. He knew the stuff the world was made of, but he knew it had a finer grain as well.

"The problem is," Carla said, stirring beside him, "that I'm a born victim, and as far as I can see I always will be."

Adam nodded. He knew about those, too. There had been a professor at school who was accused of rape and dismissed, when all the poor man had done was put his hand on a student's breast — and that so briefly he hardly felt the shape of it.

"Would you like to talk about it? Sometimes it helps to talk."

She began, and went on through the whole afternoon. "I've spent ten thousand dollars of my inheritance talking," she said. "I've talked to doctors in Geneva, in Berlin, in Lausanne, in New York, in San Francisco, and for the last three years in Beverly

Hills, conveniently close to shopping." She lay flat on the steps and closed her eyes. Adam felt there ought to be a pencil and a pad in his lap. He would hear her out with his fullest attention. If there were tears he would certainly dry them. He had once slapped a girl who was in a paroxysm of hysteria, and he had felt competent to deal with it. He would know how to make her laugh if there was a need for that. Beyond that, he would have to improvise.

On and on she talked while Adam listened and shifted from one numbed buttock to the other.

She began with her father, whom she idolized. He was a famous theatrical lawyer with offices in Paris and London. Unexpectedly, he did not shower her with gifts and attentions. He was a stingy, demanding man who questioned her closely on how she spent her allowance and why she was running up light bills by reading in bed at night. He was only generous in his admiration of her quick mind. He showed her off. He told everyone she had read Machiavelli and Strindberg and that she could work the Double-Crostics in half the time he did. He took her everywhere with him, putting her in the cheapest single rooms at the Plaza-Athénée and at Claridge's, or in little pensions if he could find them, saying she would learn languages that way without having to be tutored. Her mother followed after them and drank steadily in the gardens and on the terraces of a dozen European cities. One lovely spring in Paris she went for a walk and never came back. They heard later that she had killed herself in a luxury suite with sitting room and bath in Baden-Baden. She had not turned down the bed, unwrapped the soap or used the bath towels. She had taken sleeping pills. There was no blood, no damage. Her father refused to pay the bill.

When Carla was sick, he doctored her himself, telling her that aspirin would do the trick. He bought it in huge cut-rate bottles and carried it everywhere with him. He told her it was perfectly safe to drink the tap water in Naples and as a result she came down with typhoid. He found an Italian doctor who would care for her for a small fee. He mostly did abortions. She nearly died.

When they came back to the United States, she wanted a place of her own but he wept profusely and said he could not manage without her. They moved into an apartment at the top of the Chateau Marmont. They took it unfurnished and he accepted beds and couches from an interior decorator who owed him money. Thus, they lived in silk-tufted and gilded luxury. He had the heat turned off. He said he despised rooms over sixty degrees. If Carla had not found him so intelligent she would have thought him mad. In the end he took to eating less and less, complaining that a child's portion was too large. He died of malnutrition with instructions in his will that his coffin was to be a plain pine box. Carla's breakdown began the day after the funeral.

She broke off the narrative to go inside and make them each a large glass of freshly squeezed orange juice. It turned out that she was merely refueling for the second chapter and, before Adam had time to wipe his mouth, she was launched again.

Alone, rich, and quite out of her head, she had been prey to all sorts of sharp and unprincipled young men. One of them, who looked remarkably like James Dean and had the same loony intensity, had met her coming out of her doctor's office and with the speed of light had danced off with her. Before she knew it, she was being married by a strange young minister of some ill-defined denomination and was living on the broad high plain of Taos with an actor-husband who ate peyote for breakfast and went through her money before the first year was out. All she could remember of that time were awesome sunsets over the Sangre de Cristo mountains, the smell of piñon wood, and a headache that never left her.

Charles had been the remedy and the cure. She had met him, on a rainy afternoon, in Hunter's Book Shop, where she had gone to look at books about orgasm and the new female freedom and the right to live without all the old shibboleths. She stood there reading the first lines of dozens of such books, unable to grasp what they were saying but in dire need of a straw. He had watched her for fully half an hour and then he had invited her to have coffee, saying that her sad beauty was breaking his heart and what on earth was the matter with her.

They had compared their angst for the rest of the day, both feeling that they were good for each other and that a real nostrum could be found if they could see each other again.

Within the space of a few months, she forgot her parsimonious father and found a new and generous one in Charles. He, on the other hand, looked into her eyes and found belief. He read her every line he wrote and she said wonderful, wonderful, because she saw that it was the kind thing to do. Kindness, she told Adam, is an underestimated virtue. She was not as bright as Emma but she sensed that Charles found too much brilliance blinding. He could not find his way in so much light. For a long time, they had a mild, relieving kind of love affair, rather like warm milk taken at bedtime. He lay in her arms and confessed his inadequacies, while she dutifully concealed her own. The truth was that her mother had killed herself and her father was as nutty as a fruitcake, and she was their child. Of late her nerves rang like an unanswered telephone jangling night and day. She felt as if she were a field mouse creeping into one hole, nest, crevice, den after another, hiding from her real self. She was not the patient Griselda Charles thought her to be. No, she was not!

Adam heard the clang of her voice as it rose in protest. He began to wonder unhappily where this confession would lead. There were shadows across the lawn now and he had the sensation he had known as a child — that soon he would be whistled home. He wanted to go.

Everybody, she continued, leaned on her and she could no longer bear the weight. She wanted to pack her bags and fly to Ireland and burn peat fires and speak Gaelic. Or, she wanted a young lover on a motorcycle, brown and healthy, who knew nothing of dependence or disillusion.

"I could sleep with you," she said suddenly. "You'd be right for me."

Once Adam had gone to an amusement park and had paid a dime to ride in a wind tunnel. He had howled with fright and exhilaration but, when the ride was done, he was disoriented and could not even remember his name. He felt that way now.

"Are you getting taken care of by a doctor right now," he asked, "because I think you should be. I think maybe you've gotten yourself into a bad place and could use a little help."

She smiled. "You help me."

"Well," Adam said, trying to give himself time, "first I think you ought to discuss this with my father. He's a nice man, you know. You can rely on my father." Adam let her digest that for a moment and then, hurriedly, finished off his daydreams at one blow.

"I don't think I'd like to hurt my father's feelings by acing him out with you — although you're very beautiful. I wouldn't feel right about it. You probably wouldn't either, after you'd had time to think it over. Thanks anyway. And thanks for the orange juice." He stood up. She did not seem to hear him. She put her head on her knees, communicating to Adam implacable pain far beyond his ministrations.

He hesitated on the porch. "I wish you'd let him down easy," he said.

"Go away," she replied.

For a moment, just for a moment, Adam speculated on the dark embraces that had been offered him. He felt somehow that her skin would be hotter than any other to the touch, her mouth hotter still.

He fled from the house and across the front yard, and the latch his father had affixed to the gate closed firmly behind him.

# Chapter Nine

BARTOLOME BROUGHT with him his own set of knives — one for gutting the fish, one for chopping—and a clean white apron. The knives had been a gift from his wife, an odd present perhaps but she had known how particular, even fussy, he was about things like sharp knives and large bath towels and napkins that did not slide from his lap.

He arrived before Emma, introduced himself to Felicia and shortly thereafter they were dicing onions and mincing parsley and speaking in the friendliest way to each other in perfect Castilian Spanish. He explained his bringing the makings of dinner by saying he was finicky about food and he wasn't sure what he would be offered in Emma's house. Besides, the red snapper he had purchased had bright, shiny eyes, indicating its absolute freshness, and smelled wonderfully of the ocean; his mouth had watered and he had been unable to resist it. Felicia told him that Emma did not like fish. He pooh-poohed that. Anyone would be delighted with his red snapper, beautifully stuffed with bay shrimp, delicately perfumed with fennel. He meant to add a small salad, new potatoes in their jackets, a branch or two of broccoli, steamed and served with butter and lemon. They would drink a bottle of Chambertin and finish the meal off with strawberries and cream.

He asked Felicia about herself. How much money did she make? Was the work in this house hard? He did not ask about Emma. Felicia volunteered nothing beyond saying that her mistress was a good woman, to which he grunted. He asked her to decant the wine and to drink a glass of it with him. He set the table himself, asking if the boys would be at home. They had gone off for an evening of silent movies and beer. They always sought each other's company after any crisis and both had seemed subdued and shaken up, departing quietly. There was no sign of Cleo.

Bartolome put three plates on the table. Felicia jogged him with an elbow and said he needn't be so democratic. She would not be at the table. A man was taking her to dinner and probably to bed. She would not be back till morning. He accepted that without comment, asked for scissors and a basket and went out into the garden to cut a bouquet of flowers, which he arranged with great charm in a mayonnaise jar. When there was nothing else to do, he took a volume of Robert Browning from the bookshelf, seated himself in the best chair and read and drank his wine until Emma arrived home.

Emma, standing on the threshold, took it all in — the air rich with fish and flowers, the man aproned and absorbed, the cordial welcome of the lamplight. She was, to say the least, astonished.

"Come in," he said, carefully marking his place and rising. "Have a glass of wine with me. We have exactly twenty-five minutes to wait on the fish, no more, no less. You look tired."

Emma dropped her purse, slipped out of her shoes and accepted the drink that he poured for her.

"You did all this?" She saw the table now, replete with larkspur and daisies and a bit of flowering jasmine.

"Yes, yes," he said with faint impatience. "I live by myself, you know. I live well. You could use a touch of it." He indicated a film of dust on the table beside him. "A little beeswax wouldn't hurt that, either. That's a fairly decent table."

"I got it for fifty bucks," Emma said triumphantly.

"We all do dishonest things from time to time," he said. "Sit down. Your children, whom I wished to see, are out for the night. Your housekeeper is putting on more of her very potent perfume and is also out for the night. We are alone."

Emma was pleased with her homecoming, pleased with him. He had set exactly the right tone. There were occasions, though infrequent, when Emma could do without ardor. One did not arrive at the top of a mountain until one had climbed it, and very often it was agreeable to linger on the way up. She felt in some subtle way that Bartolome knew all this and was waiting for her to ascend. She could set her own pace. He commanded the view from the highest point. She knew that, too.

"Well, Emma," he said, "I've been in your kitchen, I've scanned your bookshelves, I've even had the temerity to look into your bedroom — and I begin to see the shape of you."

"What can you make of a bunch of clothes on the floor and a burned roaster? The place is a mess. I'm going to houseclean sometime this summer. I told Felicia to close the bedroom and bathroom doors. How did I know you were going to snoop?"

"Information is indispensable to me. How would I know on so short acquaintance that you wear cotton underclothes like a schoolgirl? That you have a truly monstrous appetite for cheap fiction? That the heels of all your shoes are run down. That you are sentimental. *Thirty* snapshots stuck in your mirror! How do you see to comb your hair?"

"I do it without looking. I suppose the dog was asleep in the middle of my bed."

"He was. Indicating to me that you occupy it alone."

Emma grinned. "It would take a brave man to climb in with him. He has fleas and possibly mange."

Bartolome took out his immaculate handkerchief, folded it twice to make a neat little pad and set it on the table for Emma's glass. "I see there are already a dozen rings here, however," he averred. Bartolome looked at Emma thoughtfully. "I think your company will be good for me," he said. "We're very different. I see that you strew the path before you. You're in glorious disorder. You remind me of my boyhood summers in Spoleto, when I lusted after my grandmother's maids, who went about with crosses dangling between their breasts and rings of sweat under their arms. I used to watch them bathe in the goldfish pond, my grandmother having the only bathtub in the house. They'd pull off their blouses and lave themselves and call to each other. And there I'd sit, hanging out the window with my sex as stiff as a poker between my legs, wondering if I could find my way in the dark to their bedroom. Have you ever been to Italy, Emma?"

"Apparently not in the right way," she said, closing her eyes. She remembered quarrels with Charles beside the fountains of Ravenna and in the curling streets of Siena. He had wanted to go to the dark and oppressive churches; she had wanted to close the shutters, swing the wardrobe mirror around to face them and make love after lunch. She saw again the impudent faces of the gargoyles. They had gone to the churches.

"I'll teach you to speak Italian. There are things I may one day want to say to you in that language." He sniffed the air. "Do you smell the butter? It's just beginning to brown now. Are you coming to the table like that?"

"What's wrong with the way I look?"

"The wine you're drinking costs twenty-seven dollars a bottle. You could put a rose in your hair for that."

"Bartolome," she said, "I've worked all day. I screamed over the long distance phone. I threw an agent out of my office. I fired my secretary. Don't talk to me of roses."

"The day is over," he said imperiously. "The office is closed. I've cooked a red snapper with shiny eyes to a turn. After dinner, we'll sit in your garden and I'll tell you the story of my life, which you'll find interesting."

"I don't like fish," Emma said, but she ate her portion and half of his and before dessert there was a flower behind her ear.

They sat in the garden, the gnats routed by the smoke of Bartolome's cigar. He had carefully washed and dried and put away the dishes before settling himself beside Emma on the porch swing, which had lost one of its glides and part of its canopy. It was just as well; the gaps made the stars visible and a section of misty moon. It was too cold for comfort. Bartolome took off his jacket and hung it around Emma's shoulders. It still held his body warmth and gave the feeling of a pleasant embrace. He said he didn't need it. He was burning the considerable number of calories they had consumed at dinner. Emma stretched her long legs before her, clasped her hands behind her head and abrogated her responsibilities as a hostess. She fell into a reflective mood, brought on by wine and the company of a man who stared at the end of his cigar and held his tongue. She was used to the tension generated by Charles, who thrashed inside his skin without being able to shed it. Bartolome's thunder would be of a different sort, rolling outrage, inflammable temper, earth-cracking passion. He would never be merely courteous. Never mild. Only at bay.

"Don't stray too far," he commanded her. "I like attention."

"I'm sure of that," Emma said, but she was willing to pay it.

"I was a spoiled child," Bartolome said, "but in a wonderful way." He blew a series of perfect smoke rings, contemplated them with satisfaction and laid out his jubilant childhood for Emma to see.

From the very moment of his conception, his parents had been convinced that he would embody dazzling virtues of mind and character. He had been gloriously beautiful as a child; he himself was astonished at the singular good looks evident in his baby pictures; himself on a pony, on his father's knee, naked on a blanket. He had played the violin at five, had mastered two languages at seven. His mother, wild with joy over his abundant curls, had secretly had one of his ears pierced so that a small diamond might glitter there amid that dark abundance. He leaned closer to Emma and, indeed, there was a small puncture to be seen.

"Well, well," Emma said, having no other comment to offer.

His mother was given to extravagance of all kinds. She had bought him a harp, arranged singing lessons. She had had his palm read, his horoscope cast. He went to sleep to the sound of priceless Caruso records and woke to the rays of sun lamps positioned near his bed to ward off colds and other maladies.

His father outdid his mother. He took him to Rome and had him blessed by the Pope. He took him to Paris and fed him at Maxim's. He had ten little suits made in exact replica of his own resplendent clothes and purchased a Vuitton trunk to pack them in when they roamed the world. Bartolome had grown up spending summers with rickety old ladies and rheumatic old gentlemen who were addressed as Duchessa Mastioni and Conte Pelegarmi and Principessa This and Dottore That. His grandmother caught the fever of adulation that burned in his parents. She left him the fortune she had accumulated by exploiting the peasants on her estate; it included bracelets of canary diamonds and a false Tintoretto. He still owned her villa, but now the frescoes were faded beyond recognition and the great halls were filled with baled hay and goats. He had her furniture in his present house. It was eaten by worms but he kept it in memory of the marvelous summers he had spent with her, sitting upright on those very chairs while an illustrious company recalled Amelita Galli-Curci and Gabriele D'Annunzio.

When he had passed his eighteenth birthday, he decided to go to Stanford and become a doctor. His parents wept with pride and ordered dinner at Perino's for a hundred members of the family and all their friends. His father offered five toasts, choking on tears before he could get the words out and crying openly after he managed to do so. On the morning of his leaving for school, his mother presented him with a portrait of herself so flattering that his roommate fell hopelessly in love with her and importuned Bartolome to introduce him to this paragon. His father gave him a Patek-Phillipe watch engraved with the words "Blessed be every one that blesseth thee." And he cried again all the way to the train station and while Benjamin's several bags were being loaded and while he tipped the porter twenty-five dollars to look after his only son.

When he graduated first in his class, his father donated a handsome sum to the library and bought Benjamin a portfolio of stocks, which later, alas, declined considerably in value.

When he married, they arrived in a caravan of cars stuffed to the roofs with late Victorian silver, hand-hemmed linen, hideous Capodimonte vases and a small bag of garlic for his bride to wear around her neck when she conceived their grandchild. His wife had worn it to bed as a joke and they spent their first night smelling like a tossed salad.

Even in death they embraced him. There was now, at this very moment, a family tomb of Veronese splendor awaiting him in a San Pedro churchyard. It was carved of rose marble imported from Tuscany, and his parents, in the form of two grieving shades bowed with sorrow, were chiseled on its facade. He thought, though he wasn't sure, that they had even purchased his casket. If so, he didn't know where it was stored. His boyhood house had long been unvisited.

"That," Emma said, "is a hard act to follow."

"Not at all. I was very happy as a boy. As a consequence, I love life, revere it. My father's tears were good for me. They demonstrated emotion, open, unashamed. Human feelings, humanly shown. Lovely. I often weep. At school they called me the Faucet. There were three suicides in my class, one total breakdown, fifteen shattered marriages. All from backed-up feelings, smothered feelings, dead sensibilities, murdered sensibilities. Laugh, cry, boys, girls, all of us. I conduct a class in laughing and crying. You must come see it sometime. It's terrific."

"Is my mother enrolled?"

"Yes, as a matter of fact. We've already had long talks about her girlhood, her past, what she can still recall of it. I like your mother. She likes me. We've talked about you." He stubbed out his cigar, stretched, groaned. "Too much dinner. Hereafter, keep an eye on me. Don't let me eat bread."

"*What* about me?" Emma was on guard.

"What did your mother and I discuss, you mean? Why your marriage failed. What's to become of you."

"Stick to laughing and crying, why don't you?" Emma said sharply. She struggled out of his jacket and tossed it at him. She got to her feet. Suddenly she wanted to bring the evening to an end. He remained where he was, looking at her.

"Let me quote the Talmud. 'If I am not for myself, who will be? If I am only for myself, what am I? If not now, when?' Do you like that?"

"Not at this late hour."

"It's only ten o'clock."

"I'm tired," Emma said crossly.

"No," Bartolome said, "you're defensed. I'll help you with that." Slowly he arose from the swing. "All right," he said, "off to bed, then. I'll put the lights out and lock the door." He took her arm companionably and walked her inside to the foot of the stairs.

"Next time will be your turn," he said and then quite lightly he added, "How pretty you look in this light, circles under your eyes and all."

"You're rather pretty yourself," Emma said. "Thank you for dinner, Benjamin."

"You're welcome, Emma. Sweet dreams."

He walked away, turning out one lamp after another as he crossed the room. Emma waited a moment in the darkness, but the door closed and he was gone.

Charles's manuscript lay on her bedside table, accusing her of indifference. It was not procrastination that had kept it there unread. Emma hated pain; she did not wish to inflict it nor to be its victim. She knew how hard Charles labored, how doggedly he sought to express the grain and cross grain of life. He was a man of sensibility but he saw life as a puzzling maze; each turn confused him. He would have preferred a straight line from entrance to exit, from birth to death. Visions, fancies, whims were all obstacles in his path. She often thought he would have been happier as a lawyer, happier still with a plow and a furrow before him. He had, in fact, wanted to be an architect but there was no money to educate him. He had loved the farm but it had been sold, leaving him homeless in place and spirit. One summer he played baseball in the minor leagues, and he had enjoyed the long, mild summer evenings with his good-natured neighbors cheering him on and the kids clustering around him after the games, asking for autographed balls. He liked the company of the players with their wads of chewing tobacco tucked into their cheeks and their jaunty promiscuity. He might have made that his niche but he tore the cartilage in his knee, and after some time in the hospital he saw that he was too old and too complicated to stand on third base much longer, shading his eyes against the sun. He wrote a little story about the ball players and sold it to a sports magazine for twenty-five dollars. It was called "Dugout" and it wasn't very good, but a fan had written him from Eugene saying it was the best baseball story he had ever read — better even than Ring Lardner's. Charles still had the letter. He tried his hand at several other things, selling haberdashery and counseling at a summer camp, and finally one day he bought a cheap Smith-Corona typewriter and told his folks he'd decided to be a writer.

He sat all day long out on the screened back porch with a dictionary and a thesaurus beside him while his father tinkered with the family car in the yard and looked over his shoulder at his son with considerable bewilderment. Those looks worried Charles. After a while, he went indoors and sat on his bed in his bedroom with the typewriter on a card table before him. It was stifling in the room — the windows were jammed with old paint and he couldn't raise them — but he stuck it out, soaking his shirts with sweat, racking his brain for inspiration, trying for a humble place in the world of letters. He doubted the truthfulness of every word he wrote, and he cared very much for the truth. He couldn't see much of a market for the stories he knew. They were mostly about deprivation and loneliness. The local pharmacist had committed suicide because his wife had left him to raise three small children by himself. One of the high school teachers was a compulsive gambler who bought pari-mutuel tickets with every cent he had and ended up selling his house and his car and his kid's Red Arrow bicycle. Charles's piano teacher was a flasher and had to leave town by invitation of the local sheriff. Charles, following the dictate that one must write about something one knows, put them all into story after story. He received twenty-three printed rejection slips and one two-line criticism from a junior editor. "Mr. Howard, I rather liked your last effort but our readership leans to the brighter side of things." He did not keep that letter but he took its warning to heart.

He wrote a screenplay about two cowhands on a spree and sold it to Paramount Pictures for five thousand dollars. He had packed up his suitcase and his typewriter and had taken a Greyhound bus south to Los Angeles. His father applauded the move. He told Charles that there were suckers born every day and, if they'd pay that kind of money for dog tracks across paper, Charles had better get himself down there and dip his bread in the gravy. His mother saw him off and gave him a box of fried chicken to eat on the way. She didn't kiss him good-by. Nobody in the family ever kissed in public.

He found a two-room apartment on Fountain Avenue that looked out on an alley and into a dead palm tree, and he lived there alone among bit players and carhops and boisterous students from U.C.L.A.

Loneliness drove Charles hard. He worked from six in the morning to six at night, stopping only for an hour's walk after lunch to keep himself in shape. He grew very silent. No one spoke to him except the mailman. He longed for the old days among the cheerful baseball players. Sometimes he awoke in the night, thinking he smelled perfume, but it was only the orange tree blossoming across the street. He tried a desultory flirtation with a girl who shopped in the same local market, but he saw that she only bought gin and cat food and he was afraid to get involved.

He wrote screenplay after screenplay. One about two policemen on a spree, another about two interns on a spree. They were not very lighthearted. They didn't sell. He thought he ought to work with his hands again for a while. He bought some power tools and began to make furniture for his living room. He made a very nice imitation Shaker bench and a hanging shelf. He made a dining room table with lathe-turned legs and a passable chest of drawers. There was sawdust everywhere, and one night he stepped on a nail on his way to the bathroom and had to call a taxi and go to the emergency room. The nurse who took care of him slept with him that night, but she was married and did things to him in bed that he did not feel he could reciprocate, so it came to nothing in the end. He felt as if he were a clock, winding down, running too slow to be of any use to anyone. He caught a cold and ran a temperature and got up to make himself canned tomato soup, shivering and desolate in his awful solitude. He wondered where the wicked life of the city could be found. When he made a casual inquiry of a fellow writer he met at the Screenwriters' Guild, the man looked at him with contempt for his gaucherie. Then he relented and gave him a sort of map indicating where orgies were held after barbecues and where he could obtain a very special massage. Charles drove by the health spa and saw a sixteen-year-old girl with a beehive hairdo smoking in the doorway. She was playing with a yo-yo. Charles fled in horror.

After that he stayed close to home, reading Dostoyevsky and Turgenev and Isaac Bashevis Singer. He grew a beard and stopped eating meat. He began to have a spiritual air about him that the girls found attractive, and soon they were drifting barefoot by his door with guitars slung over their shoulders. Some of them stayed and brought fruit and whole-wheat bread and venereal disease. He stopped writing and went to see obscure French and Italian movies, sometimes with a girl draped on each arm. Sometimes he awoke with a girl draped on each arm. Then he saw that he was too old for that, too, and he moved out to Westwood to a neighborhood where everyone made thirty thousand dollars a year and washed their cars on Saturday. He sold all his handmade furniture in a garage sale, meticulously pointing out to all the potential buyers that the stuff was not antique and that he had put the marks of age on the wood with tire chains.

He began working again from six in the morning to six in the evening, stopping only to run on the beach to keep fit. There he had first seen Emma; and the very sight of her made him glad that so much of his life was before him . . . .

Emma picked up the manuscript. It was entitled "It Will Be Fair and Warmer in Los Angeles Today." She began to read.

Emma rarely cried and then not for the reasons most people shed tears. Once, when she was at college, she saved her money and bought her mother a nine-carat gold heart on a chain. When she saw that her mother wore the locket to bed, and in fact never took it off, she wept. She cried, in privacy, leaning against a cold tile wall in the women's lavatory at City Hall the day of her marriage to Charles, tears she had never analyzed and did not wish to remember.

She wept as she finished Charles's script. It was as if everything he had ever hoped for had finally yielded to him. All his minute calculations, all his rigidity, had left him and he had written about love with such brightness and ardor that he seemed to stand splendidly naked before Emma. Gone was the touchy, estranged figure who had turned a stiff back to her through a parade of nights. Here was a new Charles who had found a joining of need and appeasement, a verdant summer for his middle years. She saw that he would brush his beloved's hair, sing in his bath, fornicate in dappled sunshine under a tree. When he turned out his pockets on the bureau at night, there would be a found penny and a scrap of verse among its contents. This Charles would spend February in Spain, cancel his health insurance policies, hang up his umbrella, go hatless in all weather. He would disconnect his phone, change jobs, vault a fence. He might even let the fallen leaves go unraked, let his calendar of religious holidays go unmarked. Charles, who had been given to penance, would no longer fall on his knees except to aim a kiss. There was no dark night of the soul; when the light failed, it would be only a lamp turned low.

Charles, who questioned endlessly, had found an answer. How moved Emma was by the largesse, the amplitude of it. How chagrined that she was not the source.

It was all there in the pages Emma read. How willing he was to be claimed, to serve his love, to set out its myriad virtues. Emma saw now that she had not secured him against himself; she had not stilled his doubts.

There was a photograph of him in a broken frame standing at her bedside table. Charles had often looked at it ruefully. He said the picture embalmed his dead youth. It had been taken on a raw, windy day and, with his hair lifted from his head and his prominent Adam's apple visible, he looked as if he had just arrived in a country whose language he did not understand with a passport that was not valid. His ongoing journey had been equally desolate. "What are you saying?" "I don't understand." "No, I have no credentials."

Emma riffled the pages of the script. He remembered a sunset in Antibes, the sun falling like a wilted rose into the sea. He remembered it differently from Emma. She recalled a disputed hotel bill and no sun at all. He had watched a pretty girl eat snails, her tongue dipping into the shells with avidity. In his mind he had followed her into a tiny room with an iron bed where she had been beautifully charitable.

He remembered a hurdy-gurdy playing after dark in Lugano. There had only been bad French records played on an ancient Victrola Emma had cranked herself.

Aloud Emma said, "I can't have been so dumb."

She hauled herself out of bed and went to study her face in the mirror. "You're a fine one," she said. She leaned closer, noting the stubborn mouth. Suddenly she was chilled and apprehensive, exposed to herself. Could she inspire what Charles had written of so eloquently? Emma questioned it in the cold air at this latest of late hours.

Your husband has written his best work and you inspired not one single line of it. Think of that, Emma the Strong. Emma the Meek bowed her head, but only for a moment.

"Well," she said, "I am what I am. I'll get him a whopping price for his script. That's more than she can do."

Emma invited Charles to lunch, packed a picnic basket, selected a pretty straw hat he had long admired. Then she grew uncertain, left it on a peg in the hallway and changed her blouse twice, settling on one he had bought her in Majorca. Charles had always given marvelous presents. One year he had bought her a white goat, which they tethered in the backyard. He learned to milk it and to make cheese out of the milk, and he had said that the sight of Emma barefoot in the garden with her head bowed against the animal's flank had refreshed his spirit. He had driven halfway down the coast to a little shop where one could buy pearls bred in oysters and had shucked fifty of them until he found a suitable one. Emma still wore it almost every day. In those days, Emma thought, she deserved his attentions. She had reciprocated with carameled apples, for which he was downright gluttonous, and out-of-print Dashiel Hammett mysteries sought after in book shops, and a bathrobe she had made herself that did not fit. He wore it to shreds although it only came to his knees.

In those days they took immense pleasure in each other's company, prodigally hiring baby-sitters so they could walk in Griffith Park or along Hollywood Boulevard. They seemed astonishingly durable in those days, with no money and stacks of bills. They were not bothered by deprivation. Charles went around the house with a pencil stuck behind his ear, making light of the fact that his bathwater ran cold (the water heater having given out), that they lived on strange casseroles, sat in odd chairs, slept under worn and shrunken blankets.

Emma served forth her messes with a flourish, concealing the grayish chicken parts under rafts of parsley. She wore Charles's old sweaters and thongs she bought at the dime store. He said she had style enough to give any clothes an air. She agreed. She said he was handsome in his old dungarees. He agreed. Sex simmered between them constantly in those days, like a rich broth. Emma said she could do it three or four times a day with pleasure. She was willing to stop peeling potatoes and hop into bed at any hour. He had only to beckon her, to lift a finger. She said she had as many varieties to show him as Heinz had pickles and God knows that was fifty-seven. He was abashed but game. Emma, he said, took the cake. He often told her how he had dreaded marrying some stalwart farm girl who would can peaches and have the neighbors in to coffee. He could hardly believe his luck when he had met Emma, who played the ukelele without her clothes on and who put her hand between his legs the very first time he took her to a movie. He found her so competent, so unexpected. She knew how to pitch a tent. She knew the verses of Donne. She could change a tire. She nursed her babies.

Emma met him in the park, lugging the basket with two bottles clinking against each other. She felt the need to fortify herself against this meeting. She wanted him to go away this time charmed. For old times' sake. For that lovely, old and almost eclipsed time.

"Hi," she said, waving an arm in greeting. "I've brought champagne."

Charles came toward her and Emma saw that his shirt was badly ironed. She had the feeling he had done it himself, probably at midnight, standing in the kitchen, testing the iron with the tip of his finger as he had seen her do. He took the basket from her and they found a spot on the Palisades, where the elderly walked in the gentle sunshine, some cradling small fretful dogs, some linked arm in arm, supporting each other.

Emma wondered, were she and Charles to go on together,

whether they would have ended up two tall, old figures lording it over the landscape of age.

They sat together on the grass. He rummaged in the basket. "Deviled eggs. You make good deviled eggs, as I remember."

Emma lay on her back and stared up into the sky. She felt suddenly that nothing had intervened in their lives, that they were here as they had been many times in the past, that they were innocent of malice or harmful intention, that they were good friends.

"Charles," she said, "I read your script. It knocked me for a loop. I was up all night, lost in admiration, bowled over."

"Thank you, Emma. With all my heart."

She hesitated and then went on. "New inspiration . . . better words."

"Emma," he said sternly, "you're peeking through the keyhole. Don't."

"Okay. I can't see anything anyway." She paused. "How are you feeling these days, Charles? Are you happy?"

"Are you, Emma?"

"I asked first."

He leaned against a tree, closed his eyes. Two sea gulls stole a crust of bread and carried it out to sea between them.

"I guess you could say I'm a looser fellow, all in all. You could call that happiness if you want to."

"How come you're so thin?"

"I do the cooking. You wouldn't like to give me some recipes, would you?"

"I'll send you *The Joy of Cooking*. Everything I make comes out of that. Charles?"

"Hmmm?" He reclined on one elbow, his face close to hers.

"Are you looked after?"

"Bodily? Spiritually? How, Emma?"

"Your shirt isn't ironed very well."

"I haven't got the hang of it yet."

Emma scowled. "Damn it, Charles," she said, "you won't tell me anything."

He grinned. "What would you like to know?"

"Things that are none of my business. Like . . . is she better in bed than I am?"

"You're right," he said. "They're none of your business."

"Is she or isn't she?"

"Emma, you're no lady."

She hugged her knees and thought awhile. "You used to like that about me."

"I still do."

Emma rolled over on her stomach. She was wearing tight and very becoming jeans. "I think," she said slowly, "that you're in a Saturday afternoon state."

Whenever else, they were always sure to make love on Saturday afternoons, sending the kids to the longest double feature they could find. Emma remembered the boys complaining to her that no matter how late they came home they found the front door locked and had to play catch in the yard until their arms ached and the light failed.

"Maybe I am," he said. "I'm in the mood for you today. Maybe it's this champagne. Maybe it's your praise of my endeavor. Maybe it's the curve of your fanny. Look across the street, Emma. What do you see?"

"A hotel."

"A very nice little hotel. Why don't we see what their vacancy factor is? Why don't we stroll across the street and make some inquiries?"

Emma sat up in the grass. "What will that prove, Charles?"

"I can't say at this distance."

"The cheater cheating." She was tart.

Charles was not deflected. "Emma," he said, "you used to accuse me of having a very tight asshole. I can no longer be described in that way. Doesn't that stir any curiosity in you?"

She sighed. "I hate moral dilemmas," she said. But there was something about Charles that induced recklessness.

"Come across the street, Emma," he said in a low tone, "just across the street."

Emma measured the distance, estimated the risks. Tomorrow she might be struck by a car or burst her appendix. She might slip on a banana peel or be electrocuted plugging in her hair dryer. She never knew when fate's glittering eye would fasten upon her and she would be beyond love in the afternoon. When all was said and done it was such a short walk across the street it seemed foolish not to take it. Emma did.

The afternoon they passed together was lovely and soothing, restorative to the ego but not a panacea. They parted with kind words but in time, Emma noted, for Charles to avoid the four o'clock traffic and for her to stop at the butcher shop and get lamb chops for dinner. If truth be told, she planned the meal while still in bed. Nothing else had been solved there. Plainly they could give each other pleasure. Charles was an assured and accomplished lover, making all the right choices. He was both mannerly and passionate, seeing that she had her fair share of the blankets and all else. But when they rose, politely sharing the bathroom, the intimacy was at an end. She felt they had each given the other the smallest part of themselves and that what was reserved might never be granted. It was very sad. They held hands going down the stairs into the cheerless lobby. Charles saw her to her car. He urged her to drive with care. He left her.

All the way home, winding down Sunset Boulevard, Emma thought of herself for the first time as really divorced from her husband. Their life together had moved into the past tense. *We used to go to the ball games. We always traveled in the summer. We knew each other when young. We were married.* It hardly seemed possible that they should make so final an end to it all. It hardly seemed bearable. It was not jealousy. Emma stopped herself abruptly. Not true. There was jealousy in it somewhere. She knew Carla bested her by simply being younger. One could not underestimate the charms of fresh young skin, pellucid eyes, little shell ears hearing everything for the first time. Could one compete with the first tonic mix of new lovers?

Very well. He needed fresh adulation. Emma was not beyond understanding that. She knew Charles, knew him in light and shade, sickness and health. She had discounted his pettiness, loved his humor, bowed, now and then, to his opinions. She even knew his shadowy, sorrowing soul.

"That's smug," she said aloud. "You're smug, Emma. And that's how you've lost the game."

For as well as she thought she knew Charles, she knew herself better. Sometimes too abrasive, too hearty, too quick to recover. It must have seemed to Charles that she was without tear ducts, without nerve ends, beyond suffering. She had felt for him, in his wavering, uncertain review of his life. She had only not said so.

And, Emma, she asked herself, what is to become of you? For a moment she lost her nerve thinking of it. She would never do good works or play mahjong or arrange tennis lessons to fill the weekends. More likely she would garden until dark, drink more than was good for her, rise in her job and sink in her self-esteem. Unwise, unhealthy, unnecessary. Suddenly she craved her mother. There was no malaise that couldn't be cured by listening to her mother's crisp voice proposing common sense and self-preservation. She would go to her mother.

There were only two people sitting in the garden watching the dazzling sky cool into darkness. Dr. Bartolome and Agatha reclined in deck chairs like companionable travelers on a calm sea. Emma heard their voices as she walked across the lawn, and saw that her mother had arranged her hair in a new way and that she seemed smaller. Her mother was gesturing emphatically, as if she were batting away an argument she would not brook.

They looked up at Emma's approach. "Hello, Emma," her mother said, "what are you doing here?"

Bartolome rose to his feet. "Ah," he said with pleasure, "you've come just in time. We were about to exchange blows.

I'm getting to know your mother. It will show me what to look out for in you. Stay and eat dinner with us. We're having a dance afterward. I'll whirl you around a time or two."

"Lovely," Emma said.

Her mother's eyes questioned her, penetrated her. "Something's wrong with you. You get a lemony color when you're not right."

Emma shrugged, detesting the tears she felt sting her eyes. Bartolome studied her as well. "I'll leave you two alone. Don't sneak off. I'll want to see you later."

He left them. Emma's mother patted the seat, held out her thin hand to settle Emma beside her.

"Well, puss," she said, "what is it?"

"Nothing," Emma said, and then, "everything."

She put her head in Agatha's lap and felt her mother stroke her hair. "Look up," she heard her say. "You won't see a sky like this every night."

Emma raised her head. There was a last flourish of color like a trumpet note and a pale elegant moon just becoming visible. "I don't know why I'm bothering you," Emma said. "I just felt low and I thought if I came and saw you you'd buck me up or dose me with castor oil or something."

"Castor oil won't do a thing for heartache, as far as I know," her mother said crisply. "It's plain to me that you're moping over your marriage. Well, it's far too late for that. If I were in your shoes I'd give up on it. Right now. Right this minute. You did some things wrong and some things were out of your hands. Your husband came into middle life and he didn't want to be there. Nothing you could do about that — beyond not staring at his bald spot when he developed one. Charles forgot that he was alive and breathing and growing. He counted his birthdays, that was his trouble. It made him angry to be middle-aged. Well, I don't like being old but at whom am I to shake my fist? God is through with me, that's obvious. Now I like Charles, I always have, but I think he's off on a fool's errand. So be it." She drew her sweater around her and looked closely into Emma's eyes. "Raise your boys, Emma, improve your mind, show some spunk and you won't lack for male attention. Now let's go in and primp a little. I intend to dance the first waltz with that Italian doctor."

The dancers swirled around the room to music provided by a slightly palsied piano player with a dead cigar clamped in his jaw and by a very old woman playing the fiddle who stomped time with an emphatic foot clad in a dusty tennis shoe. The musicians knew what they were doing. Anemic blood leapt, faulty hearts accelerated, all capacities were enlarged as the rinky-dink music drove them on. A light breeze lifted the window curtains. They floated on it like thistles, grasses, seed pods, two by two, fox-trotting, waltzing, jigging, in blithe disregard of tempo, age or the hazard they presented to each other as they collided.

Bartolome lead all the rest, partnering Emma's mother with élan, swooping this way, bending that, whispering in her ear, throwing his head back to laugh.

Emma stood against the wall and watched and waited her turn. She had waited on other occasions, high school proms, college homecomings, standing with her back straight and her gaze accusing, scowling, until, unable to tolerate it, she had advanced on an enclave of men drinking beer in a dark corner, tapped the tallest of them with a brusque, "Come on," and rewarded him with the thrust of her pelvis for the rest of the evening. She smiled a little now remembering herself then.

She had earned a reputation for being promiscuous, which was only partially true. She considered herself straightforward. She saw that not much was volunteered her unless she asked for it, and she saw no reason to be self-pitying and lonely. She was neither. She thought, on balance, that she gave good measure. She loaned money, was neither laconic nor sleepy in bed, would hold her boyfriend's head in the men's room should the need arise, and never compared, even in her mind, one with another. As a result her friendships were durable and she was invited to all-male poker games, at which she won enough money to see her through her senior year.

She wondered, were that time restored to her, if she would have done better to acquire a milder manner, to have reconciled herself to posturing and delicate lies and airs and various graces. Might she not have ended up with a husband who brushed her hair and remained faithful through every exigency of life? Might she not be his only enthusiasm, her photograph in his wallet, her name on his lips, designated his insurance beneficiary and the one to call should he be struck by a passing car?

Emma shifted from one foot to the other and yawned, accepting herself as she was, accepting her quick-stepping mother, waiting her turn. It would come. Already she saw Bartolome's head turning in her direction, offering her an unsmiling stare, an unspoken signal. He was on the watch for her; she felt it in a sudden tension that seemed to rise over the heads of the dancers as if he had sent her a challenge.

Her mother finally relinquished Bartolome with a benedictive pat on the head. Emma saw her chance and took it. She was across the room and into his arms before the first chorus of "The Indian Love Song" was under way. They danced a sedate waltz without speaking, moving smoothly together as if they were long-accustomed partners. Emma felt soothed and comforted with his hand low and warm on her back, faintly sleepy, at her ease. She liked the sense that she could talk or remain silent, that in neither case would it occasion ill will. She wanted time to dwell on her afternoon with Charles, to sort it out like a good housewife putting a linen cupboard in order. She felt that she had let things slide too long, had let dust gather and fall silently over reason and good sense. Well, she had made a beginning, she told herself as she circled and circled in Bartolome's arms. She had spoken the word "separation" aloud, testing it as she might the temperature of water, too hot or too cold to endure. When she found she could bear it she had gone a step further and said "severance" in her head, a more surgical stroke; the final one.

Perhaps she would take a house at the beach, far up the coast where something could be had at a decent price. She would walk at night, alone, and look at the ragged sky with its scraps of colored clouds. She would see about love again, or some form of it, in the autumn. Autumn was the time for it, when the close summer days were left behind and a new season began with softened light and shortened days. She would drift through two seasons and awake on the advent of the third. She would know herself by then; she would be on easy terms, brown, probably overweight and, she hoped, good-natured once more.

"You're very quiet," Bartolome said.

"I've been wrestling with problems."

"Any you want to confide in me? I'm a good listener."

"Your office is closed, or it should be. Besides, I hate it when people come up to doctors at parties and say, 'Could you tell me why my ear aches?' or, 'I have a pain just above my appendix.' "

"My patients suffer after office hours, too."

"I'm not suffering," Emma said, and then instantly, "do I look as if I'm suffering? I've eaten my lipstick off. I always look washed-out without lipstick."

Bartolome shook his head impatiently. "How did you arrive here? I'll tell you. In tears."

"Smog," she said promptly.

"What happened to you today?"

"It would be indelicate to tell you, so I won't."

Bartolome did not answer her for a long moment. He seemed to retreat into himself, and then he lifted his head and gave her a protracted look.

"I make people feel better. That's what I do. Say I'm egotistical, which I am. Say I want to show you how good I am. Other men preen in other ways. They display themselves in their clothes, shirts open, chest hair visible. They drive large cars . . . hard bargains." He smiled. "I'm clever. I want you to know that. Put yourself in my hands. You could do worse."

"And what will you do with me?" Emma inquired.

"To begin with I'll take you away for a weekend. To Coronado maybe, to that big, old, wooden hotel, which I like very much. I know where to get good oysters, so I'll feed you oysters. I'll bring along some wine that will make you sit up and take notice. I'll take you sailing. Then I'll have beach chairs set out on the sand and I'll sit in one of them with my hands folded over my stomach, looking up at the sky, and I'll wait."

"I do love oysters," Emma said.

# Chapter Ten

FELICIA SAT on Emma's bed sewing buttons on the shapeless men's pajamas that Emma habitually wore to bed. She herself slept in voluminous cambric nightgowns with handstitched hems, modest but tempting with their pale ribbons and their calculated innocence. As for Emma's tattered bathrobe, a disgrace. What woman in her right mind would be seen in torn Chinese silk with bellicose dragons showing their fangs over her breasts? "You'd do better to go naked," she advised.

Emma, paying bills at her desk, frowned over the figures, seeing herself depleted in old age, and she groaned aloud. "We've got to cut down," she muttered darkly. "I'm not made of money."

Felicia bit off a thread with a disdainful snap of her teeth. "A lady is judged by her underwear." She held aloft the offending garment. "You're going to let him see you the first time in this?"

Emma looked up, peering through her glasses. "What's wrong with them? They're comfortable. They're clean."

"Convicts wear pajamas like these." She put them aside with disgust. "It'll end before it begins."

Emma licked stamps, slapped them onto envelopes. "It's not

important. I won't be in 'em long. How did the light bill get to be sixty dollars, that's what I want to know? I'll murder those kids if they're reading till three in the morning. Lamb chops, four ninety-eight a pound. It's got to be chili till they go back to school. I can't afford to give them four lamb chops apiece." She rubbed the back of her neck, shoved her glasses up into her hair, thus ruining the frames she had again overpaid for. "The plumber makes more than I do. You know why I don't care what I look like in bed? I'll tell you why. I don't feel sexy. All I think about is what a new roof is going to cost this fall and why there's still a leak in the basement when I had two men out here at twenty-five bucks an hour cementing the whole damn thing and why I have the only Dichondra in the neighborhood that is being eaten away by blight. The money goes like water. Pack the pajamas. They'll do."

"Maybe you ought to get married again," Felicia said.

"I'm not divorced."

"A man would take care of you."

"Who says? Has a man taken care of you?"

"No. Because I don't allow it. I make my own decisions in life." Felicia was majestic. "I gave up the church, marriage and red meat all in one year. I don't miss any of them. My sister in Guatemala wants to buy a farm with me. She's very hard-working, very sweet. We'd be a house of women. She knows how to use a plow. I know how to use a gun. I'm thinking about it."

"Keep a room for me." Emma padded across to her bed, scratched inelegantly, flopped down with her arms behind her head.

"How long have we been together, Felice?"

"Since the children were born. Lots of years."

"It's been peaceful around here with just you and me." Emma yawned. "Maybe a house of women is a good idea." As she spoke, the memory of just such a time came back to her. Her father had gone on a hunting trip and she and her mother and her aunt had spent a burning August together, wandering through the house with the shades drawn, down to their slips, hair carelessly combed, eating dainty food, napping on the couches and on the porch swings like so many pregnant cats. The scent of her father's cigars had faded from the draperies, replaced by lavender toilet water and the redolence of heavy-headed roses. The days had slipped away, one after another, murmurous with chatter and tea sipped in the shade and confidences offered in light soprano voices. Emma remembered butterflies with petal-thin wings hovering over her aunt's head as she dyed her hair a defiant shade of red and her mother sat on the railing enumerating and setting aside the men of their common past.

"Oh, he came to no good at all. He married badly and died young."

"And his brother. I really preferred his brother."

"A bankrupt."

"And the Tilson boys?"

"I never cared for them."

"Still?"

"They were after money, you know."

"Did they find it?"

"I'm sure I couldn't say. Did I tell you, Agatha, I'm going to Europe in the spring?"

"Alone?"

"Yes, of course."

"You're lucky."

"Come with me?"

Emma never forgot the look of longing on her mother's face as she listened to the offer that would bear her away to strange landscapes seen through the windows of rolling trains, to narrow hotel beds and politely shared bathrooms. She could almost see her mother weigh the stamp and snort of her husband's presence against the cool possibilities of escape.

"He can't tie his shoe if I'm not here. Some other time . . . perhaps."

Emma had questioned the reply later, after her aunt had departed, carrying away with her her air of virginity and the white paper fans with which she refreshed the air around her.

"Why didn't you decide to go with her?"

Her mother had begun to ascend the stairs. She paused, her hand on the railing. Her voice when she answered was low and rich and amused.

"I don't care to be explicit," she said. "It's enough to say that I sleep in a double bed and will continue to do so. If your aunt wishes to cling to her girlhood, that's up to her."

It was not necessary to elaborate. Emma long remembered her mother's dark eyes and the knowing lift of her eyebrow.

"Are you going to sleep now?" Felicia asked.

"Yes. Felice?"

Felicia was at the door. "What is it?"

"There's a new nightgown in my bottom drawer. It was on sale. I bought it in case I ever had to go to the hospital to have my uterus out. Pack that."

She fell asleep serene in the thought that she was her mother's daughter.

From the first hour Emma saw that things would go well with Bartolome. He was capable of tact; he was not a man to take a woman to bed before he had so much as unpacked his toothbrush. He had booked two adjoining rooms, saying nothing to her about the door that could be opened between them. Nothing smacked of strategy, unless she considered the small bouquet of flowers, so artless he might have cut them with his own hand from his own garden, and a peeled and sectioned orange standing on a plate by her bedside. That touch delighted her. It was as if he was privy to her habits. She did wake dry-mouthed in the morning and often kept fruit on her bedside table. She liked that single orange, as if he also knew she would pass only one morning alone — a confident and not improbable assurance on his part.

He had also left instructions with the desk clerk that he was available for certain calls, explaining to Emma as they rode up in the elevator that he had a patient, an old man who was truly sick of life and stayed his hand only to argue with Bartolome the ethical questions of suicide and his right to commit it.

Emma, having known male cunning and contrivance, was oddly moved that he was willing to be found at any hour in any circumstance. Somehow it incorporated the intimacy to come; she could already see him rise from her warm bed, grumbling and unwilling, to grope for the phone while she stroked his back and draped the sheet over his exposed body with wifely solicitude. Emma was no stranger to men and their ways, but each time had some shyness to conquer, some scruple, some small dread. One wondered about bathroom protocol, about proclivities; how intemperate might one be without causing astonishment or retreat? She had been surprised in her time and had surprised in turn. There was so much to keep in mind or to put out of it, and only rarely did delirium sweep all before it. There were burdens both of them would bring, other images coupling with them despite death and distance. How far could Charles be banished, and what echoes of another voice would Bartomole hear when her own cried out? Well, tush to all that, Emma concluded. She would not be heartless about the past, but she would relegate it and see that the time to come was their own.

Bartolome knocked on the door and waited till she opened it to him. Good again, she thought. Though he paid the bill, he did not consider himself the sole tenant.

"Your view is better than mine," he said, and she was amused to see that he was slightly aggrieved.

"Want to change rooms?"

"No." He went to the window, leaned far out. "Yes, you can see the whole sweep of the coast. *I* catch the corner of the building."

"Really. Change with me. I don't mind."

He turned back and looked at her slowly. "You've still got your hat on," he said, "which means you're bemused."

"Yes," Emma admitted it. "I'm thinking all this over."

He came across to her, snatched her hat and pitched it out the window. "That's the mood I'm in," he said. They both watched the wind catch it and sweep it across the sands.

"That was a twenty-dollar Italian straw hat," Emma said mildly.

"The first of many grand gestures. Are you hungry?"

"Starved. But I haven't unpacked yet."

"Shall we be comfortable with one another, Emma? Shall I bring my things in here?"

"Yes," she said. "Bring them in here."

"Once established, I'm not to be budged," he told her.

Emma considered it. It was getting late for prudence, later still for lamentation. Forward then, with fife and drums.

"Don't use all the hangers. I brought loads of clothes to impress you with. I propose to change two, or even three, times a day."

"Are you squeamish about strange fish?" he asked her. "Squid, for instance? Octopus? Eel?"

"I don't like fish but I eat what's set before me," Emma said.

"Do you know William Morris?" he asked suddenly.

"I know he made wallpaper and beautiful books."

Bartolome waved aside those trivialities. "He said the following: 'If we feel the least degradation in being amorous or merry, or hungry or sleepy, we are so far bad animals and therefore miserable men.' "

"I am all of those," Emma said. "Hungry in particular. It's the holiday air. When we travelled by car, I always ate up the sandwiches before we'd gotten half a mile. Charles said . . ." She stopped abruptly.

"Never mind what Charles said." He came and stood in front of her and traced the shape of her face with his hand. "Wonderful bones," he said, "and very widely spaced eyes."

"Myopic."

"Beautiful."

He took her into his arms and Emma knew she was in the presence of authority.

"I've been hibernating," he said, "but now I think it's time I stirred around. Yes, it's time to snuffle and scratch and rear up. At your side might be a very good place to begin."

They stood close, each listening to the sounds of thaw, the shivering of ice, the release of bound springs, the slow warming.

Emma put her mouth into the hollow of his throat. "I thrash in bed," she said. "I'll throw my leg over yours. It's a habit."

"All right."

"You won't mind?"

"Not in the least."

She whispered something then, into his ear, of other services. He laughed, then kissed her lightly. She was teased and baffled at its brevity.

"In good time, Emma," he said. "All in good time."

He placated her appetite with a huge lunch, of which she ate every scrap. At first it seemed to Emma that she was talking immoderately. They walked along the beach, close to the water, trying to avoid the littered sand and the cacophony of a dozen transistor radios vying with each other. Bartilome paid no heed to the discord, turning his attention to Emma as if they were all alone on some vast open strand, unpeopled, silent, their own terrain. Emma saw, with some pleasure, that he was scrutinized as they passed by half-a-dozen lithe, sun-ripened young girls who reared up on their oil-slicked elbows to take his measure. It made her aware once again that he was handsome and that, with his vexed, satanic face and his long confident stride, he dimmed the chicken-breasted boys who looked anxiously after them, sniffing a fox in the pen.

Now, Bartolome, his head bent close to hers, searched her out, feeling his way toward her. She liked being sounded. Bartolome seemed in search of subtle signs; he was after her singularity.

He should know that she, too, was egotistical, sure of her competence, certain that her cakes would rise and her children flourish. Did it signify that she saved string? Was it significant that she was loud in a quarrel and quick to shrug it off?

Of what interest was her fear of death — her own, her mother's? Should she tell him that she saw fate as both capricious and dangerous? Might she confide that what she wanted, above all else, was wisdom? That she wanted to come, at the end of her life, to some bounteous harvest of the mind, with all the chaff winnowed away and only mellow fruitfulness left? It seemed pretentious to say so.

"I'd like to end up with an illusion or two intact," she said, "and all my own teeth."

They had walked very far down the beach, walked away most of the afternoon.

"What else?"

"I want to see my children prosper. I want to go at full tilt till I'm old, eager for my meals, still able to read. I'd like a companion. A male companion who would say, 'Look at her, isn't she still remarkable?' Is it too much? Is it too little?" Emma paused to empty the sand from her shoes and to watch the water curling in a long, fringed line and drawing away again. Bartolome hunkered beside her and sifted the grains through his fingers.

"I met my wife when I was twenty-seven years old," he said. "She was five years older."

He told Emma how he had seen her in a park on a rather gray afternoon, wearing some kind of long, rather unfashionable dress, with her hair knotted on top of her head and pinned with a wicked-looking, ivory skewer. She had been painting and he had come and stood behind her, seeing at a glance that she had talent and humor. The sketch was of a lolling nude; the model, a girl sitting sedately upright opposite them.

He had offered to buy the little study on the spot and she had promptly ripped it from the pad, accepting the large sum as her due with satisfaction. A week later they were married. They never after discussed the haste with which they came together. Everything that followed was the purest happiness. He accepted it as he accepted water or air or food or any of the elements necessary to sustain life. He seemed never to have been without her. She must have been a presence, he felt, in every day of his previous life, in the same way that trees and the sky were. He had merely failed to round the corner to discover her.

She was not a beautiful woman; he was puzzled when he sometimes realized that her hair was dry and unkempt and that her mouth was large and irregularly shaped. He felt there was some injustice done her because she was plain. She deserved astonishing beauty.

No one quite understood his passion for her. His father, used to the Oriental acquiescence of his mother, found her angular and silent. His mother respected and recognized her virtues and only worried that her son might go unfed while his wife painted through the dinner hour and on through the long night until breakfast. But they were both artists, so his mother sent eggplants for her to incorporate in a still life, with directions for cooking them afterwards.

Bartolome cared not at all that she was engrossed, a woman who lived in a dream. He would sit in her studio after his office door had closed on the tears and lamentations and woes of his patients, laved in her calm, perturbation cooling in him as he watched her work. Sometimes she questioned him, always to the point. Mostly she listened. All their life together she listened. No one could imagine the charm of that audience in a world of talkers, self-absorbed, self-enamored talkers. He emptied himself into her. He'd never had such a friend; had never conceived of friendship as a component of marriage. You were married and had friends. He lived and rejoiced with his.

That was the anguish of her death; the loss of a friend who knew more of him than he knew of himself. The images of their life together faded slowly, like snapshots exposed to the sun. There they were, eating bread and drinking wine under the trees he had planted in the garden; there stood a pile of his shirts, beautifully ironed, crisp, buttoned, still warm in the folds; there was her chair with its faded cretonne cushions holding the shape of her body. One spoke of the terrible tears and rents of death but overlooked the small cuts: her glasses, her bedroom slippers, her battered hairbrush, a scattering of hairpins lost under the bed. And there was the silence . . . that vast, interior silence that seemed like a wide, frozen plain with no end, stretching into a desolate distance. How he had stumbled and lumbered through those empty weeks. He still had to rise in the morning, put together a day. He had to eat and shop for the food, holding two peaches, replacing one, thinking of the reduced portion of his being. He lived in a litter of cans with the taste of ashes in his mouth. He went to the cleaner's. He changed the sheets on his bed with murderous rage in his heart. He mopped the kitchen floor. Slowly he dismantled his former life, burning his wife's letters and packing her clothes in cartons for the ladies of the neighborhood to take away. He read her diary, laughing aloud with a kind of manic glee at her sharpness, at her self-mocking gibes. He grew a savage-looking beard. He went to the movies and stayed till the last showing, until he was left alone with the ushers, who stepped over him to pick up the gum and candy and empty pop bottles. He wrote terrible replies in response to notes of condolence, railing against the asininity of commiseration. He was beyond pity.

His wife had a sister living somewhere in the east. He sent for her under the guise that she was needed to help settle the estate. He began to imagine that when he met the plane his wife would be on it, wearing her faded print dress and her old-fashioned crystal beads. He was so sure of it that he prepared everything for her arrival as he might have done before. He bought wine and flowers. He cut the lawn and had the windows washed. For the first time he slept through the night, his arm curved around the pillow next to him. He saw that he had lost an enormous amount of weight and went and bought new clothes, a handsome sweater and some expensive shoes. He shaved his beard. He seemed to have an unslakable thirst and his pulse was rapid. It was the same feeling he had always had when he returned to his wife, even after the briefest separation.

On the day the sister was to arrive, he phoned the airport three times to see if the plane was on schedule. He got caught in a traffic jam on the freeway and cursed and blew his horn and was sideswiped by another car as he cut recklessly in and out of the traffic. A voice in his head kept repeating, "soon, soon," and when he looked up into his mirror he found that he was smiling ferociously. He stopped to buy peach ice cream, an old indulgence of his wife's. He bought three quarts, heedless that it melted on the front seat of the car. Its fragrance rose like the air of a summer afternoon and he recalled kisses that tasted of it.

The sister was nothing like his wife. She was smaller, paler, with kind eyes and a weak smile. He kept looking beyond her, straining for the true appearance, but when she took his arm and spoke his name he felt such disappointment, so ruined, that he could barely acknowledge her. He took her home because there was nothing else to do. They barely spoke. The wine went untasted, the flowers unnoted.

Still, in the middle of the night, he got up, went down the dark hall to the guest room and lay beside her on the bed. She gathered him in without a word while he began vainly to sojourn in the past.

She had stayed on, not in the house but in the city. She was a good woman. He did not love her.

They walked along as the beach emptied and the sunlight diminished. Emma felt a strange kinship for this unknown, pale intruder. She too felt she hovered at the edge of a flaming funeral pyre, waiting for the fire to abate.

"You're thinking you'd be crazy to have anything to do with me," he said suddenly. "A man with hallucinations. A madman."

"No," Emma said, "I was thinking of your disappointment."

"I was out of my head," he said. "Then I recovered. I remember the exact moment. I bought myself a goldfinch. I've always found them beautiful creatures. I went into a shop and stood a long time before I selected the one I wanted. At that very moment, I said to myself, 'There have to be two of them.' I didn't want the one bird to die of loneliness. I remember thinking, 'Good. It's a good sign. I'm not suicidal. Good, I intend to live. To go on.' People are terrified by grief. It's necessary to grieve."

"Yes," Emma said. "It's just that my state of affairs seems so petty against yours. I'm only aggrieved. What do you want with me after such a notable woman."

"More of the same."

"What an optimist you are."

"Yes," he said emphatically. "Yes, Emma." He took her hand. "I'm confident of a favorable issue. I was an excellent husband. I was a student of my wife's moods, her whims, her crotchets. I did not marry in order to have room service or to have my tennis socks washed or because I wanted heirs or for convenient sex. At my best, I'm tender, accepting, reasonably affable, demonstrative. You can hardly afford to pass me by."

Emma smiled. "Not if all you say is true."

"I mean to have you," he said.

She was prepared to assist in that at the very least. That was the easiest part of it. Will you compare us, though? she thought, and then, being Emma, she said it. "Will you compare us?"

"No," he said. " I won't do that."

You will, Emma thought, but never mind.

"Stop wavering," he commanded, taking her into his arms, letting his hands reassure her that all was new and fresh and exciting. She was persuaded, then captured, then urgent. There'll be sand grating on my back, she thought. There'll be spectators parting the curtains in those houses, and then she did not think at all.

When they returned to the hotel, she saw Charles and Carla signing the register.

Oddly, Emma felt no agitation. There was something in the way the girl stood looking over her shoulder that spoke of unease, a harried look, as if she expected to be asked to leave for some offense against the decorum of the polished floors and the potted palm trees. She clutched her own luggage, a soiled airplane bag that could not have held more than one change of clothing. Both she and her baggage had a battered look, as if they had been tossed from hand to hand, had gone unclaimed in a dozen terminals.

Charles was engaged in some kind of small confrontation with the desk clerk. He had asked for rooms with a view of the ocean. He was being shunted into second best. His voice, raised in argument, had a cracked, defeated sound. Emma found herself stifling an urge to cross the lobby and straighten matters out for them, so forlorn did they seem, so in need of assistance.

"That," she said to Bartolome, "is my husband and his friend."

"Would you like me to get your room key? You could go upstairs if you're uncomfortable."

"No. I think I'll say hello." She did not take Bartolome's arm nor did he offer it. In fact she walked away from him as if she were striding into the wind.

"Hello there," she said. "Haven't we nice weather?"

Charles turned to her. His face was flushed and Emma saw with a certain tenderness that he looked tired. She knew that he had planned this weekend with care, that he had phoned ahead days ago, that he had a milk of magnesia bottle in his suitcase and hopelessness in his heart.

"Emma, this is Carla."

Emma held out her hand. "It's a shame you got here so late. We had a marvelous afternoon."

The girl's palm was damp, her fingers nerveless. She let her hand lie in Emma's as if she had no further use for it.

"They've put us in the wrong room," she said. Her voice was toneless and yet she made it appear a tragic circumstance to find herself down the hall, close to the elevator.

"There's a mix-up," Charles said wearily.

"The place is half-empty," Emma said and then, as she had so often advised him, "Make a stink."

The desk clerk lifted his head at the word. Emma met his gaze coolly. She won the round.

"We've found your reservation, Mr. Howard. You're in seven twenty-two."

"The same floor as me," Emma said cheerfully.

"We didn't know you were going to be here," Carla said. She bent and scratched her leg like a child, leaving nail marks trailing up her brown skin.

"Of course you didn't."

The girl seemed on the edge of tears, scratching fiercely at herself. Emma almost said, "Stop that, you'll infect yourself," the way she might have to one of her children.

Charles was stiff. "I'm sorry about this. Carla hasn't been feeling well. She needed a change."

Emma thought they really mustn't play out this little drama for the edification of the clerk, who was already looking from one to another.

"It's a large beach," she said. "There's room for all of us." She looked across at Bartolome, wishing he would come and sort them all out. In a moment he was at her side. Emma made introductions and the two men shook hands politely.

"We're all on the same floor," Emma said. "They're just two doors away."

"Well, then," Bartolome said imperturbably, "we're bound to run into each other."

Emma already saw herself waking to a false dawn, lying with her back turned to Bartolome, thinking with disquietude of Charles, who would also be awake, his thin dark face turned to the window. How close they would be and how far apart. He had the old tentative look back again, as if he had ventured too far for safety, and Emma saw appeal in his eyes that seemed to say: "Is it a long journey back?"

She wondered if Carla would know that when he ground his teeth and cried out in the night he was not sleeping. It was no longer a concern of hers, she told herself, not that or his dry cough or the fear that he would set himself afire in his bed with his pipe clenched in his jaw. You must deal with it all, she said silently to the girl who looked anxiously around the elevator as if its confines caged her intolerably.

"I was in an elevator once that fell," Carla said.

"In a dream," Bartolome told her quietly.

"No. Yes. In a dream." She looked at him sharply, as if his soothing tones were familiar. She embraced her bag as if it were some kind of support to hold her upright. Emma announced loudly that she hated elevators, that her throat closed with fear of getting stuck and that they must all walk up and down the stairs for the rest of their stay. It was good for the heart anyway.

"I forgot my toothbrush," the girl said, and Emma saw her walking dreamily through her house as she packed for the trip, holding a bathing suit in one hand, listening to the clock ticking loudly, listening to it erase her day.

"Put toothpaste on your finger."

She and Charles exchanged glances. Emma always forget her toothbrush, always cleaned her teeth ineffectively in this schoolgirl way.

"I forgot the toothpaste, too." For the first time she smiled and Emma saw that her smile was charming.

"I'll lend you mine," she said and thought, my toothpaste, my husband, whatever you need.

They had arrived at their floor and there was a little flurry while they deferred to each other getting out. Emma had the mad feeling that in another moment they would all be waltzing down the hall together in surreal camaraderie. Where might not this fellowship lead them, she asked herself — tumbling entangled on a water bed, dashing like yoked horses into the spraying surf? They separated with pleasant smiles and Carla, opening her door, cried back at Emma that their wallpaper was pink.

"Ours is blue," Emma said, and they waved at each other as they ducked inside.

Emma collapsed on the bed, kicked off her shoes, looked at Bartolome.

"A fine kettle of fish," she said.

He removed his jacket. A stream of sand spilled from his pockets. They both laughed. He went into the bathroom to wash his hands and called to her over the running water.

"How long have they been together? How well does he know the girl? She's very tense."

"I don't blame her," Emma said. "So am I."

He emerged from the bathroom and looked at her. "We don't have to stay."

I must, Emma thought, because I'm ingloriously curious and because I want to fit together all the missing parts and finally see for myself the shape of the puzzle. Already she saw that the wild blue bits were the girl's eyes.

"It's finished," she said to Bartolome and wondered if that were, indeed, so.

"Not quite, but that's to be expected. I like you, Emma," he said. "I like you and so does that girl and so does your husband."

"Why?" She put the question plainly, without artifice. At the moment she felt she had only just eased through a very narrow opening and that she was grazed and scraped by the passage.

"Well," he said sitting beside her on the bed, shoving her over rather rudely, "*I* like you because you open your mouth when you kiss. They like you because you were kind to them just now."

"Bosh," Emma said.

He laid his face between her breasts, pillowed himself there, sighed with pleasure.

"Emma, Emma, Emma," he said. "I'm sleepy." He closed his eyes.

"The first time we've ever been in a bed together?" she asked, though to her credit she asked it mildly.

His voice was muffled. "There'll be many times. All that sun . . . all that sea . . ." He trailed off, his breath beginning to come regularly. There was no question about it. The man was asleep. See, his relaxed body seemed to say, this is how I accept this French farce — husband, wife, lovers. I accept it with this infinite calm, this total repose. It made Emma laugh, but she smothered it so as not to disturb him, and then, in the same spirit, she closed her own eyes and finally, suspended in the liquid sound of the sea, she slept too.

Later she awoke to a salty wind lifting the curtains and found Bartolome lying on his side, watching her as if she were Venus reclining and he a mythic figure, helmet set aside, armor unbuckled, battle forgotten, time suspended. Emma felt that her toes might encounter springing grass and flowers; somewhere, surely, there must be a ripe pomegranate, split to reveal its wine red seeds, and above her head a less-than-innocent cherub. In an instant she knew that Bartolome's gods were pagan, that monkeys would chatter at them from the tree tops and leaf mold would tangle in her hair.

She was out of her clothes in a flash. This would be no domestic mating after the Sunday papers and before the tennis matches, orchestrated by the power mower next door. This lover had come through deep woods, stamping with calloused heels, showing his furred and muscled back and the remnants of a pert and corkscrewed tail. There would be not mouthwash on his breath but grapes and she would be commanded, not requested.

It was work, following where he led. Emma had never climbed so high, rocked so dangerously; never had she fallen so far, so long, into such exquisite relief. The sweat trickled down her back. He drank it.

"Madness," he said at last. "Divine madness."

Emma on her back, mouth lolling open, limbs splayed, could only groan. She lay with her eyelids closed, a last meteor falling, its flame fading, burning into darkness.

Finally she spoke. "How did I miss this in my comings and goings?"

"You probably got what you deserved," he said.

Emma stuffed a pillow under her head and pondered that. "We take ourselves to bed, don't we?"

"Our best selves, our worst selves." Bartolome got up and

wrapped himself in his dressing gown. "What we are on our feet, we are on our backs."

"Then how is it that today was different from any other day? Tell me that."

He sat on the bed, took her foot in his hand, licked between her toes. "It's quite simple. You're improving in my company."

"I am," she agreed. "I most certainly am."

She hesitated to ask and then could not stop herself. "Was she . . . your wife . . ."

He laid a hand across her mouth. "There are only two people in this bed," he said, "not three."

"There were two of me," Emma said, "one standing aside in amazement. Benjamin," she said, "I've never had such a time. Climb back in here. Let me compliment you. Let me sing your praises."

He came back to her, drawing her into his arms, held her, bound her, captured her. They looked into the dark blue light. Somewhere a gull cried for the last time before coming to rest with its flock. The world seemed very generous in the bosky twilight, very clement as the two of them clasped hands. Emma felt blameless, loved, full of merit. She looked up to see if his feeling was written on his face and saw gravity there. She was afraid to question it. Instead she called him away with a hundred kisses.

# Chapter Eleven

CARLA ATE TWO BITES of chicken and then set it aside. It looked like a small dead bird on her plate. They had come down to dinner after most of the other guests had finished, and the food seemed dry and unpalatable. She felt as if the ocean had risen to the French doors, depositing fruit rinds and pips and lettuce leaves and gaffed fish at her feet. She smelled rot in the air. She held her wine glass aloft, certain that there was an imprint of a mouth on it, Charles's mouth perhaps, but no, his mouth was in place, except for a strange wry slippage she could not account for.

"Isn't your dinner all right?"

She looked down into her plate to see. "Yes," she said, "it's fine."

"You're not eating. You didn't eat lunch."

She couldn't remember lunch, only the tight workings of her throat, the effort to swallow. She picked up her knife and fork obediently and began to make small cuts, stabbings, slashings. The chicken skittered from the plate and fell on the floor. He retrieved it without comment, a nervous muscle tugging at his face, and then asked, "Are you all right, Carla?"

She looked up. "I can't eat that now," she said. "It's dirty."

"I'll order you something else."

"Ice cream," she said, thinking that it would freeze the pulse that fluttered in her throat.

"What flavor?"

"Wild strawberry. Wild and free."

"They won't have that," Charles said patiently.

"No, they won't . . ."

"Carla." Charles leaned toward her, reached for her cold hand. "Darling. Are you feeling sick?"

"Are you?" she asked, and felt she had bested him.

"I'm worried about you. Very worried."

She smiled. "That's silly," she said. "It's only a headache. Like a handkerchief tied around my eyes, tied around and knotted in back." She laughed so that Charles would not look at her so oddly.

"I'll go get you some aspirin. There's a drugstore in the lobby."

"Yes," she said. "I saw it. Get a large bottle. It's a very large headache."

"I'll be right back. Order coffee."

She nodded. She saw him cross the long echoing room, saw him pass a waiter who stifled a yawn, saw him cast a longing look at the pastry tray as if a cream puff would end his troubles. Carla drank her water. There was salt in it, brine. She was surer than ever that there had been a flood and that its waves were even now lapping at her feet. She wondered if the orchestra would play something brave as they did on the decks of sinking ships; she wondered if fish would swim through her eye sockets.

"Would you like coffee, miss?" A waiter stood beside her holding a silver pot.

She held her cup up to him as if she were begging.

"Careful, you'll get burned, miss. This is awfully hot."

She lowered the cup and watched it carefully as he filled it.

"Is it a dark night?" she asked.

"No. There's a big moon out. You ought to take a walk on the beach. It's beautiful out. And there's nothing to worry about because we've got a security officer patrolling all night. We get some wild kids down from town, that's why."

"What makes them wild?" she asked innocently but by then he had moved to the next table and her question went unanswered.

It was then she saw Emma and Bartolome at their table across the room. She waved her white napkin, sending a signal. Emma waved back.

Wine cooled in a bucket at the side of the table, the bottle misted with cold. It reminded Carla of windowpanes in winter, clouded with frost, panes that tasted of dust and ice when she put her tongue against the glass. She remembered peering through those small moist spots, down into the streets of strange cities; through those tiny buttonholes she saw black dots moving under black umbrellas, like house beetles scurrying for shelter. She filled her water glass with wine, drank it off, filled it again, feeling the cold draught race to the pit of her stomach and then to her head, where it burst like a Japanese paper flower, folding outward. Her father had always been cheap about drink, selecting strange Spanish wines that tasted like shellac and left her mouth puckered. She had not been finicky. The food he ordered was worse — the least expensive item on the menu, usually thick with flour and muddy in color. The acid drink cut it like a knife. She had become a fair toper at an early age. It had given her a false joviality. She had smiled throughout her youth and thus was mistaken for a cheerful child.

She got to her feet, lifted the bottle, tucked it under her arm and moved across the room toward Emma, the wine warming slightly in her armpit. She dared not be alone another moment.

She came up to them tentatively, offering the bottle as a bribe. "Could I sit with you? I hate being alone at the table."

Emma looked up at the girl, saw her carapace of drink and misery and immediately patted the chair beside her.

"By all means. Sit down. Have a piece of
which I have no business at all eating."

"No cake, thank you." She collapsed into the
held for her.

"Charles will be right back or so he said. I ne
people are coming back." She smiled vaguely. "So
some don't."

Bartolome turned so that he faced her, his arm draped casually over her chair. It was as if he positioned himself to keep her from a draft.

"I'm intruding," she said politely.

"No, you're not," Emma said. She had decided to treat this fragile girl as she would any other child. She seemed to have no connection at all with events that led to slammed doors, to an ascending scale of discord, to cancellation. Who would want to accuse this startled, possessed girl of wrong-doing? Emma saw that she had a slightly yellowed front tooth and that her collarbones were as sharp and pointed as concealed knives. Had Charles really expected to thrust his burdens into such thin arms? Wasn't it plain from the paper white skin, the look of her, the bloodless lips, that she was at the last of her strength, clinging to its frayed ends as to a rope while she swung back and forth over emptiness?

Bartolome put the wine aside, out of reach. He exchanged glances with Emma that brought them to an unspoken agreement.

Emma said that they all ought to walk to the park. There was a band concert scheduled and a puppet show to follow.

They would all be mild and easy, Emma thought, in the company of old ladies and children and men smoking cigars to ward off the gnats. They would be coatless and bareheaded, and Carla would walk between them in her flat shoes and in the dark be taken for a daughter. Charles, Emma reflected coolly, could walk behind.

"Charles gets bitten by mosquitoes," Carla said. "He swells up. His eyes close. He looks Chinese."

,” Emma said. “I know. We'll spray him with some-
ng.”

The two women laughed. Bartolome regarded them in amazement. They had already formed the beginnings of an alliance. He saw that he might very well join Charles in bringing up the rear while the two ladies, arms linked, made common cause.

He saw Charles come back into the dining room, spot his empty table, look across at them, measure the new configuration, the three of them. He hesitated a moment. Bartolome beckoned him. He would doubtless referee the game to follow. He took charge at the start.

“Over here, Howard,” he called genially. “We're all feeding together.”

Charles could offer himself no explanation for his response. He felt a sudden lifting of his spirits, as if he were back in another time, far back, when his hair rose in a pompadour and his summer shoes were white; when some friend or other called from the leopard-spotted seat of his convertible car for him to come out into the summer night; when all was fraternity and lust and the pursuit of girls who went without brassieres and showed the round beginnings of buttocks in Clorox-bleached shorts. He seemed to have circled around to his youth again, to his young hankerings, and he remembered his older brother inspecting his water-slicked hair, giving him prophylactics and sanction as he sallied forth. How strange that Bartolome appeared to resemble that very brother, or was it merely a play of light? No matter. He felt his jaw for a downy beard. He looked into his heart. He went to join them.

“We have to go upstairs and get sweaters,” the ladies murmured, and they went, leaving the men to sort themselves out. Charles was not a vain man and yet he was pleased that his stomach was flat and that he had forced himself onto the squash court and the golf course, although of late he much preferred weeding the flower beds, with long pauses for gin and tonic and reflection. He mused tenderly on looking into the silken faces of pansies and setting bedding plants into little cups of warm soil. Sometimes he wished that was the sum total of his life, just that and no more. On those occasions words alarmed him, eluded him, lost their meanings. The sheaf of yellow paper sitting beside his typewriter seemed bedrock, inhospitable ground where nothing grew. He planted hundreds of zinnias and marigolds in avoidance of that aridity, and string beans and beets and chard and lettuce until there was no room to move in the back yard. Then he saw the worms as he spaded and was reminded of time and took up the old struggle, chopping through the undergrowth in his mind, away from the sunlight and torpor of the garden.

Bartolome was a runner, pounding past astonished housewives and alarmed dogs with a red bandana twisted Indian fashion around his head and the sweatshirt draped like a toga over his shoulders. He ran in the rain and often early in the morning when the streets were still dark. He ran to open his pores and his veins, to send blood to his brain so that he might be wise and judicious and curb his natural impatience when he was importuned for happiness, surcease, redress. He ran in the company of threatened lives, his feet hobbled in a thicket of problems, tethered by plucked heartstrings. Often he felt he ran in place.

"Should we kill this bottle?" Charles held aloft the wine.

Bartolome nodded and held out his glass. Both men drank silently, once, twice, three times. Charles thought again how much Bartolome resembled his brother. Even at this far remove he recalled him with pleasure. Then he looked across at Bartolome and saw that he was older and deeper.

Bartolome offered a cigar, huge and torpedo-shaped. He bit the end of his and Charles followed suit. "I ought to give this up," Bartolome said, fouling the air with a cloud of smoke. "I preach it for others, but I don't feel like depriving myself. A man has to draw the line somewhere."

Charles felt the wine speaking in his voice. "Where," he asked, "where do you drawn the line?"

Bartolome thought a moment, tilted back in his chair, studying the ceiling. Then he resumed his former posture, held out his glass again and watched closely till it was filled to the brim. "I would draw the line," he said, "at the farthest point . . . yes, I would . . . at the outer reaches. Now what the hell I mean by that I can't say. I'm getting drunk here. Emma brewed up martinis before dinner. She never heard of vermouth. What was I saying?"

"Well," Charles said, interpreting helpfully, "I think you're saying to get the most out of it. That's what I understood you to be saying. That's what I *hope* you're saying because I'm in total agreement with that. One hundred percent total agreement."

" 'Gather ye rosebuds,' " quoted Bartolome. "A felicitous lyric."

"Old Time is still a-flying," added Charles. "I see you know Herrick."

"The entire oeuvre," Bartolome said.

"My doctor, my psychiatrist that is, reads the *Racing Form*," Charles said. "You don't happen to have any open time, do you?"

"Who's your psychiatrist?"

"Armand Bell."

"A quack."

"You don't say."

"A fool."

"That's how I'd describe him."

"A dolt."

"Yes, he is."

"He'll never get you out of the soup."

"I don't suppose so."

"Doesn't know his ass from his elbow."

"I feel," Charles said, "that I could talk to you. You look like my brother, Tom."

"And you're fond of your brother?"

Charles got up and walked around the table, sat next to Bartolome, his chair hitched up close.

"My brother," he said solemnly, "is the biggest on the block. I'd like to read you a letter."

"I'm listening," Bartolome said.

Charles fumbled in his pocket, groped through his wallet and took out a well-worn piece of paper.

"Dear brother Charles." He looked up. "That's a good start, wouldn't you say?"

"Go on."

"Dear brother Charles. I am thinking of you today, which, if I remember rightly, is your birthday. If that is the case I want to wish you a long life full of dignity and success and health. At this distance I can tell you that I think you're as good a man as I've ever come across, without your saying, 'Oh, shit,' and cutting off my water. I would have sent you a book but there's nothing to buy around here, because books get mold and fall apart. Are you going to be forty-one or forty-two? I can't remember. Anyhow I always think of you as that handsome little snot you were when you were eleven. That was the summer you peed in my beer to get even about something. I forget what. All I remember is you didn't tell me till after I drank it. Stay well and keep in touch. Your brother Tom."

Charles sat holding the paper in his hand, smiling.

"Peed in his beer, did you?"

"Yes, sir," Charles said. "Peed the foam right off it."

"Enterprising sort of revenge."

"What does it mean?" Charles said. "What does it symbolize?"

"I'd have to look it up," Bartolome said. He poured for Charles. They saw the bottom of the bottle come into view.

"This is a good cigar," Charles said, "and you're wearing a very good-looking tie there. I might have picked that tie for myself."

"It's yours," Bartolome said. He wrenched it off and handed it to Charles.

"Thank you very much."

"Don't mention it."

"How do you feel about another bottle?"

"Receptive."

Charles beckoned the waiter. "Bring us another, please." He clasped his hands behind his head. "They're going to take all night up there. Emma's a prober. Not that I give a damn. I hope they don't get around to the length of my prick is all." He stopped suddenly. "An old anxiety," he said. "I beg your pardon."

"I suffer from it myself," Bartolome said. "It's a common worry."

"You don't say."

"It's my father's fault," Bartolome said without rancor. "He was something of an exhibitionist. Actually his was curved, like a hothouse cucumber. When I was a child I thought my mother grew it in the greenhouse."

"I took it up with Dr. Bell," Charles said, "but he dismissed it."

"He's a eunuch," Bartolome said.

"Emma is a considerable woman," Charles said suddenly, changing direction. "I've spent some of the most sublime moments of my life with her."

Bartolome regarded him calmly. Far gone in drink, he did not consider a discussion of Emma's sublimity an imposition on his time. He also liked the way Charles openly laid his life on the table, plunked it there in fact. He saw Charles in a role he much admired and rather coveted for himself. Charles belonged to a land of split-rail fences and prairie grass and outdoor privies. He seemed to have only recently strayed in out of the wind and sun. He had a range rider's face with squint lines, a horse-and-dog look about him; a slow and laconic delivery. He would sharpen his mind as he would an ax, honing it carefully, testing its edge. He did not doubt that Charles's boyhood bed had been narrow, that he had forked his way through endless apple pies, that he still looked for a wheeling hawk in the sky on a windy day. He saw Charles wrestling with his talent, roping it, hogtying it, the sweat running down his face as he grappled, tasting dust. He saw the vast, lonely distances that must have surrounded him.

A far cry from Bartolome, bred to grand opera and table grapes out of season. He still recalled his boyhood pleasure when, on a Saturday afternoon, he watched John Wayne and Henry Fonda, superbly confident as they roamed spaces too wide to conquer, and he squirmed in his English trousers and narrow Italian shoes, wanting only to be bowlegged and free. In his house the women *did* come and go, speaking of Michelangelo. How remarkable that he and Charles had both arrived at Emma and by such divergent routes.

"Emma." He said her name, rolling it around his mouth, sloshing it through the wine.

"We're not divorced," Charles said very slowly. "Has she told you that?"

"I haven't asked." Bartolome had slumped a little in his chair, as had Charles.

"I think," Charles said slowly, "that she's smarter than I am. She may be smarter than both of us."

"That would be going some. I'm very smart," Bartolome said.

"Yeah. I can see that all right. But Emma's a woman. They take things in a different way. Maybe you've noticed."

"I don't follow you," Bartolome said. He inclined toward Charles as if proximity would help.

"They come in at you at an angle." Charles made a gesture to illustrate it. "They all do. Look for 'em on your blind side and that's where they'll be."

"I see," Bartolome said. He didn't.

"I told you about my brother Tom, didn't I?"

"The letter writer."

"Right. That's the one. He was in love with Emma. Yep. Came out one summer right after we were married. Helped me rewire my attic. Fell off a ladder. Fell in love. Built her a little summer house in the back yard, carved his initials in it, told me he was in love with her and left town. And that summer she was ten pounds heavier than usual. He said she had a clear gaze. Those are his exact words. A clear gaze." Charles picked up the bottle and looked at it.

"I think we've got a dead soldier here."

"Were you jealous of your brother?"

"Now that's a funny thing. I wasn't. There we were, the three of us, Tom in his crazy rodeo clothes, Emma in baggy overalls, me in fancy Bermuda shorts, sitting out on the porch singing 'Foggy, Foggy Dew' in three parts . . . drinking Gallo wine under a big August moon. I was never happier in my life."

"Why did he leave?"

The two men looked at one another; they had come to new ground.

"Damned if I know," Charles said.

Upstairs, Carla brushed her hair while Emma waited impatiently in the hall, smoking, despite signs politely requesting her not to. Carla had said her room was a mess, by which she meant Emma must not see the rumpled bed or the panties draped over the lamp to soften the light, or the little pill bottles all lined up on the table.

"This hotel could easily catch fire," she said to Emma through the open door. "What would I reach for at the last moment, I wonder. What would you?"

"My nightgown," Emma said and then, worried by something in the girl's voice, she came abruptly into the room.

"Are you feeling all right?"

"Yes," Carla said. "I know I'm taking forever. I can't seem to hurry."

"No rush," Emma said. She sat on the bed, read the labels on the bottles. She saw that Carla was anemic, that she had back spasms, that she did not sleep. She resisted the temptation to launch into a familiar maternal litany, ticking off the possibilities of allergy, poison, childish pique: 'What did you eat? Where did you walk barefoot? Show me your tongue.' Then she saw the brush fall, saw the trembling hands, the rapid blinking.

"Let's talk," she said. "Come sit down." She patted the bed. Carla came toward her slowly; slowly sat at her feet. Then she clasped her hands around her knees and looked at a hideous landscape hanging on the opposite wall. Outside, a beautiful sea repeated its stately rhythms. She chose to stare at the sun burning off of impossibly purple sage in an unreal desert.

"It will be over very soon," she said to Emma. "I'll be traveling again before the end of summer. I couldn't say in which direction. I've been everywhere. I'm tired of most places."

Emma had heard this note of melancholy before. *I will run away from home. Nobody loves me. You like him better than me.*

"And what," Emma said sternly, "will you do with Charles after you've unplugged the refrigerator and canceled your newspaper deliveries?"

"I hadn't thought," Carla said.

It was the same with all children, Emma thought, hearing the total disregard of consequence in the girl's voice. The neighbors down the street will feed me. The police will return me. Someone will give me a cookie. I'll get back safely before dark.

And what of Charles, Emma thought, Charles discarded, seeking shelter at the Y.M.C.A., returning home to water the plants and put milk out for the cat. It made her rage to think of him coming back to lock windows, to flush rusty water down the toilets, to listen to the sound of his own heartbeat while dust rolled into the corners of the empty rooms.

"Charles says your name in his sleep," Carla said.

It gave her some satisfaction to hear it but she did not take the advantage she might have. "It's habit," she said. "He always wanted me to get up and get him a drink of water. Too lazy to go himself."

"I'd like to tell you everything," Carla said, turning to look at her.

"Don't," Emma said. "You'll only be sorry afterwards. I know all I need to know."

Besides, child, she said to herself, I have filled in all the details long since, through many a long night, till many a false dawn. Let us be sparing of each other in that regard. Emma, on principle, had always held herself aloof from exchanged confidences about marital shortcomings, hysterectomies, and the nature and scope of her sexual responses.

"You're so calm," Carla said with admiration.

"I think," Emma said, "that one of us had better be."

"The strange thing is," the girl continued, "that you were always with us. He was always saying 'Emma says' or 'Emma knows' or 'Emma feels.' I found myself wanting to please you . . . rather than Charles."

Emma could not help herself. She laughed at the notion. It reminded her of a James Thurber cartoon of a man indicating a crouched figure on a bookcase and saying, "That's my first wife up there . . ."

"It makes you laugh?"

"It does."

"I began to think I was in love with you, after a while," Carla said. Then she rose and walked to the window, pulling the gauzy curtain around her so that Emma could see her only dimly. "Yes," she said softly, "I often thought that."

An observer, viewing them sitting under the stars, would never have matched them in their proper order. Did the tall woman go with the dark man or the fair one? Did the fair girl make a pair with the man who wrapped her in his sweater or was he merely the solicitous friend? Enough to say that they were all in accord with the fine night, their faces turned upward, embraced by a light breeze and the sound of a band playing a Strauss waltz with high enthusiasm and an off-key clarinet. Next to them a man ate peanuts, stuffing the shells into his pockets. He offered his bag to each of them in turn, saying that they were salted in the shell and the baboons at the San Diego Zoo were wild about them. They proved to be delicious and soon they were all cracking the nuts in time to the music.

After the concert was over, Bartolome proposed a wine garden he remembered from his youth in San Pedro. It was a ruse. He meant to pay a nocturnal visit to the garden of his old family home, feeling suddenly that he wanted to see the loquat tree that bloomed there and perhaps even to steal its fruit. He had no idea why such a mood possessed him. Perhaps it was the suavity of the night and the sense that it had no end. Darkness had fallen so softly. It was even now the color of grape skins far out over the ocean, at the line of the horizon. Bartolome thought of his parents absorbing the last flavor of the day at a table set under the arbor, his father kissing his mother deeply, exhaling his pleasure with a gentle sigh, smiling at his son, making him part of the embrace. He remembered coming into the house in a rush of hot air and how his father, oppressed by the idea of their going separately to bed, had called them all out into the yard once more. He had turned on the sprinklers, making a small Versailles of jetting water, and they had held hands and raced back and forth until they were drenched through, shouting and calling to each other to go around one last time.

It had ended in wine. His mother did not want him to take cold, or perhaps she wanted to sustain the giddy pleasure for one more hour. They had filled kitchen tumblers to the brim and with water pooling at their feet had offered each other life, love, joy everlasting.

"All the way to San Pedro?" Emma said.

"Yes," Bartolome said, adamant, "all the way."

"I'm not sleepy," Carla said, thinking of dry powder in her mouth, thinking of the dry powdery sleep that followed as she swallowed pill after pill. "Let's stay up all night." She looked to Charles who looked to Emma who looked to Bartolome.

"I follow the leader," Charles said, "but the women have to drive. You and I are pissed, Bartolome. We have to face that."

It was admitted. The several bottles of wine they had drunk sluiced through them, lacing their sweat with the fruit of the vine, making them wibble-wobble, redolent.

"Which way?" Emma said, as they walked sedately through the quiet streets.

"To the past," Bartolome said, "via the Long Beach Freeway."

In the car, Carla sang a surprisingly robust and fairly dirty sea chanty in a deep boy's voice. A police car drew alongside them, listened for a moment and then the very young officer pulled them over.

"We're drunk back here," Bartolome said, "unquestionably drunk. But they are sober up there, officer. We are in high spirits, but not rash."

"Not at all rash," echoed Charles.

"May I see your license, please?"

"I wasn't speeding, was I?" asked Emma. She saw her insurance rates rising with the young policeman's ire.

"No, ma'am," the officer said. "It's just that you sounded pretty rowdy."

"It must be hot work patrolling on a night like this," Charles said from the back seat. "When I was your age I went skinny dipping of a summer's evening with my cousin Joyce in the town reservoir. I venture to say the water tasted sweeter for a hint of Joyce's pudendum."

The young man sniffed the air for cannabis, caught instead the lilac perfume that Emma wore lavishly.

"We're taking them home to bed," Emma said soothingly.

"Okay. Drive on. But keep it down." This last was addressed to Carla.

"I oppose censorship in any form!" Carla said stoutly.

Emma drove away before she could elaborate. Charles rolled down the window and stuck his feet out of it. Bartolome lit the stub of his cigar. "Let us hear what the sailor does in port once more, shall we?"

Carla lifted her voice in song.

The wine garden was closed and it was the better part of an hour before Bartolome could find his way to his old home. The streets seemed narrower and the palm trees crackling overhead sounded dryer, less gorgeously tropical. He did not remember any condominiums with their falsely Mediterranean fronts and balconies wide enough only to contain a single plastic plant and a small hibachi. He did not remember gardens lit with violet spotlights. He wondered if the Cartucci family had moved away, taking with them their player piano and their freckled daughters.

He looked under the street lights to see if there was a circle of boys, tumescent and attentive, being initiated into arcane rites by a tall pimpled youth who had lived two doors down from him—but there was no sign of such a gathering. Lamps burned dimly. In most houses the only light was the wan eye of the television set. The old sense of conviviality was gone, the expansive greetings from open window to open window, stilled. And yet he knew with utter conviction that his mother's garden would be vigorous still, loud with crickets, musical with fountains, beautifully burgeoning with shade trees. He would see it all reflected in the windows of the house, windows washed daily with ammonia water under her stern and peckish supervision. Yes, they would all scale the wall and come to rest on their backs in the long, uncut grass.

"It isn't far now," he said. "Around the next corner . . . at the end of the next street."

Emma followed his instructions while Bartolome leaned forward, the better to see it looming ahead of him in the moonlight. "It's pink," he said. "A pink house. My mother's folly. There's an iron gate my father bought in Toledo. You'll see it in one more moment."

The house was dun-colored. There was no gate.

"It must be the wrong street." But there was the cupola that had housed his round bedroom, no mistaking it, but what was a FOR SALE sign doing thrust into the ground like a stake through his heart?

"They've let it run down," he cried, and then, urgently, "Stop the car. I want to get out." He scrambled from the back seat and ran, not waiting for the others. He ran and hoisted himself to the top of the wall. Then he called out, called out with pleasure. "It's all right. The tree is there. It's all right."

The others followed, scaling the wall with muscles unused for years. Carla tore her stockings. Emma scratched her knee. Charles grunted with exertion. They all felt they had come to steal something, to take away something that did not belong to them; they were interlopers in Bartolome's dream. They stood in the dark while he tried the front door, watched as he went around to the back, listened to the shattering of glass as he forced a window. They could see him through the glass pane of the door, lurching through the hall, moving slowly, as if he were reluctant to rejoin them. He had other company to keep.

Carla hung back in the shadows, feeling herself a stranger to this ritual homecoming. For herself there was nothing to see when she glanced back over her shoulder — only tracks pulling away, only the churning wake of a ship, only the indifferent face of a doorman looking into his palm for a tip he had not received. There were no rooms worth recalling.

"I hate empty houses," she said. "I don't know what I'm doing here." She turned to Charles. "What are we doing here?"

Charles was irritable. "Let the man have a moment, for God's sake."

Carla flinched. "Why take that tone?"

"A man has a right to come home."

"Yes," Carla said. "It's what you want for yourself, isn't it?"

Emma walked away rapidly. She did not want to witness this quarrel or mediate it. She did not want to hear the verdict. She lit a cigarette; the game had suddenly become no game at all. The amiable hopscotch was at an end. Emma began to feel the fatigue she experienced when she was out too long with the children. The same sticky exasperation was in the air; like the children, they were not playing nicely with one another.

"Come in, Emma," Bartolome's voice called to her.

"I'm not going in," Carla's voice sounded out of the dark.

"All right. Wait in the car," Charles told her.

"Alone?"

"You'll have your thoughts," Charles said.

"I'll walk back to the hotel."

"Thirty miles? You'll walk thirty miles?"

"Someone will pick me up."

"You're crazy."

"Yes." There was a bright note in her voice, as if madness flattered her.

"Have it your way."

There was a peal of laughter. "*My* way? Have it my way? Darling Charles, my way would send you reeling."

"I'm too drunk to handle this," Charles said to no one in particular.

"I'll wait in the car with the windows up," Carla said, "but hurry . . . I might breathe up all the air."

She was gone. Charles stumbled up to Emma, stared at her in the dark. "I take responsibility for all of it," he said. "Remember that about me, will you Emma?"

She was spared an answer. Bartolome came out on the porch. "My house," he said tragically, "my childhood home — is atrocious."

He flung back the door revealing wallpaper bedecked with enormous cabbage roses running riotously throughout the hall and up the stairs. The woodwork had a nasty yellow slickness, a disquieting shine. The chandeliers might have graced an amusement pier in Atlantic City; the carpet, a whorehouse anywhere in the world.

Bartolome sat on the bottom step, his hands hanging between his knees. He surveyed the cradle of his boyhood.

"I must look upstairs," he muttered, thinking of the golden morning light falling across the tufted satin quilt his mother had ordained for his bed. He could still feel it slipping across his body like a trailing hand.

"The hell of it is," he said, turning to squint at the flight of stairs spiraling upward, "these steps seem to have gotten steeper. Can't understand it. Bounded up 'em like a gazelle. Like a goddamn mountain goat."

"We'll go up together, Benjamin," Charles said staunchly. It was his first use of Bartolome's Christian name.

"Fine. Splendid. Just give me your arm. These days the knees seem to go first when I'm in my cups. How are your knees?"

"Holding up."

"I have old football injuries," Bartolome said grandly. The two men listed together as if moved by a stiff breeze.

"Are you coming?" they asked Emma.

"There's no light on the stairs. You'll break your necks."

They turned in concert to see if it would be a loss to her. She folded her arms across her chest and fought a yawn.

"You think I'm an overly sentimental man?" asked Bartolome ferociously.

"It does you credit," Charles said.

"Let's go up, then."

"Lead on."

Emma rose to follow, thinking that perhaps she would have to defend Bartolome's dead mother should the wallpaper further disillusion him. For herself, she felt the charm of the woman who lived here; such high color could only bespeak high good humor. She felt herself in the presence of a kindred spirit and saw her lying serenely under holy pictures, her face white with powder, a beaded cushion under her head in blissful afternoon sleep. And damp from his bath the father would have joined her, and both would have listened keenly to the sound of the maids cleaning below as they began to make love. It would have been followed, she knew as a certainty, by an enormous dinner, beginning with clear soup and ending with spun sugar.

"The round room . . . the round room was mine. You can see the harbor from twelve different windows," Bartolome told them. "I saw the evening stars from here. I saw callers arrive and depart in Packards and La Salles and green De Sotos. I saw the autumn leaves fall. I hung over the sills till my hair curled in the fog."

He opened the door, turned on the light and promptly burst into tears.

"I loved my youth," he wept. "I loved my mother and my beautiful father."

He circled the room, running his hand over the mantelpiece in search of the remembered wax flowers, the stuffed bird, the drooping china Niobe. Then he stopped in his tracks, lifted his shoulders in a gesture of grief and futility. "Gone," he said. "Gone."

Charles nodded in deep sympathy. Without hesitation, he walked to Bartolome and drew him into a fraternal embrace.

"I'm not ashamed," Bartolome cried. "Don't think I'm ashamed."

"We had a lot to drink," Charles said and patted his shoulder.

"No, no," Bartolome protested, "it's not drink . . . it's suffering. Susceptibility. You Protestants don't know anything about susceptibility."

"That's true," Charles said. "We don't." He looked to Emma for confirmation.

Emma did not bother to confirm or deny it. She looked instead for a pocket handkerchief, drew it forth with a flourish and handed it to Bartolome.

"There's nothing wrong with a good cry," she said. "But it's five o'clock in the morning."

Bartolome blew his nose emphatically. "Comic opera. I inherited a propensity for it. We communicated in arias in this house. Bless them for it. Well." He sighed. "Done. Finished. Over. I'm ready to leave now."

He went to the window. "One last look. Come, you two; look out here. It's just beginning to get light."

Outside the small boats rocked gently on their moorings. In the garden the hibiscus were still in tight furl. No bird had risen. All up and down the street decisions were forestalled, dreams finished, bones cracked as sleepers turned in their beds.

"I won't come here again," Bartolome said.

A horn blew insistently.

"That's Carla," Charles said. "I'll go down and see if she's all right." He paused in the doorway. "It's a fine house, Benjamin," he said and went quickly down the stairs.

Bartolome looked at Emma. "Before long," he said, "Charles and I will be friends."

They were silent on the way home, each thinking that bed was where he wanted to be, under cool sheets, against cool pillows. Emma thought with longing of aspirin. The furious morning traffic was already moving north, a long crawling worm of cars eating its way into the heart of the city. There were clouds lightly powdering the sky over the ocean.

Emma wondered who would get to use the shower first and if Bartolome would shave before they climbed back in bed together like a suburban couple after a long night of gloomy sociability with next-door neighbors.

She knew what Charles would do. He would thrash for an hour, feeling his uncomfortable proximity to her, and then dress again and try to find a morning paper and a crossword puzzle, which he would work against his watch, folding the paper with satisfaction if he could do it in less than eighteen minutes. Eighteen minutes was his best time. Emma thought a trifle smugly that Carla would be no help if asked the definition of metempirics or opsonin, but it was more likely that Charles would ask her to turn into his arms and define love. Emma rather hoped that they would not all meet later at lunch with the grainy look of a sleepless night on them. She felt they had extended tolerance like a rubber band and that, at any minute, it could snap free and sting them.

Not so Bartolome. He hummed under his breath, ushered them through the lobby as if he were rounding up sheep and saw them upstairs with a cheerful, "Good night, good night, an end to revelry."

Oh, well, thought Emma, if it's to be that way let's have some more of that plummy lovemaking before we call it a night. Tangled limbs, tangled skeins, what did it matter? — it was a long summer's eve fading away into morning, gone in a few more moments.

She dropped her dress on the floor and found a place to claim for her own between his chin and shoulder.

His head rested against her hair and he was reminded again of the garden they had just left behind. There was a spill of sunshine from under the blind. They both closed their eyes to it.

"Up all night," she said dreamily. "I haven't done it in years."

"I had a grand time," he said. "A good bawl, catharsis. I feel warm and cheerful now, nourished." He bit, he kissed, he fondled.

"I want to talk," Emma said.

"Only if you're brief," he said.

She turned her face against his chest. "Benjamin," she asked, "were you faithful to your wife?"

"Totally."

"Tell me why."

"Why was I faithful to my wife?" He pondered the question a moment. "I dare say Matthew Arnold can speak for me as well as the next man. 'Ah, love, let us be true to one another, for the world, which seems to lie before us like a land of dreams, so various, so beautiful, so new, hath really neither joy nor love nor light . . .' " He was silent for a moment, reflective. "A trifle dark, perhaps, but close. I have to ask myself: Bartolome, look around you. What edifices stand? What traditions endure? My last year's car won't run this year. I've traded sheep's wool for polyester, which makes me sweat. I've traded paper for plastic. I've traded orange juice for colored water, peace for war. I'm denied God by Reason, Imagination by Science. All the shrines are empty. What am I to do, then, with my misplaced confidence, my passionate heart? Love is the last certainty, Emma."

"Love away, then, Benjamin," Emma said, and she added, "but don't talk of certainty. Your wife died and my husband left me."

"And we are here together," Bartolome said, looking down at her, "cupping our hands around the sacred flame."

"Florid," Emma said, "but true."

"In that case," he told her, "turn out the light and give me your attention."

In another room Charles said the word "hurry" in his sleep. He had fallen across the bed immediately, flinging his arm across his eyes. Some change from his pocket spilled onto the floor, a little spatter of coins running into the corners of the room. Carla sat bolt upright in a chair, turning her gaze to the beach where a boy marched toward the sea, carrying his surfboard over his head. He would stay there till evening, rolling and tumbling in the waves, seeing dark and then light and then dark again. He would be weightless, his hair would stream behind him in the water; he would be borne and lifted and dashed. She got up slowly and went into the bathroom. She took half the pills from each bottle, cupped them in her hand and then gulped them down, bending to drink from the faucet like a schoolgirl with someone next in line pressing her on.

When she came back into the room she did not look at Charles, not even briefly. She opened the door softly and closed it behind her, pausing to stare at the DO NOT DISTURB sign. Then she picked it up and hung it around her neck.

Two doors down she stopped, crouching over. She used the remaining pills to make neat letters on the carpet, bending low, working intently, finally leaning back to look at her handiwork in the way a child examines a sand castle. When she had finished she went down the fire escape, listening to the iron ringing under her feet and the iron clanging in her ears.

Emma slept till noon. When she rose and went to the door for the morning paper that the hotel deposited there, she saw her name spelled out in Dexedrene and codeine and Parafon Forte, brilliant and poisonous pebbles. EMMA. The last "A" was widely spaced from the rest, like the dying note of a scream.

"Oh, my God," she said and ran to Bartolome for help.

# Chapter Twelve

THE SUMMER moved on — day after day of brilliant sunshine, the light relentless, the air as still as if it were all contained in a stoppered bottle. Grass turned the color of urine and there was the constant danger of fire. A crack widened in front of Jessup's house and palm fronds rattled and fell into the street.

Every day Cleo removed another article of clothing. She abandoned her head scarf and a necklace of shells. She removed a little vest embroidered with mirrors and left off her stockings. She took off her rings and an ankle bracelet, which left a thin line around her thin ankle. When the temperature soared over a hundred, she took Jessup's razor and carefully shaved back her hairline till she resembled a portrait of Queen Elizabeth, high-pated and autocratic.

At first Jessup had been charmed by the sight of Cleo exposed in this way. He grew accustomed to the little patches of her person revealed by her cotton shorts and the scarves she tied around her negligible breasts. She was like a white larva wriggling here and there through the house, glimpsed on the stairway, in the hall, in the kitchen where she could hardly be seen against the white tile.

At the same time, it seemed to Jessup that as she stripped her body she divested her mind. In the beginning he had been amused by the I Ching, the pricking smell of incense, the prayer shawl, the herbal tea, the incantations that preceded bedtime and heralded awakening. He had once spent a week in a Tibetan monastery where the monks giggled like children when he snapped their pictures. They had put a flower in his hair when he left, and he sometimes thought of returning there when a film of his failed to make the cost of its negative. On mature reflection he knew he could not live with such purity, with such bad food. Cleo served him grains and nuts that he could not chew and raw carrots and other uncooked vegetables. He began to feel like a caged monkey with these unpalatable bits thrust through the bars. Her conversation was equally indigestible. She quoted from Timothy Leary and the Reverend Moon and lines from *Howl* and other Ginsburg works.

He tried to take her in hand. In bed, while she lay with her legs wrapped around him, he recited poetry. "Just listen," he said in the dark.

*I sing of brooks, of blossoms, birds, and bowers:*
*Of April, May, of June, and July flowers.*
*I sing of May-poles, Hock-carts, wassails, wakes,*
*Of bridegrooms, brides, and of their bridal cakes.*
*I write of Youth, of Love, and have access*
*By these, to sing of cleanly wantonness;*
*I sing of dews, of rains, and, piece by piece,*
*Of balm, of oil, of spice, and ambergris.*

She snored in his arms.

He began to think longingly of his second wife, a stolid German actress who cooked pot roast and washed the kitchen floor twice a week on her hands and knees. He regretted his unkindness to her and called her long distance to see if she would come for a visit, but she had moved to Stuttgart and remarried. She wished him well in a voice like rough wool.

Desperately, he offered Cleo lessons, tap-dancing and photography, Italian and cooking. She was delectable — but he was a man of worldly tastes. He had directed Strindberg. He knew Chagall. He had been awarded the Golden Bear at Venice, an Oscar in Hollywood. Monographs and doctoral theses had been written on his work. Two Swedish film enthusiasts had crossed two continents to meet him. He had lunched at the Vatican.

"You're tired of me," she said.

"Yes," he replied. "Oh, yes!"

"You're too complicated," she said. "You must stop eating meat."

"My dear," he said firmly, "try as I will I cannot explain your presence here. Some weeks ago you spent the night. At my age, it couldn't have been very memorable. Now. You're a dear child and I'm fond of you. So fond that I'm prepared to send you to a fine girls' school or to Paris or wherever, but away from here. I don't want to hurt you but I must lay an old shibboleth to rest: Mere youth is not enough. Milk teeth are all very well and rosy knees and fresh breath are delicious, but my first wife was a Jungian analyst, my second a Duse, my third a nun returned to the secular world. I, myself, am an attempted suicide and a genius. With no malice whatsoever, I tell you you must take your Pablum and go."

Cleo hummed under her breath.

"I will call Emma," he threatened.

"She's not in charge of me. Let's go up to bed."

"I've become impotent," he said.

"When? You were all right last night."

"Just now."

"I'll fix you something," she said, and he shuddered, knowing her weedy concoctions, her bran and algae. "I'll put it in orange juice for you." She started toward the pantry. "And it's not true about the nun," she said. "She was only a novice." She disappeared behind the swinging door. Jessup rushed to the phone. His lawyer, called away from a squash game, was irritable.

"How old is she?"

"I haven't asked."

"Is she a minor?"

"Probably. She has warts on her fingers."

"You'd better take it easy, Jessup. Don't make any sudden moves. Has she got family?"

"A mother, somewhere. I haven't gone into it. I just want her out of here. My work is suffering. My health is suffering."

"It's tricky. She's been there all summer?"

"Forever. Forever and ever and ever." Jessup's voice squeaked with strain.

"Intimacies?"

Jessup snorted. "Fornication. There's a marked difference."

"Bad business," said the lawyer. "Tricky."

"You already said that."

"Well," he warned, "the first thing is to stop dipping into the honey pot."

"I am sexless from this moment on."

"Okay. That's all right for openers. Listen, you got me off the court. I'll have to give this a little thought, fella."

"Shall I move to a hotel?"

"Nope. That puts her in charge of the premises. Anybody in the house beside you and the girl?"

"My cook quit. The houseboy fled. George, help me. I'm fifteen days behind schedule. I have no completion bond. George, are you listening?"

"Yeah. I'm all sweated up and I'm getting cold standing here. Tell you what. Get someone in the house, right away, someone reliable. Get a niece, a nephew, dig up somebody. I've got to head for the shower. I'll talk to you later. How's the picture, by the way?"

Jessup slammed down the phone. He thought a moment. Then he telephoned Adam, who said he would be right over.

Adam was pleased to be called away from his home, which had altered so strangely in the past few weeks. His father and mother, returning from a weekend where they had met one another, had unexpectedly assembled the family; and, sitting over a meal of burned hamburgers and watery ice tea, they had told the boys of some sea changes in the tide of their lives. His father began bravely by saying he hated to trouble them; he would have liked this summer to be like all others, a time of respite and evenly distributed suntan, a time of pleasant idleness. In the past he had made their good times, knocking balls wildly across vacant lots for them to shag in the long grass, plowing through Sunday traffic so they might eat sandwiches gritty with sand and plunge into a salty sea.

It was shock enough to see him sitting in his accustomed place with a look of immense gravity, his hair cut in a strange new way. His hands gripped the sides of the table and it reminded Adam of Sundays in church when his father clutched the pew in front of him in contrition and humility.

He spoke slowly, in a voice they had to strain to hear. There had been a new tragedy, he said, averted only because a doctor had been with them. Then he raised his head and looked directly at the boys, first at Moses, then at Adam, and even as he did so Adam felt himself second in his father's love. His friend, he said, had tried to kill herself. They had found her in time and she had been sick on the gravel path and repentent, unable at the last instant to relinquish life. She had put her finger down her throat, eaten dirt, vomited forth her despair and the pills she had taken. Dr. Bartolome had assumed responsibility for her, putting her among his old patients at the clinic, where she had been comforted and scolded for hastening toward the death they so assiduously avoided.

The rest of the story was stranger still. A young divinity student, his pockets full of jelly beans and his heart full of light, who visited the infirm on a regular basis, had seen her sitting in the garden with a lap robe over her pretty knees. He, who had forced himself to accept the knots and whorls, the frailties and the sorrows of old age, had seen her as a miracle of renewal, an inexplicable and lovely stroke of charity by the Most High.

He sat at her side on the little camp stool he carried to rest his fallen arches and, in a garden not too far removed from Eden in its peace, he had the story of her life. His long sad face became charged with tenderness and before long he would have tested himself in fire for her. He brought her gifts of root beer and ice cream. He prayed for her and for himself, that he might be a worthy shepherd, leading her to safety. He demanded from Bartolome the name of her seducer, biting his nails in his eagerness to kill him. When it was not forthcoming he cashed in a savings bond, told his superior he no longer believed in organized religion, wrapped Carla in a fringed shawl and carried her away.

A postcard arrived from Watsonville saying they had married. The following week Charles received a letter written in a spidery hand thanking him for all he had done for her, adding that life was a constant series of good-bys and that she could not live without Dennis, for that was his name. She wished Charles to keep her books for himself and not to think of her anymore. As a final offering she said he must think well of himself because he was kind and deep, if sometimes morose. Could she keep the jewelry he had given her, not out of greed, but because they, she and Dennis, were going to be very poor and it undoubtedly would have to be pawned. She wanted to be remembered to Emma, who had so impressed her. She was sorry she had discommoded Emma's life, but then we all unwittingly do harm to one another in the name of love. Perhaps Emma would not agree but that's the way matters appeared to her.

When Charles finished his account of these events, he took a sip of water and said that he would be gratified if his sons could accommodate his imperfections and blemishes because he loved them very much and would do the same for them as they rounded out their lives. He said further that they would do well to look to their mother if anything puzzled them. In the matter of his transgressions, as in all else, she had been forbearing. He added that no disposition had been made as to his future with Emma, if there was to be one. He then refused a slice of apple pie, which was his favorite dessert and, shortly after, left the house.

Moses, made cowardly by these awesome revelations, went to his room and lay face downward on his bed. Adam had walked to the gate with his father.

"Would you like me to come over there and mow the lawn or anything?" he asked, offering with this commonplace balm and amelioration.

"It needs cutting. I've let it go."

"I guess Mom would let me have the power mower."

"Yes, I guess she would."

"Well, I'll drop by Saturday morning, if that's okay."

"That would be fine. I'd be glad to see you on Saturday morning. On any morning at all."

"Father," Adam said.

"Yes."

Adam hesitated, seeing his father as hapless and unshielded.

"She invited me over to your house once."

"Did you go?"

"Yes, sir." He wanted to absolve himself of betrayal and yet he felt he must stand by what he had done. "She gave me some lunch."

"I'm surprised. She rarely cooked."

"She gave me an apple." Even as he spoke he thought how the fruit had been poisoned by his desire.

"Well, that's an old story," his father said with a faint smile. "What else?"

Adam thought passionately of what he would do if he saw his father in jeopardy. He saw himself rushing into a burning building, flinging himself into the path of an oncoming car, surrendering one of his kidneys if the need arose. He saw his father victimized by a divinity student and his own love of beauty.

"I thought she was crazy," he said and waited for the blow to fall on his bowed head.

"Come early on Saturday," his father said. "I'll make flapjacks."

Jessup habitually removed the strains of his life by distributing them to others as if they were gifts generously bestowed. He had insisted that his wives manage his financial affairs, as he was prankish with money, prodigal one moment, capriciously miserly the next.

In the same way, he wanted protection against the mutability of his affections, expecting people to come and go like hotel guests, stealing nothing in transit.

He wanted to work night and day, sloughing off all but the simplest bodily needs — food, evacuation, scant dreamless sleep. He often went days without changing his underwear and his beard grew brindled and untouched. He had been refused entry to restaurants, and where he was admitted he was made to suffer someone else's jacket and hideous tie. His agent had made provident arrangements for his funeral, fearing that he might die in some far-off place, Durango or Wittenburg, and be laid in a pauper's grave.

Emma was his one close friend, chosen with deliberation because she asked nothing of him and could be called at three in the morning if he were struck by either inspiration or indigestion.

Her son seemed the perfect choice to assume the burden of Cleo. Jessup had already conjured the scenario in his mind, replete with the swirls and vapors of the soft-focus lens. He would give Adam a job answering the mail — a mix of adulation, claims of paternity and mendicancy. He would have him organize his vast library, rich in pornography and obscure South American poets. He would direct him to take a brotherly and tutorial attitude toward Cleo, knowing that they would soon stew in their own juices, made helpless by fecundity and temperatures over ninety. He would be free again, enclosed in the stale darkness of the cutting room, rooting among reels of film for those moments of finesse undamaged by over-acting, by camera noise or the flight of planes overhead.

He walked Adam through the tinder-dry garden, arm draped paternally over his shoulder.

"My dear boy," he said, "You can do me the greatest of favors. There is some talk, loose talk, that my picture is in disarray. I was forced to show footage before I was ready. It was a rough cut, hurriedly assembled, no music track laid in, the sound out of sync. I was forced to bow to pressure because the costs got a wee bit out of hand. No fault of mine. There was some reshooting, some words with my actress, some film ruined in the lab. This is not *Jaws*, you understand, this is not *Star Wars*. I'm doing serious work. They're threatening me. They've mentioned some young jackanapes or other. They actually talked of replacing me. Idiocy, of course. No one can finish this picture but me. No one *will* finish it but me. I'll burn it. I'll destroy the negative. They know that."

He stomped down the path, dragging Adam with him. "Do you know what has happened to this business? I'll tell you. They've given it to children playing with Tinkertoys. It's Christmas morning and the little brats are firing off their rockets. My Martians are bigger than your Martians. Lunacy. Where is the human heart? Who speaks for the grape pickers? Who looks into the ghetto? Who affirms life? I do! Put my films in a time capsule and a hundred years from now people will know what the dust bowl was, what sinew forged this country, what crises destroyed marriage and God and the cities. They dare threaten me with pip-squeaks who make Chevrolet commercials? I'll see them in hell first!"

"Maybe you ought to sit down, sir," Adam said. "You're pretty red in the face."

Jessup clutched Adam's shirt. "I am my work," he croaked. "All else is silence."

Adam steered him to a cracked and peeling wooden bench,

carefully lowered him. "Just stay put. I'll get you a glass of water."

"No water. Sit beside me."

Adam complied, saddened by the sight of the old man turning his head away to cry. He wished Moses were here in his place, Moses of the ready tears who knew how to gentle pain. He reproached himself that he did not understand the thrashings and lashings of the artistic temperament. He liked movies about outer space very much indeed and was delighted with robots that walked and talked. He liked slightly dirty movies, jaunty licentious ones that made him want to follow girls on the street when he emerged from matinees. What he thought wrong was that this old man should be reduced to tears that dripped off the end of his nose, taking from him his rightful dignity.

Jessup drew a large handkerchief from his pocket and mopped up. "Emotion is cleansing," he said. "What was I saying?"

"About your picture."

"It's beautiful. I'm exposing myself in this picture, my childhood, the landscape of my youth. If it fails it will be a personal humiliation. I am like a man showing himself to strangers, flapping open his overcoat so they see him naked. Some will say, 'See, he has an appendix scar.' Some will say, 'Call the police.' A man who is brave enough to do that should be respected, eh?"

He jumped to his feet. "You will be a great help to me. I want you to come to the house every day. Come early. Stay till after dinner." He mentioned a large sum of money. "Enough?"

"More than I've ever seen in my life. What will you want me to do for it?"

"Keep me from delusions," Jessup said.

"Sir?"

"I'll find work for you."

The old man looked toward the house. Cleo was visible in the window, her long hair trailing over the sill. At this distance she appeared, in her white diaphanous dress, to be naked, thin, a tubular scroll, her mysteries to be unrolled and read in the future. Adam followed Jessup's gaze. For a moment, but for only a moment, he felt the jerk and squeal of the sacrificial lamb shudder through his body. Then she called to them in a mellifluous voice and he was the first to answer.

Jessup was too far removed from youth to understand its circling dances, the feints and retreats, the pawing and whinnying, the bows and curtsies that accompanied its measure. He thought half an hour after his departure would see Adam and Cleo coupling under the roof beams of the attic, bedding down on old legal papers and abandoned winter overcoats. He did not see how Adam in his prime could resist the tiny cup that was Cleo's navel set in the flat table that was her belly. He devoutly hoped he could not.

Jessup had asked Adam to examine his library with a view to cataloging it, at the same time directing Cleo to take a dustcloth in hand and wipe the shelves and the books. He had blocked the scene with care, placing Cleo on a kitchen stool so that the tender flesh of her inner thigh would be visible; an offering in reach of a simple upward gesture. He himself had been blistered by that sight. The onset of all his current difficulties could be laid to the path that led from her ankle to the grassy mound above, verdant as clover. There his head had rested, there he had idled while lesser men plotted his ruin.

"I'll be late at the studio. Don't wait dinner. Be industrious."

Cleo floated toward him, knotted her arms around his neck, hung like a garland for a long moment. Framed in the doorway they appeared to be satyr and nymph . . . domesticated.

"Have a good day," Adam said.

Jessup's glance scorned him. He detested that counsel, offered by gas station attendants and grocery clerks. In a world where, even as they spoke the words, some man beat his wife, a hurricane struck, a sniper aimed, Jessup would have none of it.

"Too mean in its aspirations for me," he said curtly. "I intend to exult in it." He departed.

Once they were alone, Cleo rounded on Adam, heaping coals

on his head as she ascended the stairs, he following at her calloused heels.

She flayed him to the bone with accusations. "You know why he brought you here, don't you? To *distract* me! To flummox me."

Adam adored her use of the word, adored the bounce of her tight little buttocks as she sashayed ahead of him. Chagrined though he was at the comparison, she reminded him of a small dog he had had as a child — yappy, distrustful, all asperity and tooth.

"I'll try not to flummox you," he said, mindful that he had taught that very dog to fetch and carry in less than a week.

"It's all a misunderstanding," she told him with a compressed mouth. "He's always been surrounded by ambitious women, women of low character. Actresses!" She spat the word. "I had a taste of that and it's dross. What I want now is much deeper."

"What would that be?" he inquired politely and with genuine interest, for he could not fathom where her higgledy-piggledy mind would take her.

"I want to have eleven children," she said, "with an older man. With Jessup. I want some of every kind. A violinist. An ice-skating champion. A weaver, a ballet dancer. I want us to say family prayers with everyone on his knees in his pajamas. I want to wash the girls' hair in rain water. I want to give them lovely names: Lucinda and Failya and Cosmo and Porticus."

"Porticus Jessup," Adam said, trying it out. "I don't see a running back there but he'd sure stand out in a crowd with a name like that."

"We're not going to get along," Cleo said. "That's clear. Why don't you go home?"

"No. Listen. Tell me some more. Why so many kids?"

She suddenly sat down on the steps, a sigh lifting her small chest. "I have no brothers or sisters. No one in the whole world resembles me in physiognomy or spirit. I think I must have been adopted, though my mother denies it. Children would be a dream come true."

She laid a delicate hand against her breast. "They would draw from their mother's milk what I never had . . . *tendresse*."

Adam, disquieted, sat down beside her. "I bet your mother was crazy about you." Visions rose in his mind of Cleo toddling after a flight of birds, rubber panties sagging to her dimpled knees; Cleo pulping graham crackers in a rosebud mouth while spilling her milk on the floor; Cleo in talcum-powdered, scented sleep. Adam, who had fathered no child that he knew of, fathered Cleo as he patted her hand. She withdrew it sharply.

"I'm the best judge of that," she said. "If my mother had loved me I wouldn't dream of death by drowning. I wouldn't have moles. My teeth would be straight."

"I'm sorry," Adam said, and he was.

"Sorry or not," cried Cleo, "if you spoil my plans you'll live to regret it."

"Hey, wait a minute," Adam said. "Have *fifty* kids. Have a a hundred. I'm just here for a summer job."

"Your nose is sunburned," Clea said aggressively. "You smell of tennis shoes."

"What's that supposed to mean?" He thrust his jaw out pugnaciously.

"I don't find you attractive."

"I'll go right upstairs and cut my throat."

"I've slept with boys like you," she continued. "Their hip bones are too sharp."

"Where's the library?" Adam asked. "I want to get started."

"They go home to their bunk beds right after they sleep with you. They don't call the next day." She stared at Adam with accusing eyes.

"It's a big house. I'll put a lot of it between us. Okay?"

"For the moment," she said loftily. "For the moment."

They did not speak another word to each other for the rest of the day.

Across town, in Millie's cavernous kitchen, Moses fried two eggs to perfection and laid a tray with a clean cloth for Millie's breakfast. He had taken these duties on himself and other light tasks as well to right the balance between lechery and domesticity. He cleaned the swimming pool and the dog run, burned the trash and raked the leaves. He picked Millie's clothes up off the bathroom floor and turned down her bed. He washed her hair brushes, twisting the loose golden hairs into love knots that he stuffed into his pockets, feeling faintly foolish for doing so. He cleaned the refrigerator, remembering to leave an open box of baking soda on the back shelf to sweeten it. He was, he felt, restored to self-respect by making himself useful to the woman who was now indispensable to his life.

"Very nice," he said aloud, regarding his handiwork. Steam rose from the coffee cup, the toast was golden brown, the eggs spit and sizzled in their butter. "Very, very nice," he hummed and lifted the tray above his head.

A rap on the windowpane caused him to drop it. He looked across the room into the squandered face of Alan Hammer, who pressed his nose against the glass and tapped his nose conspiratorially.

"Hey, kiddo, open up."

Moses stood transfixed in egg yolk and marmalade and broken crockery. He had paid out a goodly share of his weekly allowance on many a Saturday afternoon to see this very actor booted and saddled, and now here he stood at Millie's back door, far shorter than he appeared on screen, his skin crosshatched with broken blood vessels, his grin mean. Moses crossed the room, his tennis shoes squelching, to admit the idol of his youth.

Hammer drifted into the kitchen, skirting the mess on the floor with a skittish little two-step. He saluted Moses with two fingers raised to the level of his eyebrow and in a voice of gravel inquired after Millie.

"She's not awake yet," Moses said. "She watched *The Late Show.*"

Hammer grunted. "I haven't been to bed in two days," he said.

Moses' mind leapt forward, embracing all the meaty possibilities, but he felt it improper to comment.

"Is that coffee?"

"Yes."

Hammer helped himself, selecting an unwashed cup from the drainboard. All the while he studied Moses with the unwavering stare he had made famous. Moses felt the wax in his ears, the fluff in his navel, the very loops and coils of his colon laid bare.

"How old?" said Hammer suddenly.

"Sir?"

"How old are you? Seventeen, eighteen?"

"I'm seventeen," Moses said with reasonable dignity.

"They'll get her on the Mann Act," Hammer said in an amiable way and ate the toast Moses had made for himself.

"I suppose you've got a rod of iron," Hammer went on. "All kids have."

Moses' glance raced downward, fearful that his fly was unzipped. He felt an urge to cup his hands over his private parts and to cower.

"But it's got to be more than that." Hammer reflected. "There's something cheery about the young. I can see that. I can see a woman going for that. I recall an older woman myself back somewhere around sixteen. Maybe fifteen. God, I was nice to that woman. Washed her underwear for her. Took her to the dentist. Poor thing died of cancer in Waco, Texas. Hell of a place to die. Left me some money, too. Lou Jean McClellan. That was her name. Taught me everything worth knowing about women. Nothing dirty. Just everything worth knowing." He swished the remains of the coffee through his mouth and sat down on the edge of the table, staring morosely at the floor.

After a moment's silence, while Moses tried furtively to wipe up the spilled eggs, he spoke again.

"Gable started off with an older woman," he mused. "Always spoke well of her. Always respected her. Told me once that most women expected too much of him. They expect too much of me, too. Hell, I'm better at handball than I am in the kip." He looked at Moses with friendly blue eyes. "You don't have to spread that around, but it's so. I'm not ashamed to say it. I'm not saying I don't have lead in my pencil or anything like that, but I'd appreciate it if I didn't have to prove it every time at bat. Don't see why a man has to put a notch in his belt every single goddamn time, do you?"

"Puts a little pressure on you," Moses mumbled. "I guess . . ."

"You're a nice-looking kid," Hammer said, "but do something else with your life, son. Raise pigeons or something."

Moses remained silent.

"I'm going to retire next year," Hammer went on, "and leave off my rug and buy a ranch and eat chili and let my toenails grow. You can come on down and visit if you want to. I'm going to write a book of verse and raise hogs. How does that sound?"

"Fine," Moses said. "Just fine."

"I'll only relieve myself of my poisons on Saturday night in the local crib. No emotional involvements. How does that sound?"

Moses was stumped for an answer so he coughed and cleared his throat and smiled politely and said nothing.

"Yes, sir, I'm going to hang up my boots and saddle and my codpiece this time next year. And I tell you, honcho, I can barely wait." He pulled a crushed pack of cigarette papers and a bag of tobacco from his pocket, rolled a cigarette and hung it from his lower lip. Moses marveled at his dexterity.

"Let's get Millie up," Hammer said. "I want to take her for a ride on my Harley-Davidson. I'd ask you to come along but there's only room for two."

"Millie doesn't like to get up much before ten," Moses warned. He looked anxiously at the steel and rubber monster tethered against the wall outside. "Is that safe? That seat looks pretty small for her."

"You wanna be safe, you ride a streetcar."

"Well," Moses said, full of misgivings, "if you're going to

wake her you'd better take some coffee with you. And don't come up on her right side. She doesn't like that."

"I know," Hammer said.

Moses stood very still, listening to an inner voice telling him a hard truth. It was no blinding revelation and yet he felt his Adam's apple bob in this throat as he tried to swallow it. "You and Millie . . . you've been lovers," he said quietly. Hammer squinted uneasily and hunched his shoulders. He had the look of a man caught in a hotel fire with another man's wife.

"Do we want to get into that?" he asked, stroking his chin in search of a sage and considered gesture.

"Well, I'd just like to know," Moses said. "For my peace of mind. No details or anything."

"I never go into details," Hammer said, and then he saw the misery before him and he relented.

"A long time ago," he said. "One shot. We ended up friends. Millie keeps her friends, which says a lot for her, for the kind of woman she is."

Moses was plagued by what remained unsaid. Had Millie turned on her side, flushed and rejected? Had she cried in the bathroom? Had Hammer been kind, cruel, flippant, flagrant? Had he honored her with silence or had she been spread out for the edification of his cronies on poker tables and bars amid potato chips and pretzels?

"I wouldn't want her talked about," he said.

Hammer rubbed his hands over his face and shook his head. "Son," he said, "don't you know that's a two-way street? God, I've been *flayed* by the women I've bedded. Hell, two of 'em I know about took *rulers* to me. That's right. *Measured*. Everybody was hee-heeing all over town! Look. Millie's a peach. The woman's a pearl. Enough said."

"Why did it end?" asked Moses, who could not conceive of such joy being set aside. He made a hasty catalogue of his happiness, from briny mornings trotting over the sands of Malibu to midnight meals gobbled on a bed sifted over with matzo crumbs. He had heard Millie, full-throated, at the Dodgers' games, hurling pop bottles and epithets with the beer drinkers who called her by her first name. He had walked with her through Griffith Park, where old men ran past them in orange warm-up suits and lovers embraced on army blankets like living sculpture. She had treated him to an expensive haircut at Vidal Sassoon's, prowling around the chair, a nervous mother, until she was satisfied with the fall of his new-washed locks.

She had led him through the haunts of her girlhood — second-hand book stores and ice cream parlors, where the confections made him faintly sick to his stomach and where she relived the past with concoctions of chocolate and whipped cream still named after her. In the summer twilight she sang old songs in a high jazzy voice, leading him through the three hundred lyrics she knew by heart.

On Sundays they drove past the building where she had nearly joined a Communist cell and an apartment house where she had first slept with a gentile.

Did they not have the habit of each other, curved together through the long nights, breathing in the same easy way? Were they not meshed and bonded together forever — or at least for a while longer? Hammer must be a cynic or else a stranger to Millie.

"It always ends," Hammer said.

Moses knotted his fists, sniffing a slur, a cowardly disparagement.

"She's a wonderful woman," he cried, "she's honest, she's fine."

"Drink your fill," was all that Hammer said.

Suddenly Moses saw the transiency of it all, the veering wind that would inevitably blot out the sun. Treachery lurked somewhere in the landscape. His heart grew heavy at the antic changes of love. He felt his knees shiver with doubt as he studied his predecessor. He could only be a feeble echo in Millie's ears after this great roar, the rabbit after the lion.

Hammer heard the bottomless sigh. He practiced cunning. "I bombed out, " he said, "and I never got another chance."

Moses lifted his head, color and virility restored. It was not to his credit but he preened ever so slightly and struck a blow. "Mr. Movie Star," he trumpeted.

He was immediately sorry. Hammer's good humor made him despise the cheap shot, nor could he bear the sad and lopsided smile on his rival's face. "I apologize for that remark," he said contritely. He wanted to explain that he had been struck by a seismic force, that even now the ground trembled under his feet at the thought of returning to his old, dense, unknowing state, without Millie.

"Yeah . . . you should." Hammer fumbled in his pocket for a handkerchief that had seen better days. After he used it, he tucked it up his sleeve with a dandy's gesture. Moses had never seen a man do that before; he was enamored with the stylishness of the flourish.

Then Hammer settled onto a chair, scratched the abundant hair on his chest and warned Moses against losing his humanity. "We all get old," he said. "You will, too. Hard to believe it now, but your fires will bank in due time. At your age I never got thrown from the saddle, but I've been bucked off plenty since. I hardly take my pants down at all anymore in the service of love. Not that a man is just his sex. That would cancel some of us out pretty early in the game. But there's no denying . . . when old Dick dies a little of you goes with him. These days about all I do is ride that bike out there; that's about as prancy as I get. Makes a helluva 'vroom,' though. Wakes up a lot of sleepers."

"You sure as hell woke me," Millie said and stood before them, rosy with sleep, one huge breast visible like a globe of the world. "What's going on down here? Who broke the dishes?"

Moses took the blame. She absolved him with a smacking great kiss and then turned to rummage in the refrigerator. "Ummm," she said, "there's a little cold duck in here. That's breakfast. Pour me some coffee, sweetie." She plunked the platter on the table and licked orange sauce from her fingers. "What're you doing here, Hammer?"

"Came to take you for a spin."

Millie peered past him into the yard. "You expect me to straddle that thing?"

"Yeah, I do. Expect you to ride the hills and the dales. It'll set you up for the day."

"You're not supposed to be on a motorcycle. It's in your contract with the studio . . ." She held aloft a bit of brown skin. "This is the way I like this. Crisp. No fat. No grease." Her glance swept from one to the other, sensing secrets recently exchanged, reading the flush on Moses' face with uncanny accuracy.

"I've gotta take a bath. Mo, come up and wash my back for me." She skewered Hammer with a brief and bruising glare. "You wait here," she commanded. "I'll deal with you later." Then she hoisted the platter and thrust it at Moses. "Bring it upstairs. I'll eat in the tub."

She padded from the room, Moses following in a position of privilege where he could study the white slope of her shoulders ahead of him.

She floated on a sea of bubbles, little islands emerging here and there like a lovely archipelago. She held a roasted joint clear of the soap and waved it in the direction of Moses, who sat on a bath chair, his head reeling with scent and steam.

"All right," she said, "let's clear the air. I don't make explanations but I don't want hurt feelings, either. So. Just this once. Never again. Yes, it was an affair. Not Tristan and Isolde. No big arias. Something to warm up with on a cold night. I think I went to bed with him because he didn't wince when I ordered dessert. How do I know? I was glad to be asked. What do I mean, 'glad.' I was *grateful.* If he had been the Pope I would have kissed his ring." She snorted and waved a disparaging hand. "Do you think they line up six deep, waiting for me? And I'll tell you something else. He was cold sober. If he saw two or three of me it wasn't because he was drunk. Big point in his favor from a lady who tips the scales where I do. So. He was sober, he was decent, and he left the light on. It didn't last but I like him and I make a big commission off him. End of discussion. Turn the hot water tap a little . . . the water's cooling off."

Moses complied and took his seat again, watching her as she scrubbed vigorously under her arm.

"I'm not upset," he said, trusting he had achieved an insouciant tone.

"You're upset, all right, but you have to live in the real world. Right now you look like you've bitten into a lemon."

Moses assayed a feeble smile. "I just wondered about you and him."

She soaked her ears, using a finger to dig into the crevices. "You're not the first," she said. "Well, listen, this business makes strange bedfellows. Is it any crazier than you and me? You should be off chasing a little skinny *shiksa* . . . you should be in love with a chicken breast. But you're here. As my grandmother would say . . . *gans meshugge.* He did me a favor. You're doing me a favor. I'm a happy woman."

She chortled and submerged, rolling like a porpoise beneath the surface. A hand rose from the waves. "A towel, a towel."

He stood holding one spread wide to receive her. She stepped into it and his arms closed around her.

"Millie," he said, inhaling her. "Ah, Millie."

"I left the duck bones in there," she said as she rested against him. "Fish 'em out. If they go down the drain the pipes are ruined."

He clasped her stubbornly. "I don't want you to put yourself down," he commanded. "I don't want you to say it's a favor if a man goes to bed with you."

Millie cupped his chin, turned him so he faced the mirrored wall. "Open your eyes, boychick. Is that a sylph? Is that a gazelle? That's a double feature! Some day, if I have a heart attack, I'll diet. Till then, the motives are suspect. They've gotta be."

"Not mine," Moses said.

"You," she said tartly, "what do you know? You still suck

your thumb. Look, you got crooked teeth to prove it." She prodded his jaw, then cupped it. "What do you tell your mother you're doing all summer?"

"I said I had a job."

"She should know what kind."

"This has been the best summer I ever had. And that's up to and including scout camp."

Millie released him, took a powder puff and shook it. "After summer comes winter. We'll have to talk about that."

"Millie," said Moses, "don't treat me like a kid."

"How should I treat you?" She turned her luminous blue gaze on him. He picked up the bath towel, folded it, hung it neatly on the rail. He did not look in her direction.

"Seriously," he said.

"I just got out of hot water. Now you want to put me back in." She snatched up a hairbrush and built a pyramid of curls high on her head. "When you were born," she said, "I was already taking typing and shorthand at Fairfax High School. How's that for serious?"

"I don't care."

"You don't care."

"No."

"I care."

"Why?"

"Because I'm older and smarter. Because my mother used to talk about Sonny Wiscarver."

"Who was he?"

"A kid with an older lady. It wasn't so appetizing. Not then. Not now." She pushed past him into the bedroom, selected boots and a caftan. "Can I wear this on a motorcycle? Why not? I can't get into my slacks. Why did you let me eat duck for breakfast? Grapefruit, that's what I should have had. Grapefruit and a glass of water. Tomorrow. Don't forget."

She rummaged furiously in a drawer, came up with a peasant skirt. "Get behind me. Pull the zipper. Don't catch the skin . . .

Go slow." Moses took a stance as directed. He found himself perspiring.

"It won't close."

"Shit." She whirled on him. "Look what you're crazy about," she wailed. "Look!"

"I am looking," said Moses and kissed her cheek.

Millie shoved him away. "I have to think what's good for you. When I decide, I'll let you know."

"I'll have something to say about it," Moses said stubbornly.

"All of a sudden you're in charge?"

"I'll have something to say," he repeated.

"Hah. Seventeen and he's on the board of directors." She put a drop of perfume between her breasts. "I bought this stuff in Tijuana," she said, examining the bottle critically. "They water it. It's all water. Bargains!"

She started to pull her boots on, cursing her compliance with a fashion that swaddled and confined her. "Give a hand!"

Obligingly Moses turned his backside to her, felt the thrust of her foot against him. He was ashamed at his sudden tumescence; more ashamed when she noted it instantly.

"You're not the first," she said dryly. "Don't worry."

"Let's lie down," said Moses urgently. "Leave the boots on."

"No," she said crossly, "that's too Nazi Germany for me. Anyhow I'm late. Where do you get such ideas?"

"This one just came to me."

"A month ago everything was kindergarten. Now it's boots. I don't know who's the teacher here anymore." She gave him a long, slanting look. "If I didn't have to meet Lew Wasserman this morning . . . but I do." She put her arm around his waist and thus entwined they walked to the bedroom door.

"You should be wearing a crash helmet if you're going to ride that bike."

"That's all I need, to be a regular Hell's Angel. No helmet. I only hope to Christ nobody from C.M.A. sees me."

She slid on a pair of oversized dark glasses, kissed Moses

juicily. He made a futile grab at her as she descended the stairs.

"Will you be back for lunch?"

"No. I'm eating at Hillcrest. A raw carrot — unless they have chicken fricassee."

She clumped on, her perfume wafting upward to him, widening his nostrils, flooding his heart.

"I love you," he called after her.

"I don't insist on it," she retorted and called to Hammer that she was as ready as she would ever be.

There is a blind corner at the intersection of Beverly Glen and Sunset Boulevard where the oleanders grow tall and signs are posted warning of children at play. Whether Hammer was intoxicated with his Pegasus or there was an uneasy confluence of his stars or whether Millie's great weight destroyed the equilibrium, he crashed into a wall going eighty miles an hour and died on impact.

Millie made an arching trajectory and landed in a ditch, where the bees sought to draw sweetness from her pooled blood and a traffic signal washed her face in light as yellow as butter.

Moses, who was raking a flower bed, stopped and lifted his head. He thought for a moment he had gone blind, so white was the landscape. Then he remembered he had not eaten breakfast and that he was often giddy when his stomach was empty. He would have been the first to decry any gift of clairvoyance. His god did not deal in terror. He went inside and cooked ham and eggs, which he ate with good appetite, and was on his second glass of milk when the phone rang.

Adam stood with his head in one of Jessup's books, ingesting the rich sexual brew with considerable pleasure. For an hour or so he had tried in his mind's eye to accomplish the various couplings and straddlings he saw, and felt that the figures before him, while Japanese, must also have been samurai and in great shape at that.

So lost was he in libidinous thought that he hardly recognized

Moses' voice imploring him to come at once. He barely made out the name of the hospital and asked twice to have it repeated. The rest of his response was immediate and visceral, as if Moses had shifted in the womb reaching out to his twin. He ran.

St. Mary's offered a small waiting room and the comfort of *Reader's Digest* and the *Catholic World* as well as a highly colored lithograph of a Madonna and Child. A game show flickered on the television set as a housewife tried to formulate the answers that would bring her a Dodge Dart, a trip to Hawaii and the wrath of her sister-in-law who had not been chosen from the studio audience.

Adam held Moses' hand in his, feeling the warts that afflicted him every summer. He had asked a nurse for a sedative and had offered it but Moses said he was all right and he'd just drink the water. His shoe had come untied and Adam knelt and knotted it and then sat beside him again. After a while Moses said he had to go to the bathroom and Adam walked with him, holding onto his arm until he stood at the urinal. He forgot to wash his hands and Adam forbore to remind him. When they got back to the waiting room the game show was over and a rerun of *Hawaii Five-O* had replaced it. As the hours passed, Moses' face grew haggard and severe and Adam, looking into it, saw what he himself would be as an old man.

"Mo," he said, "we ought to call Mom."

"No, I don't think so."

"Dad?

"No."

A Catholic priest walked by and gave them a tentative look but, as he saw no tears, passed on. A patient wearing a red bathrobe shuffled in and switched programs, and after a moment Groucho Marx appeared and told a funny joke. Moses laughed. Then he put his head in Adam's lap and cried. The patient in the red bathrobe looked kind and unhappy.

"Got somebody in trouble?"

Adam nodded.

"Hope for the best," he offered.

Groucho made another joke and Moses lifted his head to hear the punch line. He laughed at it and Adam foresaw a crazy hour and wondered bleakly where it would lead.

The man in the bathrobe was disturbed; he feared hysterics unless they were a woman's.

"I got to get back," he said. "I'm only supposed to walk up and down the corridor. I'm just out of bed the first time. Gallstones."

Adam rocked Moses to and fro.

"They get you right up. The first day. I'm in a lotta pain. Is it his wife?"

"He doesn't have a wife."

"His girl, huh?"

"Millie," Moses said and got to his feet. He walked blindly down the hall while Adam raced after him. He bumped into a nun who drew back indignantly and told him to look where he was going. He caught up at the door of Millie's room and tugged at Moses.

"Don't go in," he cried. "They've taken her leg off."

Moses looked at him blankly. Adam clutched his brother to him, heard him gag and retch, supported him.

"Hold on," Adam said. "Hang on."

A nurse emerged from the room and pointed irritably at a sign commanding quiet that hung just over their heads.

"I think he's going to faint."

"Head between his knees," said the nurse and held a warning finger to her lips admonishing silence.

They ended up together on the floor and for a while they crouched in the blissful darkness of their childhood when they had sheltered in closets and under beds. But then Moses stood up and took a comb out of his pocket and combed his hair and straightened his shirt and with the gay and false smile he assumed to confront his worst fears, he shook Adam off and walked into Millie's room.

At first he saw only the welter of tubes and bottles, as if an artist had constructed some surreal fantasy of saline solution and plasma and dextrose. Grotesquely he named it Millie Feeding and thought how none of it would be to her taste. There was also a tent raised high over her, so that he imagined for a moment she was at play somewhere in its folds. There was the hiss of oxygen, sibilant as a whispered warning, and on the wall a rapt and inattentive Christ. Moses searched the corners of the room for the menace of death but it was not there. Millie's groan was deep, resonant, resolute. His heart beat braced to meet the sound and then slowly, manic with his own impetuous courage, he came close to her.

Some final storm roared in his head and then cleared, and he saw her eyelids flutter and finally the unfocused but not empty gaze.

"Well," he said, "this is one way to lose weight."

# Chapter Thirteen

JESSUP WAS DAZZLED by his own gifts, drugged by them, out of his head with admiration for the work of his hand. No detail was too small to linger over with the sated smile of a lover. He ran the dailies again and again while his cutter, cold and cramped, wondered if he'd ever see a fairway again and if the old man had not twigged out altogether.

"Da, da-da," he sang, "that's good. That's delicious. Something almost genuine there . . . not quite but we'll cheat by going to the long shot. Yes, the tight angle's good but I have something better. Where's Take Five?"

"You didn't print it, Mr. Jessup."

"Are you getting senile, Lyle? I printed Two, Five, Seven, Ten. It's there. Keep your wits about you. Stay awake. It's the shank of the evening — it's only ten o'clock."

"It's twelve, Mr. Jessup."

"Is your wife waiting for a hump, Lyle? Is the beer getting warm? Don't tell me the time. I deal in lifetimes. I want Take Five. Find Five."

Lyle thought frantically of his need to urinate, of his need to retire. He thought of his kid at Northridge and his large mortgage.

"Mr. Jessup," he said, "you didn't print Five because there was a hair in the aperture."

"There's a hair in your asshole, Lyle. It's on the moviola upstairs. Fetch. Fetch, Lyle."

Lyle gulped air. The old shit was right. It was on the moviola. He'd seen the fucking film hours ago . . . years ago. He wondered if his brother-in-law would take him into the auto parts business. He would humble himself. He would ask.

"On your feet, on your toes," ordered Jessup.

"How can you use it with a hair in the aperture?" asked Lyle numbly.

"By twisting it and curling it, by tweaking it and twirling it. They'll think's it's a tree trunk. It'll look like Kurosawa, dolt. Your pardon, Lyle. Ignore the invective. Five's the ticket. It's the only real moment I got all day from that woman. In Take Five the lines show on her neck."

"She looks pretty old in that particular shot, Mr. Jessup."

"Like the steppes of Russia . . . geological layers, rings around redwoods. Realism. She *is* old! Get the shot."

Lyle hesitated. "Excuse me, sir?"

"Excuse you for what? What, Lyle? Are you about to be foolhardy? Are you about to be rash? It's a game of inches we're playing here. Don't step out of bounds. Is it wise to have an opinion?"

Lyle, a man who wanted only the life of Jack Nicklaus under clean skies in fresh air, cut his own throat.

"Mr. Mason came upstairs around five o'clock. He looked at some of the stuff on the machine. He was pretty upset. In fact, he went ape shit, Mr. Jessup. He ate you out. He ate me out. I thought he was gonna have a stroke. He called up Hilary and chewed his ass out for an hour. He said the lighting was shit. He said he couldn't see a goddamn thing, and what he could see made him want to puke. He was dancing up and down pretty good there."

Jessup hummed a bar or two of *The Bartered Bride.* "Go on," he said. "Go on with your story."

"He said he'd seen better movies in a Mexican cat house. He said you fucked your mother. He said your head was up your ass and that's why the film was so dark. You want to hear the rest?"

"Certainly," Jessup said with aplomb. "By all means continue."

"Well, it was pretty much of the same thing. He said he was going to call New York. He said what he really wanted to do was call Detroit for a hit man. He didn't like the movie, Mr. Jessup."

Jessup snapped on a work light. The upward beam revealed a satanic eyebrow, a stiff and horned thrust of hair, a prosecutor's ferocious smile.

"And what did you say, Lyle?"

Lyle teetered on the edge of the precipice, looked down on the savage rocks of debt and dismissal. "Mr. Jessup," he said, "I don't know whether this goddamn picture is good or a turd from Reel One. What I do know is I've worked on it for six months, from seven o'clock in the morning till you let me off the leash, which is usually two or three the next morning. I've got a new grandson, named after me, that I haven't even seen yet. His daddy isn't talking to me. I'm up to three packs of cigarettes a day, and the one Sunday I got to the links I had to ride the golf cart and watch the fucking caddy play." He gulped air and felt the sweat sting his eyes. "Someplace, Mr. Jessup, at home, under my socks, I've got the Purple Heart with a special citation for bravery signed by General Dwight David Eisenhower. That was in defense of my country, and I'd do it all over again, against the Commies or whoever. But I wouldn't pop a hemorrhoid for *you* or *Mason* or any part of this whole fucking factory!"

Acid roared into his belly; he embraced himself and rocked like a shawled old Jew on a park bench.

Jessup let some time pass in respectful silence. He knew the value of a full moment; a dying fall. Lyle must have his due and he accorded it. When at last he spoke, his voice was rich with appreciation; he was an audience stirred and mastered.

"My very dear Lyle," he said. "What a remarkable monologue. Really extraordinary." Then he bethought himself. "And of course you're right. I've abused you shamefully. Would you accept an apology offered with the greatest humility? I had no idea I'd taken such advantage of you. What a strain you've been under." He clucked sympathetically. "But then . . ." he said, pausing delicately, "so have I. I must ask you, who has the ultimate responsibility? It's *my* reputation they will shred. My eyes they will pluck out. It's my anus naked to my enemies, my dear Lyle. Yes, it's that cleft that will take the rod all the way to my forelock, though you've had your share of the burden. What I think we must do is soldier on together. Not in hope of citations, my dear Lyle, not in the expectations of medals or honors, but because it's what I hired you for in the first place. Now if you'll just toddle upstairs and bring me Take Five I will be most beholden to you."

"Go take a leak, Lyle," Mason said, appearing in the doorway. "A long one."

Harry Mason was accustomed to viewing himself as others saw him. He had long been the victim of lampoons and profiles, of scoffs and jeers; students of cinema had worked him over in underground journals, and boyish critics in weekly magazines had aggrandized themselves by pelting him with epigrams and insults. Once every three or four years he was consoled by being awarded a scroll from the Conference of Christians and Jews, and during the Johnson administration he had been invited to the White House.

He had known William Jessup for thirty years, had accepted two Academy Awards in tandem with him, draping his arm around his shoulder as if they had been born in the same cradle and had nursed at the same maternal breast. Jessup adored him, adored his vulgarity and his vitality, borrowed money from him, bullied him and seriously considered making him the hero of his next opus, on the principle that this country had been formed by bumptious, irritable and unlovable men in Mason's mold.

"You've gone too far this time, William," said Mason, seating himself at some distance from his target. "The fucking jig is up."

As they had played this scene at least a dozen times over the years, Jessup remained unperturbed.

"I begged to see a script," Mason raged. "What did you tell me? Truffaut doesn't work from a script. Fellini doesn't work from a script. Bergman makes up his mind the night before." He wagged his head in despair as he considered it afresh. "Try that out in New York sometime. Try telling that to the Bank of America in a conference room." He massaged his tortured chest. "The publicity department will put out a story. It can either be bronchitis or artistic differences. With artistic differences some other poor schmuck will hire you. Bronchitis makes you an insurance risk. Pick. Robert Walpole is taking over as director in the morning. Please God he's not in jail for kissing little boys."

Jessup chortled, rose and made his way toward Mason with little sparrow hops. "You find a point or two in the footage unclear? Bound to be at this stage. You remember the babble in *McCabe and Mrs. Miller* — everyone speaking at once? Lovely touch on Altman's part. And the muted color — a little muddy but rich with authenticity?"

"You're off this picture," Mason said. "I'll keep your cutter, I'll keep your A.D., but you're bounced!"

He was seized with a paroxysm of coughing. Jessup pounded him helpfully on the back and was flung off with a wild gesture.

"Let me choke," Mason cried. "Better I should die now before the board gets a look at this dung." He put his knotted fists against his forehead. "*Where* did you spend twelve million! She's wearing clothes from Sears, Roebuck. He's naked to the waist through the whole fucking mess. Two kitchen chairs and a table. One set. The only time you get outside is if he walks to the outhouse. Show me twelve million dollars. It looks like twelve cents. Oh, God, why didn't I put a fink on your set to report to me. 'Trust me,' you said. 'Don't look at the dailies,' you said. 'Trust me to surprise you with something original and stupendous.' In nineteen seventy-eight, you have a leading lady who doesn't shave under her arms!" He moaned aloud. "It's the pits. I'm ruined."

"You're beginning to offend me," Jessup said majestically. "Not seriously yet, but enough for me to warn you that my patience is not limitless."

"On top of everything else," cried Mason, "he's deaf. I just fired you, Jessup. Tomorrow your set is locked. An armed guard stands at the door with orders to shoot you if you put a foot on that sound stage. A big marine with a low I.Q.!"

"If," Jessup said, "you will stop ranting and behaving as if you were Harry Cohn while he was alive and unconscionable, I will lead you through this film, shedding light on whatever darkness you perceive. At this point there is, I admit, some pardonable confusion. The raw clay is there; it will be shaped, it will be molded, it will be stunning. Go to your office, my friend. Look at the Oscars I won for you."

"I know," Mason said heavily. "I'd like to turn the clock back." His tone lamented past triumphs, the old camaraderie. "We all stay in the business too long. Chaplin stayed too long." He looked uneasily at Jessup. "You've stayed too long. Look. You're a brilliant man. Go teach somewhere. Pass on what you know to the kids. Be a professor. A Mr. Chips." He hurried on, trying to enrich the prospect. "It can be a nice life. No reviews. No stockholders. Pretty little girls in T-shirts coming in for conferences. Jessup, they'll kill you with this picture. I'm doing you a favor, believe me. If you're short of cash, send the bills to me. For a while. Not forever. I'm not made of money. Bow out gracefully. You make the statements to the reporters. I can be the villain. I'm right for the part."

He heaved himself upright with a grunt and started for the door.

"That's all you have to say to me?" cried Jessup. "After a

lifetime of my best efforts? 'You're too old'? 'You're fired'? 'Go lecture to nymphets'?"

"I'll say one more thing," Mason said. "I'll say thank you. I know who really won the Oscars. I'm not a total putz." He lumbered on, paused at the door. "Take some advice, Willie. If you can't face retirement, get German money. A sausage maker looking for a tax loss. Make a picture in Munich." The door closed silently behind him.

Jessup stood on trembling legs, and then he cried out, shaking his fist, "I'm not Leni Riefenstahl . . . I'm William Jessup!" His voice sank to a whisper, an old man's croak. "I'm William Jessup."

In the small hours of the morning when the rest of the world had the good sense to surrender to sleep, leaving the battle unjoined until the sinews and the cells could renew themselves, Cleo made cinnamon tea and offered broken oatmeal cookies to staunch Jessup's psychic wounds.

He gummed the cookies distastefully and pushed away the fragrant cup. He was in no need of mewling or cat's licks by way of comfort.

Jessup said, "He threw Chaplin at me but he picked the wrong man if he intended to discourage me. Chaplin went off and fathered eight children in a cold climate. He was knighted by the Queen of England. Swiss banks bulge with his money."

"Yes," Cleo said, still warm and musty from her crumpled bed. "His wife, you know, was much much younger than he."

Jessup would not be anchored with domestic details. "I hope," he said, "that the last image on my eyelids as they close in the final sleep will be of that adorable little tramp, spurned and friendless, marching valiantly down the road to a new day. I can remember standing on my feet in a darkened theater calling to him: 'A few more steps, Charlie, and you'll be eating oysters . . . a pearl in every mouthful!' I met him once. He kissed me on both cheeks. A generous man . . . a lovely man."

He marched through the cold and silent kitchen with a turkey strut of confidence. "I thrive on crisis," he declaimed. "I do not intend to snooze my way into old age. For one thing, I'm already there. For another, I'm as fertile as the Nile Delta. I have dozens, scores, hundreds of ideas. I'm not fond of the Germans, but their money is respected and they work hard. I'll make use of them." He fixed Cleo with an electric eye. "Walpole will make a disaster of my picture while I go off to do something splendid with the krauts. There's nobody there but Fassbinder, and he makes patchwork quilts, not cinema. Call the airlines!"

"How many tickets?" whispered Cleo.

"How many tickets? One, of course. First class. No smoking. Close to an escape hatch."

Cleo twined her thin legs around the kitchen chair. "I speak German," she said. "I speak it fluently."

"I have all the German I require," Jessup said cautiously. "*Achtung* is all I need. You're not thinking of joining me?"

"I am," Cleo said. "What happens if you cross the water and get turned down?"

"But my dear child, I'm an international figure. Monographs have been written about me — books! You've failed to grasp that. Naturally enough, since you've only been privy to my diminished sexuality, my spindleshanks. I will be welcomed, hailed, embraced." For a fraction of a moment he considered that his reputation for extravagance and temperament might have been exported. "Of course they'll be thrilled to have me." But now a crackle of doubt was heard in his voice, a faint quaking. "Unless . . ." He stopped. "But no. They understand me in Europe. They appreciate complexity."

Even as he spoke the air escaped from the dream. Doubtless the tribal drums already sounded through the lobby of the Plaza-Athénée, the Dorchester, the Hassler. Men in Gucci shoes and silk shirts would even now, like recording angels, be scribbling figures on the backs of envelopes. Twelve million bucks into the toilet. A big dunk.

The specter of a German winter rose before his eyes. He saw

himself walking the streets while the cold thinned his blood and the chill of death crept like fog into the crevices beneath his California overcoat. He would hurry back to his pension, where he had not settled his bill, to ask for phone messages. He would sit in windy parks reading newspapers he could not understand. He would wait for a call from his agent, which might never come.

"Child," he said to Cleo, "the cream is off the milk. I've really nothing to offer you. The truth is you're only as good as your last picture in this business. And I didn't even finish that. In due time, because I'm only human, I'll begin to feel sorry for myself. Then what will you have? An old man snuffling into his pocket handkerchief. Here, alone, in the dark of the night, I'll confess something to you. Mason may have been right. Perhaps my ear is no longer to the ground. I'm not at all certain I understand these times. I'm not at home with the violence . . . with the phallic lashings. Like Chaplin, I live with little girls with flowers in their hair . . . with flowers for eyes. In a fairy tale. And I'm often bored with that." He smiled. "You must find another daddy. This one is quite suddenly a grandfather."

"Germany isn't the place for you," said Cleo briskly. "What we want is a warm climate, where you can show the grizzled hair on your chest and wear a straw hat with ribbons on it. We'll go to Mexico. They have modern studios. Make a picture with brown babies in it. John Huston is living there now. He'll write you a screenplay that will really be about something, because he's had an aneurysm and it's made him thoughtful. I'll do the marketing and boil every drop of water you drink. Maybe we'll become Catholics. I love those dark, passionate churches, don't you? As for boring you . . . I'm not the least bit worried about that. By this time next year I'll be reading Hegel and Juvenal."

"Mexico?" murmured Jessup. "They make light of death in Mexico. Stoics. Indian blood. Enviable resignation." He munched a cookie with sudden appetite. "What an interesting notion."

"I'll play castanets," cried Cleo. "I'll get pregnant."

She looked so radiant Jessup could not disabuse her. In any event, he rather fancied himself in Gauguin-like exile, eating spiny fish and smoking ropy cigars while chickens pecked in his front yard and night bloomed in a purple sky. Yes, Huston would sit on his hacienda and they would tell lies to each other and drink Mexican beer and he would have a friend and compatriot who had been to the same wars. He would speak a softer tongue and live a softer life, liquid with indulgence.

Cleo flew to the phone. He heard her breathlessly asking information for Aeromexico, and already her voice sounded deliciously foreign. He felt the warmth of an ancient sun on his back and an easing in his heart, as if some stricture had loosed its hold. He must remember to tell Cleo something.

"Take Lomotil," he called. "I am subject to diarrhea." He could think of no other complaints.

Millie had said, "Bring cream cheese, I've got the lox," and Emma carried it in her hand, past the car boy with the Casanova eyes, past the desk clerk and along the corridors of the Beverly Hills Hotel. It was in a little container like a child's sand bucket and Emma swung it by its handles in defiance of the slick agents and the oil Arabs who turned to admire her ankles.

For some reason known only to herself, Millie had taken up residence in one of the shrimp pink bungalows, where assignations customarily took place and where there still lingered in the air the smell of semen and struggle. Her quarters were jammed with flowers, each of her clients having given instructions to his florist for the full treatment. There were threatening bouquets of tiger lilies and modest ones of violets. There were branches of willow rising out of fresh moss and arrogant orchids displayed one at a time in little hooked vials that resembled urinals. The florists were sometimes guilty of malice in consideration of unpaid bills.

Millie was enthroned on the patio under a pink, silk coverlet. Two spots of rouge dollared her cheeks to match the high color that ran like racing stripes from her forehead into the deep cleft of her breasts. She had the look of a woman who had just consumed a huge meal, so that now all her metabolism labored mightily like a stoked furnace, causing her to gasp and pant. She wore many rings. Her eyes were bright and contentious.

"Out here, baby," she called as Emma came into the living room. "I'm out here going over my goddamn hospital bills. You know they charge for aspirin? I get amputated above the knee and they charge me for an aspirin tablet. It's a *shanda*."

Emma suffered acutely as she saw the ominous slope of the blanket over Millie's lap but Millie would have none of it.

"Don't look over my head," she said. "Look at me. Take a good peek and forget it. Listen," she went on, "a few parts are missing but the engine's running, so what the hell." She waved Emma into a chair. "How are you, darling?"

"Millie," Emma said, "you don't have to be stalwart for me."

"Yeah, I do," Millie said. "For you. For everybody. Mostly for me." She fanned herself with a sheaf of bills. "Did you bring the cheese from Nate 'n Al's? I've been crazy for lox and their double cream cheese. Open the little refrigerator in there, will you? There's a package of belly lox and some bagels."

Emma rose to comply.

"Moses brought it," Millie called. "Seven ninety-five a pound and he brings three pounds." She raised her voice slightly. "Did you hear me? Moses brought it."

"I heard you."

Emma returned, carrying the lox.

"He's here *every single day*," said Millie, emphasizing each word, "so let's talk about that first."

"Let's make sandwiches first," Emma said. "You're sniffing like a cat around a tuna can."

"Spread it thick. I hate it when they give you a little smear like on a slide in a laboratory. I wish I had an onion."

"You can't get an onion in this luxe hotel?"

"They're already going crazy with me. I've had a couple visitors. A couple *hundred*. You ever heard of anybody sniffing coke while visiting the sick? Jesus. I had a rock group in here last night — I think one of 'em is still sleeping in the bathtub. Nobody's brought up right anymore. You visit the sick, you bring coffee cake, you stand around and *shmoos* for a while and then you go home. No! These punks are dancing and singing and making love standing up. Did I have a headache! The truth is I don't want to see anybody but you and Moses. Speaking of whom . . ." She pointed Emma into a chair. "I want to talk."

"All right," Emma said, and she settled herself to hear her out.

"It's not easy. If you want to know . . . losing the leg was easier."

"I know most of it already," Emma said. "Moses confides. It's one of the nicer things about him. He confided all night long last week, holding my hand like he used to on the first day of grammar school. He said he was merry, he said he was happy. He said a lot of other things but I think that's all I heard. That he was happy."

"So am I," said Millie. "Believe it or not. The rabbi from the Wilshire temple came to cheer me up and I said, 'Rabbi, I don't need you. Why don't I need you? Because I have Moses.' I think he thought I was delirious. 'Moses,' he said. 'The patriarch?' 'No,' I said, 'Moses the kid.' He wanted to go into it but I just gave him a big check for the U.J.A. and got rid of him." She put her head against the back of the chair and stared up into the gauzy clouds. "All the time I was in the hospital I kept asking myself questions. 'Millie, what are you doing with this baby? What will his mama say? You're older, you're a gimp. Maybe worst of all . . . you're an agent. He has a life of his own — his education, his own friends his own age.' You know what I decided?" She looked calmly at Emma. "I decided I wouldn't give him up for a million dollars. Not for two million."

She waited defiantly for a protest from Emma and then she hurried on. "That kid of yours never left my side. Night and day, day and night. I'd open my eyes. He was there. I'd close my eyes. He was there. Did he tell you he stayed when they fitted the prosthesis? 'Get out,' I told him, 'this is nothing for you to see' — but he wouldn't go. He said he'd have to know how it worked . . . like it was a bicycle or something. I couldn't look; *he* asked questions. He was telling the doctor all the time how we'd be dancing in a month."

"He told me," Emma said.

"I bet he left something out."

"I don't think so."

Millie pinked the color of an August peach. "You'll excuse me for discussing it with you, but he got into bed with me." Her voice trailed away. "He held me. He loved me. He saved my no-good life."

Emma wept. Millie wept. They clung to each other. A waiter swooped down the path beyond, a tray held high above his head. A girl in a nightgown appeared on the patio opposite, saw it was still daylight and retreated. The women's tears intermingled, flowed.

Millie surfaced first, sniffling and snuffling. "Who's got a hankie? I need a hankie." She used the back of her hand while Emma rummaged in her bag.

"I've only got a used Kleenex."

"Give it to me," she said. "I'm one of the family."

They blew their noses. They leaned back and regarded each other. "I've told him," Millie said, "he stays in school. He studies. He lives at home. No moving in with me. No futzing around throwing his future out the window. I'm a busy woman. I've got a lot of *meshuggeneh* clients. One week I've got to run to Cap d'Antibes. The next, I'm in New York. Either we keep a sense of perspective or it's no deal. Also, if it happens he sees a girl at school he can't live without, the door is open. I live in the real world. Otherwise . . . we take tap-dancing lessons as soon as I'm on my feet." She looked anxiously at Emma. "Talk," she said. "Level with me."

"Could I say no . . . even if I wanted to?"

Emma sat and mulled over her son Moses. Had she, she thought, refused him his broken-winged gull, his mangled hamster, his second-grade love with the crossed eyes? She had known from the beginning that Moses trembled in his innermost being for the unattended, the unhallowed, the unblessed. He would find an altar of need and there he would kneel and serve as surely as he splinted a dog's tail or asked a knock-kneed girl to waltz.

"It won't last," Millie said.

"But won't it be lovely while it does?" Emma said.

# Chapter Fourteen

EMMA DREAMT she lay back in a flower-strewn donkey cart drawn by Charles and Bartolome; Bartolome was the animal force devouring the path before them with bunched and powerful muscles, while Charles, untypically pert in a thistle cap, held the reins. How jauntily did the three of them trundle through the countryside of dreams, a Watteau landscape, rockless and roseate — nature served prettily at very turn. It came to her in her sleep that her life, finally, would brook no ordinary solution but must have curlicues and embellishments — a point of view she ascribed to having eaten a rich roast and drunk a half bottle of hock the night before.

The telephone woke her. It was Charles, sizzling with excitement and hot to see her. Millie had called him to say that Mason had bought his script for a whacking sum of money. He was rich, and already racked by the conviction that he was unworthy. His voice held the jittery note of a man who had floated false stock issues or passed a bad check. He was now isolated from the hard-working poor, the deserving of the world, a chasm of money separating him from the virtues and values of scarcity.

"My God, Emma," he said, "it's six figures!"

"Well, Charles," Emma said with the fuzz of sleep still on her teeth and brain, "that's wonderful. I'm very happy for you."

"What will it mean, Emma," he asked gravely, "in the long run?"

Emma lay flat on her bed and did some back exercises, propping the phone against her ear. "I don't know, Charles," she said. "I expect it will mean cars and travel and leather jackets from Dick Carroll's. I hope it means you'll get my garage door fixed. And that you'll do something impressive for the boys."

"I'm very depressed," Charles said. "When I was young and had good fortune, it seemed my due. Now it seems obscene — to have so much. May I come over?"

"I have to go to work."

"Emma, please. I'm not able to handle this right now. I know I've got no right to impose on you but I'd like the benefit of your advice. Just a cup of coffee. No eggs."

"I'm out of eggs, but all right. Come over."

She threw herself into the shower and gave her hair two hasty licks, thinking all the time that Charles was made for renunciation and bad luck. He wanted anxiety — the anxiety he had for the good of the world, for the ultimate victory over materialism. He would have been happy with barter, giving a cord of wood for a poem, paying his dentist with sweet corn, tipping with seashells. Except for their one European fling, he had remained innocent of collateral, interest payments and bank rates, content with his twenty-dollars-a-week pocket money, which accumulated unspent in his chino pants. Only when an indigent friend put the bite on him for a loan would he ask for more, and then he went beyond all bounds, offering some down-at-the-heels novelist the use of his car for three months, the key to his safe deposit box, his watch to hock if the friend so desired. He had borrowed money only in the name of love and then in great shame. What he longed for was success, that coin like no other. In all else, he was satisfied to be a pauper.

He arrived looking like one, in tennis shoes and a tweed jacket he had purchased fifteen years before. Emma wondered if his arms had grown; they seemed to have attained a simian length — or else the jacket had gone to a cheap cleaner.

Emma had not bothered much with breakfast, as she felt they would feast on metaphysical food cooked in Charles's mind. They would munch ethical questions, crunch solipsisms, wash it all down with the cold tea of self-denial. Emma felt the pangs of indigestion as she opened the canned orange juice and apportioned the corn flakes.

At the same time she was struck anew by Charles's great good looks. He had the pure countenance of a man who drank bottled water, shunned meats and sugars, all pills and adulterants. She remembered that his sweat smelled only of salt, as if he had labored in and risen from a clean sea. In a flash she was as horny as an armadillo. She put the table between them for safety's sake.

"You're looking well, Charles."

"So much has happened," Charles said. "I can't quite take it in. Emma, do I have you to thank for this sale?"

"I loved your script. I said so. That's all."

"We haven't really talked since Carla . . . since the end of that."

"No, we haven't."

"I know Bartolome is in your life now." He ran his fingers through his hair. "Am I entirely out of it?"

He sprang this change of heart on Emma like a magician fishing for one really astounding trick before stuffing his rabbits back into his beaver top hat. Emma was stunned into silence. Was there a false bottom here? Mirrors? A confederate in the audience? What did this return of Ulysses portend? For a moment Emma felt as if she were an astonished Penelope squinting over an ancient, burnished sea, straining myopically to see if this traveler with sand between his toes and seaweed in his hair had once in truth carved the Sunday roast, trained the ivy, assembled the mailbox following directions on the carton. It was Charles, no mistaking him, sad eyed, celestially handsome under the dust of the journey. Remarkably unchanged, despite the shoals and the eddies, the storms and the waves.

She thought of pride. She tried it on, rebelled against its stiffness as if it were a corset imposing a false shape. She thought of indignation — a better fit but last year's wear. She wanted to be comfortable, sloppy, at ease, out at the elbows, buttonless, down at the heels, comfortable. Big, windy Bartolome came to mind and lifted her like wash snapping on a line. She balked. "I don't know, Charles. Nothing's resolved. I'm still backing and filling. Don't know where I'm at."

"Ah," Charles said. Then: "Well, I have the wherewithal to woo you now, if you'll permit it. I can get rid of my riches that way."

"Get rid of it?" Emma queried.

"Emma," cried Charles, "William Inge committed suicide. Tennessee Williams went mad. John Berryman jumped off a bridge. Success is a deadly potion. I've had one sip and already my gut is twisting and griping."

"Look on the bright side," Emma said mildly. "The picture might flop. The government will take half the money in taxes. You might get writer's block. Charles, Charles, why must you always chin yourself on a cross, as part of your daily exercise regimen?"

"I don't know. I think I need professional help, Emma."

He poured milk onto his corn flakes and ate a soggy bite or two. She resisted an impulse to tell him to stop playing with his food. "Bartolome seems very sound," he said with his mouth full. "I like him. How would it strike you if I talked to him?"

"What about?"

"Entirely about this feeling I have about money. About feeling so overprivileged."

"Well, he seems a curious choice . . . but I don't see any harm in it if you leave me out of it."

"You have my word — I have a sense of propriety. What do you suppose he charges?"

"I don't know. He's not treating me."

"Am I being a jackass?" Charles leaned across the table and laid his hand on hers.

"You're being you. Morose. Guilty. Heaping coals on your head."

"You provided all the joy, Emma. All the warmth. I always knew that — even at my thickest. Emma shining on the snow." He kissed her palm.

"Charles, dear," Emma said, but he cut her off.

"Don't answer. Let's start seeing each other again. Make our way slowly. I'll get on to Bartolome. He's a jolly fellow. Maybe some of it will wear off on me."

"You have considerable merit the way you are. I've always thought so."

"I feel better," Charles said. "I think I can put the check in the bank now. Emma, it's wonderful to talk to you again. I admire you. I love you. I'm going to put up a fight for you. Knees in the groin, rabbit chops to the throat — whatever it takes."

She was afraid it would be an uneven match; but for the time being she said nothing.

Bartolome bent into the wind, pumping furiously, his leg muscles as hard as apples, his mouth open to catch the ocean breezes. Charles labored after him, his bike wobbling, the handles already slick with sweat.

Bartolome wore a tomato-red headband that gave him the look of an angered Indian chief; Charles, with his neat hair scarcely rumpled, appeared to be a pious settler about to rook him.

"Keep up, keep up," Bartolome bawled, his voice floating back richly. "The object is to raise the heartbeat and keep it up!"

Charles made a feeble gesture of acquiesence and was shamed when a girl, scarcely sixteen he thought, sped past him, a baby slung papoose-style on her back.

He wanted desperately to dismount, to sink into the grayish

sand, to lie haggard and waxen near the tender-breasted girls who would plunk their guitars all around him in two maddening notes. But no, he must clatter on, the hard prong of the seat ruining him sexually for life. Bartolome was already half a block away, swigging from the curious, leather water bottle he wore slung across his broad chest, splashing his head with the remains. Charles had an instant vision of Bartolome in the forest, felling trees as if they were matchsticks, fording unfordable rivers, stealing fire from the sun, setting rabbits atremble in fear of their lives. He felt rabbity himself — meek, prostrate before the terrible energy forging ahead of him.

"Hey, wait up," he called and tried for a winner's smile.

Bartolome's head swiveled. "Winded?"

"Dying," Charles said.

Bartolome came at him in a racer's rush, stomping himself to a halt by dragging his Atlas leg on the ground. "Well," Bartolome said, "we're not here to prove anything. Let's stop and have a beer."

He steered his bike against a wall, kicked it into submission as if it were a balky steed and warned a pimply boy not to steal it if he knew what was good for him. Charles padlocked his own bike and smiled at the kid.

The waitress who served them was beautiful — a gliding, whispering wraith with Garbo's hooded eyes. Both men looked prayerfully after her as she swayed away to get the Miller's High-Life, both busy with a hurried dream of possession.

Bartolome rose and helped himself liberally to the pretzels on the bar, although they were intended for serious drinkers. He proffered some to Charles.

"You need the salt," he said. "Eat."

Charles obeyed although he hated pretzels. He was committed to whatever was good for him; Bartolome had been sought for advice and he would receive the pretzels as the host itself if this priest of the mind conferred them.

"I don't know why you called on me," Bartolome said, crunching and munching as if he were knocking down a building with his teeth. "I'm involved with your wife. Why pussy-foot? I've slept with her. I'm swept away by her. Anything I say to you would have to be to your disadvantage. I don't believe in self-sacrifice. Also, just because I'm a psychiatrist, it doesn't follow that I know how to get out of a straitjacket, a muddle. Clearly, we're in a muddle here. You're not an ignoramus, so you know that. Your feelings are valid. My feelings are valid. They oppose each other." He took the last pretzel for himself. "I can recommend a man to you. Max Goldfarb. Not a charlatan. Not a genius either, but well-trained."

"Suppose we leave Emma out of it," Charles said.

"Evasion," said Bartolome. "And that's not the point. I'm a man before I'm a doctor in this case. I'd be uneasy with you. Take today for example. You're aware of my superior physical stamina. I'm aware that you accept it gracefully. Already I've begun to make decisions in your favor. You're not a small-minded man. You're not adolescent in your perceptions of me. Already I have to reckon with you. In another hour you will begin to charm me. We're in danger of friendship. I'm not a dramatist, but I can see where that would lead. No. It's ridiculous. On a personal level I'm interested in my own life. I know that it's healthy to function well, to garner assets — beauty, enrichment, not dollars. Emotion is crucial to me. I still taste my mother's milk in my mouth. Emma revives that memory and others equally delicious. No, it won't do. I'm a suspicious fellow. I think you're slipping a Trojan horse into my camp. And you're inside it."

The beer arrived. Bartolome insisted on paying and, since Charles carried no money as part of his Weltschmerz, he allowed it. "Goldfarb is the man for you," Bartolome said as he blew the foam onto the table. "Take your troubles to Goldfarb." He grinned. "He doesn't like me. He'll defend you in every action."

"Why did you agree to see me this morning? Why did you invite me to go bike riding?" asked Charles.

"I'm not always logical. I do things on impulse. For a moment I felt compelled to be a nice guy. There are probably other reasons. Goldfarb will tell you what they are."

"I don't want Goldfarb," Charles said crossly. "I think he's a brother to a producer who gypped me out of a credit. In fact, I know he is. He talks about his smart brother all the time."

"I know a Jungian Swede. Lindquist. But he's cold. Not right for you. Let me think. How about a woman? A Viennese with skin like whipped cream. Good credentials, superb ass. You're not a chauvinist, are you?"

"I don't think so."

"Helga Mitroff. I can't be in the same room with her without an erection. She loves writers. She smells of cinnamon. It drives me wild. Once I was pushed up against her in an elevator. It was like having your face pressed into schnecken. I'll call her."

"Don't call her." Charles set his beer glass down firmly. "This is getting out of hand. Look. You're right about my sneaking up on you. That's exactly what I had in mind. It was childish. A trick. Okay. I wanted to see how tall you were, what your range was. I wanted to see what I was up against." He glanced moodily at the last of his beer, sloshed it and drank it down.

"Perfectly human," Bartolome said, "perfectly reasonable. To tell the truth I was very pleased to see you cave in after two blocks on the bike. A baby's gratification. Unworthy. Incidentally, you're not in good shape. Now I'm speaking from a purely medical point of view. Don't you get any exercise?"

"Golf."

"For bankers. What else?"

"Chess."

"You play chess?"

"Not in a master's tournament. But I have some moves."

"Do you? Chess is my passion."

"We could have a game sometime," Charles said.

"We're having one right now," Bartolome said. "All right. Let's examine the situation. You want to look into me. I want to look into you. The outcome? Uncertain. The experiment? Interesting. In my own estimation, and remember that it's an educated opinion, I'm a secure man. I don't have to establish my position by standing on your back."

He beckoned to the waitress and ordered two more beers. While he waited he propounded his theories. "When man rose from a four-legged crouch to a standing position, he was immediately vulnerable. But, and this is important, he could look upward, outward, his head was raised. More important than safety was an expanded vision of life. I accept that vulnerability. Be my guest. See who I am. See what I am. We'll go swimming at the Y next Wednesday night. You need to tone up."

Charles did not mention an infected right ear. He intended to brush up on his crawl and a swan dive he used to do to perfection.

Emma reposed on Bartolome's bed, luxuriating in its extra length, pressing her toes against the footboard elaborately carved with heavily buttocked cherubs and vine leaves. Bach filled the air. Itzhak Perlman and Pinchas Zuckerman reminded them that the body only existed to house the soul. Rain fell lightly past the windows, greening the crab grass and filling sodden birds' nests left from other summers.

Dr. Bartolome made love like a hot-shot intern, determined to bestow all the remedies at his command, whether homeopathic or pharmaceutical; here a touch of dissolving warmth, there a caress designed to speed the blood; kisses inserted into crevices like letters into envelopes, swiftly carrying messages of lust.

"I hear you thinking," he said.

"I'm not."

"If I lay my hand just there, I hear you debating and arguing. You have a pulse in your temple that is throbbing in defense of your being in my bed. It's saying, 'It's right, it's wrong; it's wrong, it's right.' "

"Wrong," Emma said. "There's nothing in my head at all

except Oriental potentates, fiery meteors, silken banners, falling stars."

"You have bitten your lip."

"Indeed I have," Emma said.

"And we have torn the sheets."

"I'm not surprised."

He threw off the cover and looked down at her. "Whoever took out your appendix should be horsewhipped. He has put a mustache on the Mona Lisa."

"With all the stretch marks, who sees it?" said Emma.

"You nursed your children."

"I was too lazy to make formula. Are my breasts ruined?"

"Roman fountains," he said passionately.

"I used to hate my pubic hair," said Emma. "I either wanted to straighten it with hair straightener or shave it off. Doesn't it feel like a hair brush?"

"Certainly not."

"It does to me."

"You touch yourself, then."

Emma grinned. "I'll tell you nothing."

"I know what I need to know," he said. "I know you're a woman of uncommon generosity. I adore women who are prodigal in bed . . . who groan and shout and yip and yelp to express their pleasure. A man likes to know where he's at. You give ample measure. Was I mistaken or did I hear you cry out 'Huzzah!'?"

"I couldn't say," Emma said. "There was a roaring in my ears the whole time." She laid a friendly hand along his flank. "You're a caring fellow . . . everything geared to me. You dance a stately measure, Bartolome." She rolled against his chest and lay there listening to the deep, healthy thump of his heart. "Where do you suppose we're getting to, you and I?"

He smoothed her hair. "Well, just now we spoke to each other without words. But I can put into language what I feel. In fact, I insist on doing so." He turned the music off and settled himself back, bringing her close to him. "I was a spoiled child — spoiled in the sense that I was raised in anticipation of happiness. I was taught that it was attainable. Not perfect felicity, but something approaching the Ideal — as Bergson, Spinoza, Plato saw it. When you appeared some weeks ago in all your Junoesque proportions . . ."

Emma hooted, "Junoesque!"

"Hush. Don't interrupt. When you appeared, I foresaw a sexual encounter, perhaps many. Now I see the dimensions of joy, very nearly perfect joy. Think about that while I whip up some *oeufs durs farcis aux asperges vertes*."

He rose and wrapped himself in a robe, which had stenciled on the back the name of a boxer he greatly admired. ESTEBAN DE JESŨS said his bathrobe; Bartolome was partisan in everything.

Emma hauled the bedsheet around her, reached for her glasses, donned them. She felt a frumpish pleasure in sprawling like a milk-fed cat while she examined the past hour. It seemed important to see what had rooted, what flower was growing inside her mind. She thought Bartolome over, turning him this way and that.

He was at home on this planet, charmed by it, untroubled by its bucking and thrashing, hospitable to its poets and dreamers, charitable to its failures, busy with its madmen. Temperamental and volatile, he swept all before him. Emma felt herself tumbling over and over in his frothing wake. She saw caution, along with overturned ash cans, dry leaves, dampened newspapers, bottle tops and orange peels, skitter before her. In vain did she clutch a lamp post . . . already her hat had flown into the sky.

But what was this? In the very eye of the maelstrom Charles appeared, buffeted, whipped, balanced precariously on his heels but standing. She saw the plaid lining of his coat bought on a Scottish journey; she saw his fountain pen flip through the gusty air. She skidded, she slowed. She came to a sudden halt against his braced and handsome legs. She looked up into his ardent eyes. She bethought herself. She reconsidered.

In a moment the wind died down and there was another kind of weather to reckon with.

Bartolome was prey to a terrible and debilitating angst. He felt compassion for his fellow man. It bored through him like an awl through wood, reaching for the living sap. He felt it must be as visible as eczema or pockmarks, cutting him out of the herd, an easy mark, a tsk-tsk-tsker who could be dumped on any time, any place. He was not safe in the dentist's chair, nor at his barber's, his proctologist's or with his peer group. He had looked so long into aching and unquiet minds, had cocked an ear for so many years to the sound of weeping, that the slightest pressure on his sensibilities, a tear-reddened nose, the cracking or quavering of a voice, even a hangdog look about the jowls, and he was alert and on the ready. He was not pleased to be so burdened, but it was not in his power to control it. Regularly he wrote to prisoners in faraway jail houses, to elderly Talmudic scholars and to plump and grieving widows. He had become a psychiatrist in the hope that he would at last have his fill of the woe, the tribulations, throbbings, cricks, stitches, clonic spasms and general wretchedness of the human race. This ministering urge was his hair shirt, the pebble lodged in the toe of his brogues, the mote in his eye.

He saw instantly that Charles was in need; he recognized the shadow of melancholy, the Abraham Lincoln cast to the face. As he swam after him through the mouth-wash green of the Y.M.C.A. swimming pool he knew that he would once again be laying on unguents and emollients, if not evangelical hands. He opened his eyes under the water and in the wavering pool lights saw the foreshortened figure of Charles beat him to the far end of the pool, bob to the surface and rest. It took Bartolome a while to get there, as he favored a powerful but old-fashioned breast stroke. His father had taught it to him, and he still remembered the figure his papa had cut in his tank suit and rubber cap, his feet protected against fungus infection by cunning, Japanese paper slippers. He looked like an Australian lifeguard adorned with an Italian mustache. Such memories softened Bartolome. He decided he would treat Charles to a sandwich, to his attention, his concentration, his focus.

"Are you busy tonight? Let's eat together at Cantor's."

"I don't know about the ethnic food," Charles said. "Lately I've had a lot of indigestion."

Ah-ha, thought Bartolome. I know about that little bit of suffering that will not pass the uvula, that's hell-bent for the windpipe, that will, if not dislodged, occasion spiritual death.

"You're in good physical health?" he asked, beginning on the long familiar road of inquiry.

"The best."

"But something sticks just the same."

The two men bobbed like celluloid ducks on the calming water of the pool.

"That's right. Nothing helps."

"Let's see. Before we eat we'll take a walk. Say, from the May Company to Fairfax High School. It's pleasant on a summer evening. I have friends in the neighborhood."

"Fine," Charles said. "I think I'll go off the board once before I dress."

Of course you will, thought Bartolome. A two-and-a-half gainer off the platform. I've been expecting it.

Fairfax is a neighborhood of confidences. Half the strollers walk on a tilt from inclining their heads to one another. They have much to say. There are hysterectomies to be discussed, rent increases, justice for Israel, pinochle scores, loneliness. The elderly stay up past a suitable bedtime to sit on benches provided by mortuaries and discuss life. For a brief period the hippies came, gnawed by a sweet hunger to eat marble cake and blintzes with strawberry jam, but they saw their ultimate fate in the soft-breathing old people turned ashen by the street lights and they went away again.

"The only parks are in Beverly Hills, where every house has a park in the back yard," Bartolome said. "Here they have to sit at bus stops. They go out like children after supper because their sons and daughters are having people over, are playing bridge. Some nights it's too cold for them. Some nights too hot. A wooden bench hurts old behinds. Good evening, Mendel," he said as he passed. "Good evening, Sarah."

"Doctor," they replied. "A good Shabbes to you."

"They think I'm Jewish," Bartolome said, "so they give me the best they have to offer."

Charles studied his companion. "Why do I feel alien?" he asked.

"Because you were corn fed. My first food was *fettuccini*. What time did you eat in your house? I'll tell you. At six. Sharp. Am I right?"

"Six sharp," Charles said good-humoredly.

"I ate at nine, at midnight, at two in the morning if my parents came home from a party. I ate on their bed, on the floor, in the grape arbor. I can even remember being fed in the bathtub."

"Is that why I'm having trouble swallowing?"

"No," Bartolome said. "You asked why you felt alien here."

"I think you're saying I have a tight asshole," Charles said. "I do. I don't want one but I have one."

"You think you're expressing self-acceptance, don't you?" Bartolome said as he strode along rapidly. "You're not. You don't like being rigid. You judge yourself for it. A mistake." He paused. "How I wish I could charge you for my time," he said. "Too late for that. Walk a little faster . . ."

Charles stepped out smartly. "Go on."

"Of course, 'go on,' " Bartolome said crustily. "You are benefiting by *my* neurosis."

Charles politely inquired what that would be.

"I must help. I'm compelled to. It's like a man washing his hands a hundred times a day. Where was I?"

"I've lost the thread," Charles said.

"Never mind. I know. To admit something — in this case your rigidity — is a baby's step, a toddle, nothing more. Anyway, we are not in the business of self-hate. We are in the business of self-love." He stopped in his tracks. "The smell of that pickled tongue is killing me. Could you eat now?"

"I'll have a glass of milk," Charles said. "Maybe they'll warm it up for me."

"If you want it at body temperature, why not go to the source?"

"You're losing patience with me, doc," Charles said. "Don't do that. I feel I'm making headway."

"You will. You're in my hands now."

He took Charles's arm and steered him into the delicatessen, announcing loudly that he would not be seated near the swinging kitchen door.

Before the meal had progressed very far, Charles attempted a corned beef sandwich. He took a good bite and nodded his approval to Bartolome, who sat watching him like a closely observing hen with a chick.

"Good, huh?"

"Not bad. But I think I'll skip the pickle."

"That's like saying you'll have sex but skip the climax."

"I've been very depressed," Charles said suddenly. He put down his sandwich and pushed away the plate. "I'd like to talk about it." He glanced uneasily around the crowded restaurant. "Maybe this isn't the place."

Bartolome spread his hands wide. "As good a place as any. Why not a rich atmosphere? Why a sterile one? If I order a piece of strudel it doesn't mean I'm not attentive. It means I want a piece of strudel." He beckoned to the waitress and then folded his arms on the table and addressed Charles again.

"Some of my colleagues would say I have no business getting involved with you on this level. They talk a lot of crap about impersonality, cool judgment, dispassionate evaluations. Little gods with advanced degrees, some of my colleagues. I'm interested in health. I'm interested in relationships, in caring and communication. Your depression interests me. Tell me about it."

"I promised Emma I'd leave her out of any discussion with you . . ."

"Impossible," Bartolome said. "We are three human beings. We are involved with each other. Wouldn't you say it was civilized to be concerned with the common good? Do we leave our humanity behind us because we're a troika?"

"I would hope not," Charles said.

"We're not buffaloes, butting each other at a waterhole for a lady buffalo. We're men. I'll speak for both of us: decent men. By a stroke of fortune and my father's generous assistance I happen to be a head doctor. You have a problem. Lay it before me. I've taken an oath to minister to the best of my ability. And as I'm not a priest and this is not a confessional you may speak up, it's noisy in here."

"I feel displaced," Charles said. "I miss my home, my children, my tool chest, my filing cabinets. My wife. I've lost my center. I love Emma. I admire her. To this day I can't totally explain why I left . . . some damn fool feeling that I needed to appear to someone starting from scratch, without all my failures hobbling and crippling me."

Bartolome shoved aside the cutlery, the salt and pepper shakers, the impediments that kept him from thrusting his face close to Charles. His breath came across the table as hot as a pot belly stove.

"What did you talk about in your household when you were a kid? At random. A conversation at the table, for example."

Charles smiled. "Weather. The spark plugs in my father's Chevy. Pie crust . . . whether it was soggy or not. Time. Was the clock five minutes fast or not? Followed by silence. Liberal helpings of silence."

"No one shouted, argued, laughed, belched, farted, at this table of yours?"

"My father picked his teeth behind his napkin."

"And your brother? The one whose letter you carry in your pocket?"

"He didn't come home for meals. He picked up a hamburger and a malt on his way to work. Are you asking if I was emotionally deprived?"

"Let me lead," Benjamin said. "You just keep time."

The waitress appeared with dessert. Bartolome divided it and put half before Charles. "They make marvelous strudel here, full of cherries. My father used to pick the cherries out of the fruit bowl and hang them over his ears. Like jewelry. He loved adornment. It's too bad he died before he could drape himself with gold chains and keep his shirt open to the navel. It wasn't the style in those days. So how did you clear the air?" he asked, segueing so rapidly that Charles barely heard the question. "In what way did you express pleasure, displeasure, your longings, your anxieties, your dreams?"

"I kicked the dog," Charles said.

"No, I think you sat on the edge of your bed with your hands hanging down between your knees. I think you looked at a spot on the carpet."

"On the wall," Charles said, "at a water stain the size of a quarter. What's that got to do with this feeling that I've checked out of the hotel, out of my own skin?"

"You have a train to catch?" asked Bartolome. "You're in some kind of a big hurry? Relax. If you're hot for a computerized answer I'll throw you a bone." He took back the piece of strudel, which Charles had left untouched. "I shouldn't eat this," he said as he forked a mouthful. "All right. Now nibble on this notion. Don't have so much difficulty with emotions. You are both flesh and spirit, saint and sinner. God rules the world with a right hand and a left hand — the right being Christ, the left Satan. So reconcile your opposing forces, become integrated, become whole. How? By making contact with other people, living side by side with them, sharing your deepest emotions with them. When you're pissed off, you can show it. When you love, you can show it. You're not walking around with a hand grenade of repression in your pocket that can go off and kill you or someone close to you. You are open; you rush outward, like a geyser. Too simple-minded for you? The world, my friend, is full of people who don't know what they feel in their most private selves. They know box scores. They know stock market numbers. They know a good buy in hog bellies. Ask them: Are you mad at your son? Do you love your mother? How do you feel about your wife? Not a word. The silence of the grave. The atrophied twentieth-century man. My friend Goldfarb calls it introversion. How can we live unless we talk to each other? It's necessary, without embarrassment, without cruelty, to express anger. Equally it's necessary to express love." He wiped his mouth and folded his napkin. "I think you should get the check. A little sense of obligation on your part doesn't hurt."

"I don't have my wallet."

"Subterfuge. But I'll pay." He stood up. "Something very interesting goes on near the Palisades where I live. I won't tell you what, but you'd enjoy seeing it. Are you game?"

"This whole experience is very strange," Charles said. "The long twilight, a dab of psychoanalysis, strudel, pickles. Could we stop on the way for an Alka-Seltzer?"

"We'll drink a little champagne at my house," Bartolome said. "The bubbles are slightly more elegant."

"I'll come," Charles said. "I don't quite know why, but I'll come."

"You'd be insane not to," said Bartolome. "It's Dom Perignon . . . a magnum."

The whole outline of the man was in his house — the contradictions, the exuberance, the fidelity to the totems of his past. Who else would have preserved the hideous sideboard, the impossible gilded mirror? Who would have set out row after row of cut glass, his dead mother's delight, to catch the setting sun?

Charles thought of his own childhood home with its thin, grayish pallets, its empty book shelves, the curtains with irregular hems pulled out of shape by countless washings and a heated, digging iron. Here beneath his feet lay a Persian carpet of glorious warp and woof. The walls were dense with paintings — scimitared Turks assaulting captive maidens, amorous Bedouins, bloodied pheasants hanging upside down in engorged still lifes — each raping the senses with purples and reds blinding to the eye.

"Kitsch," said Bartolome, flinging his Cavalier's hat on a chair. "But come out into the garden and I'll show you something extraordinary."

In a sky the pink of cheap underwear, men flew like Icarus out over the sea. Girdled in harnesses, winged like biplanes, they burst the restraint of their ordinary state and bobbed like kites, sailing above tendentiousness and tedium. In their butterfly glory of acid blue and green, of vermilion and ocher, of violet and azure, they filled the air, a regatta of fantasists rocking on the wind.

"The birds follow *you*," said Bartolome softly.

Both men stood captive to the sight, expanding in muscle and mind as they watched the flight, feeling a capacity for daring rise in them like a column of mercury.

"Jesus," said Charles, "I'd like to try that."

"What are we waiting for?" said Bartolome. "We're getting older every minute."

They leaped a separating fence in unison, pounding toward the park where the bird-men and their vans were assembled, Bartolome already with wallet in hand to strike a bargain. They found a willing, bandy-legged boy.

"Fifty bucks? Hell, yes. We'll fit you out. Ever gone hang-gliding before?"

"Never," said Bartolome, the possibilities burning in him like released gases in space.

"Well," said the boy, "it's your necks. I done it by doin' it and I guess you can, too. You got anything sharp in your pockets I'd take it out. And if you got any last words, say 'em. You go right off the cliff. Once you're up you can stay up for hours, but remember there's no place to take a leak. Hey, Carl, these guys want to lease our gear."

A tall man with mad eyes loped up to them. "Goin dreamin'?" he whispered.

"Right," Charles said, feeling a corned beef sandwich lob up into his chest.

"Good thing to do," said the man. "Jesus Christ is out there and other things."

The bandy-legged boy lived in the real world. "Watch out for down drafts," he said, "and landing is tricky. You got to catch the current just right if you want to set down easy. Otherwise somebody'll collect your insurance. Carl, show 'em how to strap up while I count over the money."

They left their worldly goods on the grass. Charles deposited his glasses and a faded Polaroid of his family; Bartolome a dog-eared notebook, his pipe and a Mexican amulet his wife had bought him on a trip to Guadalupe. Thus divested they could go naked and trusting to a distant shore.

They were escorted to the cliff's edge. The sand below was cooled to the color of steel, and empty.

"Look up," said the madman, "and step off. And be easy. It's like gettin' born."

They hesitated, their glances mingling.

"Together," Bartolome said.

They went in the same instant, the tides of the sky waiting to receive them.

They had both known bliss and other ecstasies. They had loved women. They had topped a mountain, they had gone alone in search of their souls. Now they were returned to the elements, dropping through the air that had carried Lucifer in his headlong flight. Ordinary thought was gone, transmuted to instinct. They were ferociously free, uncaged under the final flare of the sun. They were beyond debts, boredom, bacilli. Who could screw them, fuck them, cheat them, in this wild blue yonder? They went bananas.

Bartolome sang from *The Barber of Seville.*

Charles recited "Diddle Diddle Dumpling" as he skimmed over the sea.

They felt their cellular structure; they knew life after death.

"The daring young man on the flying trapeze," vocalized Bartolome.

" 'Hope humbly then, with trembling pinions soar; Wait the great teacher Death, and God adore,' " recited Charles, flinging Pope at a postman with red wings who skimmed blithely past him, his arms behind his head.

All through the failing day they swooped and undulated, nimble as cherubim, hearing the peal and boom of the surf below them, accounts settled, in a state of perfect peace. Only when the edge of darkness appeared did they turn back, seeking the current that would begin their descent. Charles touched down first, knelt on the sand, turned his face upward. Some part of him sailed on in a larger dimension. He knew it. His inner self had been released like a visible breath on cold air.

Bartolome lit heavily and in tears.

Charles hurried to his side. "Are you okay?"

Bartolome knelt on the strand, looked up into the sky and evaluated the unacceptable. "If there are moments sucn as we just experienced, then our religious brethren have minimized the loss of Eden. Man did not merely fall from grace; he fell from Te Deum to negation. Help me up."

Once on his feet he marched along as if spurred, Charles hustling to keep at his side. He took the path with a goatish spring, grumbling under his breath, "I must have more of it . . . in one form or another."

He paused till Charles caught up to him. "I tell you," he declaimed, "there is something reductionist in our standards. We're playing a penny ante game when we should be throwing our lives on the line. On reflection, I don't know if that's good sense or not. It's possible I have the astral bends."

"If a man doesn't go out of his mind once in a while," quoted Charles giddily, "then he has no mind to go out of."

They had reached the top of the bluff. The light toasted the landscape to brownish hues. A curtain had already begun to descend on their sense of drama.

"I invited you to drink," Bartolome said, "but I don't think it's wise. I think we should separate to our several beds, huddle under the blankets and brood."

"Agreed," Charles said. They had made the doorway of Bartolome's house. They shook hands formally. Charles foresaw the rest of the night. He would lie in his bed and consider his dilemma. He was charmed by Bartolome as he had been charmed all his life by men who made things clear to him. Once it had been his mechanic, who balanced the wheels on his old pickup; once his doctor, who drew illuminating sketches of his spleen; another time an Indian shaman he had met in the Oregon woods, who explained the workings of good and evil spirits while hunkered on his heels drinking Olympia beer. Even now he could feel Bartolome at work inside his skin, a lively tick. Bartolome, the educator, had said: "Don't give up the search . . . even if it's in the dark." For Bartolome, the rival, he had this response: "All roads lead to Emma."

He turned to wave at the edge of the garden but he was gone. Bartolome had gone inside to make dog circles around his own enigmas and would doubtless sleep no more than Charles.

# Chapter Fifteen

ADAM ATE LAMB CHOPS but Moses, who had already tabulated the bill twice over in his head, had lentil soup and enormous quantities of bread and butter. Emma tactfully ate only salad and drank a single glass of wine. She had read the signs like a hunter spooring. She was certain they didn't have twenty bucks between them.

Nonetheless they had brought her, with ceremonious attention, to Musso & Frank's, steering her carefully past pimps in gorgeous hats, boys wearing earrings and other exotics. They had chosen a public place to say farewell to Adam who, in preparation for his return to school, had already had his hair cut, had filled his car with gas, had left to Moses the least reputable of his undershirts. They were all a little desperate, a little batty with longing to arrive at dessert in stylish gaiety. At one point Moses excused himself and went to the men's room and stood disconsolately over the dry ice in the urinal, wondering if tears would melt it. A fat man in a pretty, embroidered vest looked at him covertly and finally asked in a chirpy but kindly way if something was amiss.

"Family matters," said Moses, who was never surprised at the solicitude of strangers.

"Ah," said the man, "family matters. I don't have one. No

kin. It's lonely on Christmas and New Year's but I do have hundreds of friends."

He asked Moses then if he would care to join him at the bar, saying that he mustn't leap to conclusions; the embroidered vest was a gift and not his thing at all. When Moses made a polite refusal, the fat man nodded and, in passing, bestowed a fatherly pat.

"Whatever it is," he said, "it's not cancer."

Moses thought that over while he washed his hands and tried to compose himself. He was still in a state of shock and alarm.

Watching Adam pack, sorting their clothes, each garment shaped exactly alike, one inseparable from the other, he had felt unswaddled and naked. Adam was carrying away not only the best sport jacket but a special knowledge of Moses, known to no other. In an excess of emotion, he had demanded that Adam settle old debts, return his borrowed library books, surrender a stamp collection that no longer interested him. He grew quarrelsome over the tennis rackets, insisting in a passionate, breaking voice that his game would be ruined on wood. He snatched an old baseball cap out of the suitcase and claimed a pair of shoes, darkly pointing out his initials inked onto the canvas. Adam suffered him with perfect patience, balking only once when Moses exacted a red cashmere sweater with which a lovely dental assistant had tried to ensnare Adam's love and which clearly belonged to him.

Unable to bear the inner storm, the sacking of his heart and his worldly goods, Moses had gone into the back yard and there had composed a final letter to his twin, leaving it on the dashboard of the car, along with a gift of five dollars. He began by saying that it was insupportable that Adam should have exclusive use of the car. Then he said that on balance he would have to say that Adam had been a pretty good brother. He had never disappointed him, never let him down. He trusted that the feelings of esteem he now felt would endure for the rest of their lives, unless Adam did something to fuck it up. He would advise Adam to read more, as he was in grave danger of ending up a Philistine, albeit a rich one. He cautioned him not to rely on other people to write his term papers. If he got in a bind, he, Moses, would consider abetting him by authoring a draft. He was only willing to do so because he had always considered them a halved world. He would like to be in on any erotic adventures that befell his brother, the more detail the better. He had Millie now — he was going to devote himself to her night and day — so it was probably a good thing they were separating, because what he didn't need in his life was some kind of unhealthy sibling dependency. He had no intention of ending up as a psychiatric basket case because he happened to be a twin. It wouldn't kill him to call long distance once in a while. He said he loved him. He didn't elaborate on that as the pen went dry. Finally, he signed his name in full, as to a testament — Moses Dayton Howard.

"What the hell are you doing in here?" Adam remarked, appearing in the toilet. "We just got the check and you've got the money."

They returned to the table together, figured the minimum tip they could get away with and sat in silence awaiting the change.

Emma's sporting bravado, her organized smile, her maternal calm, deserted her. She looked at her offspring, ill shaven and tight lipped, and sought for some way to preserve the farcical notion that they were men.

"Let's all have some brandy," she said. "I'll pay."

Moses asked what if the waiter wanted to see their drivers' licenses.

"I'll lie," she said. "I think we all need bucking up." They consulted over a choice — Adam opting for some unspeakable chocolate liqueur, Moses for something masked with apricots.

"Courvoisier for me," she said. "A double."

When they were served, Emma lifted her glass. "I want to make a toast," she said, "and I'll tell you up front that it's going to be sentimental. Here it is: To my sons: my comfort; my pride."

Moses flushed. Adam went white. Rose red, snow white. Emma laughed, "My darlings," she said, "let love be heaped on your heads. It's not going to make your hair fall out."

She swallowed her drink in two large, unladylike gulps. She suddenly felt tired, as if she had returned to an upended house, comestibles spilling onto the floor, the cat rolling in flour. She had an urge to tidy her life, to close windows against tumult, to sort and throw out, discarding old emotions like old medicine that was no longer efficacious.

"Let's have another," she said.

"Who'll drive?"

"We'll abandon the car," Emma said. "We'll dance home."

"Okay by me," said Adam.

Moses, too, saw the virtue of anesthesia. "I could use another."

"Three more," Emma called to the waiter, "of the same." She kicked off her shoes under the table and laid an arm along the back of the booth. "Well," she said, "just where are we on the bumpy road of life? Tell your old mom."

Adam spoke. "I'm not sure I can answer that but I think I'll know more in a minute or two, because Dad just came through the door."

Charles began by saying that he was not Stella Dallas, to sit across the room eating his soup and staring at his unfolded newspaper while his family went out into the night. He said "his family" with a kind of swagger that pleased Emma. She saw that he had a newly hatched look about him, as if he had just cracked some fragile but confining shell. Before she could weigh her situation with a housewifely hand, putting ambiguity on one side of the scale and a definite excitement on the other, he had invited himself home for coffee. Emma's first question to herself was not the state of her hair or her dress — she was, in fact, wearing a very nice little French copy that concealed a slight gain around the hips — but, rather, whether she had cream in the house.

The thought of sheets, whether they were clean or not, followed promptly; the ghost of remembered sensuality arriving like an old friend asking leave to stay the night. She was reminded that she had not called the plumber and that the toilet keened like a castrato. There was something wrong with the hot water heater as well. Somehow she knew that this returned and handsome fellow would spend the first fifteen minutes with wrench in hand, head thrust under pipes, searching like an explorer for domestic order. She could find no resentment at the thought; she had long hated her tepid bath and her apathy. Let the beginnings be humble.

He was exceedingly tactful with the boys when they got home. As this was Adam's last night before departing, he supposed they would like to walk along some back fences. He provided a fatherly amount of money, putting it into Adam's pocket. It was not lavish enough to embarrass them. There followed a poignant silence while they all stood together in the living room and then Moses, the child of impulse, grappled Charles with awkward, straining arms and held him close till he was nudged aside by Adam. He was cuffed and kissed and battered and Emma saw how quickly young pain is annealed.

Charles placed a hand on each boy's head. "I'm here on sufferance, gentlemen," he said. "I feel like a hippopotamus on an ice pond. It can all go at any minute." He took a deep breath and groped for his pipe, struck a match along the edge of his fingernail and puffed on the mangled stem. "It's been my lifelong habit to bare my breast and beat on it pretty good, once I got it exposed. At this point in my life it seems like kind of a bootless thing to do. I'd like to present myself here in a new guise. Same features, same tan gabardine suit — new tie. Why the change? I don't think I can say. Why did Rip Van Winkle wake from his sleep? Maybe it was just time to get up. Anyhow, I find I'm eager to go perch fishing. I'd like to put in some petunias and insulate the attic before winter. I feel the urge to get drunk occasionally and maybe get into a fist fight. I'm not too interested in church-going anymore or any kind of piety that brings on an attack of remorse. I'd like to do useful work in the world but not too much of it. I think I've worn the look of a wronged man, a cheated man, ever since I came to my majority. I want to be rid of it. I would like to keep my health and my hair. I'd like to leave you kids some Iowa Gas and Electric shares and a conviction that life is a considerable gift, sometimes gratifying, frequently festive. I would like to re-establish the nuclear family in defiance of cynicism and because I hate spending my birthdays alone. And now I'd like to hear your mother say something, and I'd like you to get lost for the better part of an hour while I listen to her."

"Take your house keys," said Emma, "and don't look so anxious. Your father and I were friends before we were lovers. Come in the back door when you get home. Quietly."

Emma supposed there would be some inherent drama in the forthcoming scene with Charles, but her pulse was calm and she had a faint desire to yawn and scratch her head with a hairpin. She would have liked very much to stretch out in her old place on the faded paisley sofa, with her feet bare and hanging over the ends, her arms crisscrossed behind her head, unruthless and relaxed. She was not inclined to roam the fields of their marriage, picking up stones and barbs and old boots to lay at his feet; the thought of reproaches bored her. She wondered if he would bristle if she suggested bed and then egg sandwiches eaten in companionable comfort: she did not see any of this as passivity but rather as an amiable and reassuring arrangement, her legs tangled over and under him and his hand on her breast. Had they not wintered and summered in this special peace of body on body?

And, anyway, who was this other Charles, this partial stranger, splendid and springing, putting forth shoots and new green like a flourishing bay tree? Indeed his tie was new and there was a new look in his eye to go with it. She felt as if he had been off drinking some blood-enriching elixir from a crystal pool. He blazed like a log fire and she was moved to warm her hands.

Charles sat on the edge of his chair watching her. "You're thinking about bed, Emma. The tips of your ears get red when you think about bed. I remember that."

"You wanted coffee," she said, "and I haven't got any."

"*Were* you thinking about bed?" he persisted.

"Bed's so easy. We've always said nice things to each other there."

"Let's put it off for a while," Charles said. "Let it ripen."

He came over to her, lightly laid his mouth against her eyes. "How mild you are," he said in a gratified voice.

He was too close to her; he did not see the little shrug that said, "I am weary of attack and defense; let's find something more amusing."

"I've always been good-natured, Charles," she said. "Easily pleased. Give me a good dinner. Take me to a movie. Buy me a daisy. Give me a baby. A bargain. It doesn't take much."

"Is that enough for you?"

"Why all or nothing? I have Postum. Would you drink Postum? With skimmed milk I'm afraid."

"You're defrauding me, Emma." He draped an arm around her. "Here I am, a twice-born Christian, a snake shedding its skin, a butterfly rising from a larva . . . I want to show off. Let me show off."

"Suits me," Emma said. "How?"

"Come out into this particularly soft summer night. Put perfume between your breasts. Take a sweater. Give me your hand."

"I've got a new hat," Emma said. "Want to see my new hat?"

"It's the first order of business," he announced.

She gave him a little shove. "Sit there. I'll be down in a jiffy."

Upstairs she flung boxes and bags out of her disordered closet, coming at last on a wad of tissue paper. She emerged with something brimmed and Guatemalan and popped it on her head. "Charming," she said looking at herself in the mirror. "That's a good hat for a dollar ninety-eight." She marched to her dressing table, pawed in the litter and came up with a bottle of musky gardenia bath oil. "Smells like a tart," she said, "but it'll do."

She was at the door when the phone rang. "Damn — and damn again," she said but was unable to let it go unheeded.

"No one's home," she said into the receiver.

"Don't be silly," said Millie. "I recognize your voice."

"Hello," said Emma, "and good-by. I can't talk. I'm not alone."

"Coitus interruptus is fun," said Millie. "Who is it?"

"None of your business."

"Is he right there beside you?"

"No," Emma said.

"Is it just sex or something important?"

Emma pushed her hat back on her head and sat down on the floor. "It's Charles," she said, "and you're butting in at a very inopportune moment. Be quick. What do you want?"

"I want to hear all about Charles," said Millie greedily. "I'm sick of television. I've eaten a whole pound of fudge. I'm bored. Are you taking him back?"

Emma closed her eyes. "I am trying, if my friends will let me, to live from moment to moment."

"Go straight to bed," commanded Millie. "I'm serious. There are no big scenes after you've bedded down. Everybody's happy. Do what I tell you."

"Maybe you'd like to stay on the line and coach," Emma said.

"Don't joke. This is a serious moment. Listen to me, *bubeleh*. I see all the ladies in this town with big settlements and Joel Park nightgowns, and they're all alone. My line's been busy all night. 'Millie, I'm taking sleeping pills.' 'Millie, can I borrow a quart of Scotch?' 'Millie, talk to me, I've been crying all day.' If you throw Charles back in the water, forty of those piranha broads will eat him by morning. Also he won't work if he isn't happy and where's my commission? See. You'll kill a lot of birds with one bang. Jump into bed. I'm hanging up."

The line went dead. When Emma came downstairs, Charles was oiling the front door. He looked like a man who had found the root of the trouble.

"I'm ready," Emma said.

"It's the top hinge," Charles said. "One more minute and I'm yours."

They arrived at the planetarium just as it began to empty. There was a sense of agitated fluttering as children were herded toward waiting cars by their bare-legged mothers, all with the hectic look of a long afternoon on their faces, the children intoxicated with wonder and too many ice cream bars. They made way for lovers — boys with young girls resting heavily against them, as if some tide had washed them together — looking at each other with opaque eyes as a guide cajoled them with the delight and lure of the galaxy. One girl lifted her head from a long embrace and looked disdainfully around her, her world conquered. She held back from the crowd, a boy detained in her strong grasp, determined to create marvels of her own.

Charles and Emma passed them as they moved into the auditorium and took their seats under an artificial heaven spangled with a thousand artificial stars. Emma remembered two seats on the aisle that had been theirs for a hundred weekends of their courting. Charles had been charmed by the infinitude; Emma by the cheapness and warmth of the place. Charles had placed himself with awe as a tiny speck under the great strewn path above his head; Emma read her fate there, deciding she would marry and have two children in the heat of the summer when she could quench her thirst by biting lemons and iced melon. They had never asked each other what they were thinking. Charles asked now.

Emma laid her head against the back of the seat and stared up into the kindled ceiling. "I'm thinking how fixed they are and how far we've traveled."

"You mean strayed," Charles said soberly.

"No. You went in search of something, and, as I'm as lazy as they come, I sat still and something came to me."

"Emma," Charles said urgently, "for me it was a midlife passage. It surprised me. It saddened me. It ended."

A busty little woman positioned herself in the adjoining seat and leaned over them with a breath of geranium exuding from her powdered breast. "When does it start?" she inquired, as if she were here for some Dionysian mystery. "Have I missed anything?"

The question echoed in Emma's head while Charles reassured the lady she had come in good time. Had she missed anything? Bartolome rose before her like bread dough — yeasty, warm and redolent, thieving her peace of mind. Bartolome the stranger. Charles likewise the stranger. She turned to look at him and saw that she had almost forgotten the set of his ears, the appeal of his long, straight nose. She had once ordered her life around him. She had desired him. More on the occasions when he had a cold in the head or a slight fever than when he was robust. She had admired him. More when he wrestled with himself than when he was smugly sure. She was touched by this new gaiety with which he smartened himself, putting a flower of joy a trifle uncertainly over his ear. She was sure he had had his teeth cleaned for this meeting, his shoes polished.

"It's cold in here," Charles said.

"A little." She threw a fold of her sweater across his legs, and the gesture reminded her how she had eased and coddled and seduced and spoiled in the name of love, and how doubtless he had done the same, overlooking her indolence, her horny feet, the wax in her ears, her raucous laugh, the untidy meanderings of her mind.

"Thank you," Charles said. His fingers circled her wrist. The gesture seemed to ratify their trust in each other.

"I think I'm getting a cold," he said.

"I'll give you some vitamin C. Don't you take vitamins anymore?"

"There's nobody to put them out."

"That's no reason."

"I don't do well alone. I live on Campbell's soup because I can open it and add water. Emma, doesn't the pathos of Campbell's soup night after night move you?"

"You know how to cook eggs. I've seen you do it."

"I've developed an allergy to eggs. My bed is never mitered properly. I sleep with my feet sticking out. On rarely changed sheets."

"There are white sales going on right now," Emma said.

"Let me go on," he said, and the woman next to them inclined her ear. "I talk aloud. I watch television now. *Starsky and Hutch. Baretta. The Late Show.* Terrible things. I think about making a will. I think about robbers. I'm sure my heart has an irregular beat. I dream of you. Splendid soaring dreams. You become transformed into trees, flowers, clouds. You are the dark wall of caves, the nacreous heart of shells, agates, pearls."

"You've been eating Bombay curry late at night," she said, but she smiled.

"I've taken to sleeping in the afternoon." He bent toward her. "I'm making love to you."

"I know."

"How 'm I doing?"

She was unable to answer. The room darkened and the lecturer began to lead them through the skies. Afterward they walked onto a terrace and peered through a giant telescope. Emma saw the rings of Saturn — wedding bands — like some mystical sign urging her to think. They walked down the path to their car, smelling the dust of sagebrush from the still warm hills. The night was like a grape sucked of its juices, its fragrant skin thrown aside. They sat on the grass in the dark.

"The thing is, I know you," Emma said. "And you know me. It's no little thing . . . to be familiars."

"Then you don't believe I've changed?" Charles said.

"Not for a moment. Oh, you're spruced up . . . keyed up. In your summer mood. We'll see what you're like with the first rain. You'll complain about drafts. You'll look for your old hip boots in the basement. You'll read Dostoyevsky and have insomnia. You'll fuss about an insignificant cough. You'll talk less and less at meals. You won't want any sexual extravagances on my part till spring."

"Right," Charles said with satisfaction.

"There's comfort in it," Emma said, "in not having to be up to the mark, nervy, brought to the edge by a lover who's bound to make irritable discoveries with every passing day."

"My God, yes," Charles said.

He sifted dirt and rocks through his fingers as if he were a farmer determining the worth of the soil. "Emma," he said, "can we end this uncertainty?"

Emma rolled onto her back, thus ruining a new blouse with grass stains. "How did I get into this fix?" she questioned. "Charles, you know me. I'm not a woman to sit and bewail my fate. When you left, I gave you a few sleepless nights, a few red-hot rages and then, to be honest, there was a hopeless time when I said, 'Emma, my girl, it's all over. There's a gray streak at your temple, you have two enormous gawky boys, you're no great beauty, pick up a crochet hook and resign yourself.' You can guess how long that lasted. Fifteen minutes. Maybe twenty. Then along came this irascible fellow Bartolome, grouch and philosopher. You know the rest. Now you're back, imperfect and lovable — and again everything is on its ear, altered and unrecognizable, and I'm going straight out of my head."

"Don't," Charles said. "Listen to me. Let me preserve the balance. I don't consider Bartolome a rebuke to me. He's a considerable man, a formidable adversary and very nimble in the bargain. But I have the edge, Emma, the history, the strategy and the lay of the land. Also . . . I love you."

He pulled her to her feet. Once in the car Emma made a cowardly retreat into silence, overwhelmed with choices and mad to know the outcome.

"Are you out of your skull?" said Adam, pulling up to the curb before the darkened house.

"I'm going," Moses said stubbornly. "I've been thinking about it all night and that's what I'm going to do."

"It's none of your business," Adam said.

Moses' smile was mild. "Everyone thinks you're an activist," he said, "because you're always front and center. Not true. Are you going to drive me over there or not?"

"Not. Jesus. It's two o'clock in the morning."

"I'll wake him up."

"You'll get handed your head."

"Give me the keys, then."

"Okay, buddy. It's your ass. But you get back here before five. I'm leaving on the stroke and I want this car here and waiting."

Adam opened the door and put one leg out. Then he hauled it back. "Shit," he said. "All right. I'm driving you there but I'm not coming in. I don't want any part of this. I'll just wait outside till you get the heave-ho and then I'll take you home."

"I'm willing to consider that moral support," Moses said. "Drive on."

Bartolome was making a chocolate cake with every intention of eating it as the sun rose. He had been sleepless for hours, had prowled through his wife's studio, volcanic in his emotions, unable to endure his bed. He was made haggard by his thoughts, assailing cosmic questions and human shenanigans with dark concentration. He often ground through the night in this way, examining sorrows and abnormalities, war and peace, while he made Toll House cookies and rhubarb pies. He sought these nights of riddles and nettles; he detested sleep as a little death. Sometimes he rang his colleagues — Goldfarb being a prime target — at the most ungodly hours, craving stimulus and argument. Goldfarb had threatened to have the phone company tear his instrument out by the roots but he succumbed to Bartolome's monologues much as if he had been lifted from his bed by the scruff of the neck.

"Listen," Bartolome would command the hapless Goldfarb over the phone. "Listen to this, my friend. 'Our lives are like islands in the sea, or like trees in the forest, which co-mingle their roots in the darkness underground. Just so, there is a continuum of cosmic consciousness, against which our individuality builds but accidental fences, and into which our several minds plunge as into a mother sea or reservoir.' Are you awake, Goldfarb? Do you hear what William James is saying?"

"Go to sleep, Bartolome. Take Seconal. Take Valium. Only, I beg you . . . go to sleep." He would hang up the phone only to have it ring again.

"Goldfarb, do you agree to this: 'Not the absence of vice, but vice there, and virtue holding her by the throat, seems the ideal human state.' "

"You're a terrible man, Bartolome," Goldfarb would respond weakly. "You are sapping my life with these calls. Drink warm milk."

Then, alone and cut off, Bartolome would repair to his kitchen and in a flurry of flour and spices he would think on. Goldfarb was a small man, afraid of his thoughts. Not so Bartolome. He mulled over James as he broke eggs and measured sugar. Yes. Yes. The transition from a state of puzzlement and perplexity to rational comprehension is full of lively relief and pleasure. "Pleasure," he shouted at the sleeping Goldfarbs of the world.

Moses knocked on the back door just as Bartolome put the cake in the oven.

"Come," said Bartolome, hoping that if it were a disturbed patient it might at least be an interesting one. "Come in, the door's never locked."

Moses stepped into the light. "Maybe you remember me," he said. "I'm Moses Howard."

"The pugilist," Bartolome said. "The father slayer. Sure. I remember you. You're up late."

"I came to talk to you," Moses said.

"I'm making a chocolate sour-cream cake. How does that sound?"

"Pretty good."

"It'll be out in forty-five minutes. We'll frost it and eat it."

"I haven't got that much to say," Moses said, "only about ten minutes' worth. And I don't see how I can in good conscience break bread with you."

"It's not bread," said Bartolome crossly, "it's cake. And why not?"

"Would it be all right if I sat down?" Moses asked.

"Any chair," said Bartolome, who had already straddled one himself and was licking butter from his fingers and even from his hairy wrist.

"You might ask what I'm doing here in the middle of the night," began Moses.

"I never speculate," said Bartolome, "I wait to be surprised. I like turns and twists . . . pretzel discoveries, if you will."

"Well," Moses said, "I thought I'd come and give you a peek at my family's life and then you can do whatever you want about it. Could I have a glass of water, please?"

"Help yourself. They're all clean. I'm not a slob who lets the dishes pile up in the sink. Bring me one, too. I had herring for supper, which was terrific, but I'll drink and urinate all night."

Moses filled two glasses and bore them back to the kitchen table. They drank reflectively as if they shared old wine of good vintage.

"You were saying . . ."

Moses put his elbows on the table and stared down at his knees. He seemed to be searching among memories, trying to unearth the telling one. Finally he nodded his head. "I think I'll tell you about the tree house," he said. "My brother and I built it a couple of summers back. It wasn't much but we rigged up a platform and four walls and a galvanized tin roof. We swiped the stuff from a building site and told the folks we bought the lumber out of our allowances. They never check on how we spend our own money. Anyway, it was a pretty neat little perch, only not too stable if there was a wind. We tried to get a couple of girls up there but we didn't have any luck. We were too young to do anything with 'em anyway, so we smoked and read a couple of dirty books and talked about the future and the space program and cunnilingus. Well, one night we were going to spend the night up there. I don't exactly know why. It didn't smell too good . . . there was a lot of resin coming out of the boards and a lot of loose nails but we just wanted to try it. We took some beer up and some candles and we'd just settled in when all of a sudden out come my mother and my father with a box of corn flakes and some bananas and a couple of old pillows. They asked if they could come up and spend the night. I think they had had a couple of martinis but they weren't drunk. We said okay, if they didn't mind a tight squeeze; there wasn't much room. My mother came up as if she had monkey blood. We had to haul my father up. He kept laughing and sliding back down but he finally made it. We all stretched out side by side, packed tight and up close. About five minutes later it started to rain. It didn't just rain . . . it really poured. It came in on us but we all stayed put up in that shaking tree. After a while my father started telling stories about his boyhood, which we had all heard before, but it didn't bother him and it didn't bother us and, when he finished, my mother sang some Cole Porter songs and we all ate corn flakes and bananas."

He looked at Bartolome, who tilted back in his chair.

"That's all. That's the story."

"Nice story," Bartolome said. "My mother and father used to get into bed with me. Same thing. My mother's hairpins kept shooting out of her hair. My father had a little net over his mustache. Every night he looked as if he'd caught a little fish on his upper lip."

He got up and went to the oven, opening it a crack. "You're not supposed to do this," he said. "They say it makes the cake fall. But I do it anyway. The suspense kills me." Having satisfied himself, he returned to Moses. "So. You stayed up very late at night and came a long way to tell me a tale of family life. To illustrate what? That a family is a felicitous and comfortable thing to have. Well. You came to the right man. By chance you hit on a vein that is easily tapped in me. I'm like a puppet, you see, held by a hundred strings. Who pulls them? My dead. My beloved ghosts."

He tasted the icing which was already stiffening in a bowl before him. "Tree houses," he said reflectively. "We all lived in tree houses once." The force of his gaze caught and held Moses, who felt himself mesmerized by this chocolate-smelling man. "Do you know what I sniff out here? Yes, sniff. I use my nose as much as my head. I smell delicacy. Tact. Diplomacy. I'm heartened to see that there are still kids with feelings for something besides their genitals and their credit cards. They're in short supply, except maybe in Methodist summer camps.

"However — we have a problem here. My position is prejudicial to yours. It's further complicated by the warm feelings you engender in me. While you were talking I was fantasizing you as my son. I said to myself, 'If his eyes were dark he might even look like me.' I went beyond that. I said, 'If he were my son we would go to Paris together and listen to lectures in French. We would buy cases of wine and send them home. We would look at etchings and books and women together. He would buy me something as a surprise and bring it back to the hotel in his pocket.' In short, you became a member of my family. Instant complexity. Now I am defensive of you. Interested in your well-being. Anxious that you should not feel unnecessary pain. In the vernacular, I'm in a bind. You sit there like a young Galahad, waiting for an answer. You want things settled. You want the tree house to stay in the tree. But what's this? Down by the roots is a dog with its teeth in the bark shaking the tree back and forth like a bone. You look down. It's not a bad dog you see, not a vicious dog . . . a little wormy, a little mangy, but really a charming pooch. What do you say to this intruder? You say, 'Go home. Shoo. Get lost.' Well, we can lose this metaphor. In short, you want me to disappear."

"I smell something burning," Moses said.

Bartolome sprang to his feet and wrenched open the oven door. "I always fill the pans too full. They're running over.

It's nothing." He came back and saw the tired sag of Moses' shoulder, the glassy brightness of his eyes.

"Would you like a glass of milk?"

"Okay."

"You want it hot?"

"I don't like it hot," Moses said. "It gets a skin on it."

"I like that skin," Bartolome said. "But then I like all skin. On milk. On turkeys. On women. Where were we?"

He was at the refrigerator and then at the stove, sloshing the milk into a pan. "I'll take it off for you before anything repugnant happens," he said, watching it closely. "So. You want an answer I don't want to give. There's something about me I should tell you, my son-if-your-eyes-were-a-little-darker. I avoid decisions as long as I can. Why? Because that way I maintain the illusion that there is a way to keep everything."

"Well, then," Moses said, "I guess I'd better go."

"Listen," Bartolome said, "if you won't have milk and you won't have cake, have a little comfort. Neither I nor anyone else can long hide from the truth. So good night. Sleep well. I'm going to make a phone call now and discuss ethics with my friend Goldfarb. He needs a little stirring up."

The wedding was a human interest story since the bride was close to eighty and the groom only one year younger. News of it brought two photographers from the *Herald-Examiner*, one of whom wore disreputable tennis shoes and a high-smelling leather jacket.

Bartolome refused them permission to enter the garden or take pictures, on the grounds that they were obviously disrespectful of the event; he cited the shoes and told them to leave. He would brook no interference from anyone. He meant to launch this marriage in defiance of actuarial tables; he meant to see the old bride decked and arrayed with trembling earrings and a small sprig of heliotrope tucked beneath her diminished breasts. He meant to see the old man to the altar with his feet slid into new, warm and smartly clocked stockings. He brought the wine from his own house and paid dearly for six dozen carnations that were the pink of a young woman's open mouth. He invited Emma, to show her how he served Hymen. Let her marvel with him that the ground was never too frozen to produce a flower, the blood too sluggish to leapfrog through the veins. He would himself preside over this hopeful event, make the toast, hymn the beauty of this old love. He would speak without notes, holding a glass of nut brown sherry in his hand; his kiss on the forehead of the bride would be winy and Bacchic.

Emma stood beside her mother, leaning against a sun-warmed wall garlanded with a Virginia creeper beginning to show the first rusty-nail color of fall. The assembled company rustled like a sea of grass in dresses fresh from the cleaners, in old fringed shawls, in boas here and there that lifted in the breeze like the feathers of ruffled owls. There was a spirit of hurrah in the air, as if a retreating army had found two generals in its ranks still ready to do battle.

The wedding gifts stood displayed on a table, along with plates of cookies and plastic bowls of cut-up fruit. There were no silver platters, no Waring blenders, no creamers in the shape of cows, no table mats, candlesticks, waxed fruit or deep-fryers. There was instead a dog-eared volume of Dante's *Inferno*, a dented gold broach, a used checkers set, a jar of cascara, a twenty-five-dollar savings bond and a sex manual of recent vintage.

The amount of loot was surprising since the couple were more or less despised by the others. She was thought to be dry, caustic, stingy and learned; he was dismissed as clever, arrogant, totally lacking in consideration. He was known to read Kafka in the toilet while his roommate stood on one leg and cursed him; she was notorious for taking the largest slice of cake for herself and for quoting Montaigne when the ladies wished to talk of their absent children.

"They're well-suited," said Emma's mother. "They've already slept together. He's still fierce. I heard him groan through the wall. I wish I'd seen him first."

Emma pushed back her hair and chewed on a corner of her lip.

"What's the matter, Emma?" She looked long and hard at her daughter.

Emma shrugged. "I'm between a rock and a hard place," she said.

"Just tell me who has to be dealt with," said Agatha, who was more and more given to maledictions and rage.

Emma looked across the garden to Bartolome, who had raised his hands above his head and was speaking in a loud and emotional voice.

"A toast. Lift your glasses with me but not for the usual platitudes, I beg you. Let us dispense with health, wealth and assorted good wishes. Let us instead laud what is truly laudable. Endurance. Survival. Passion. Appetite. I urge you to emulate our newly married friends. Forswear the hot water bottle. Clasp another human being. Throw away the painkillers. Find someone to make you laugh. Marry and be merry. There'll be no children. So! At this time of life sonnets are as important as sons."

"What about you, doctor, hah?" cried a cynic from the first row.

"I'm waiting to be asked," said Bartolome. His gaze burned across the grass like a lit fuse and found Emma. He thrust his glass in her direction. "Bad cess to mere existence," he shouted. "Life — or nothing!"

The wedding party advanced on the food and wine like wasps, buzzing their pleasure. Bartolome appeared at Emma's side. He told Agatha he would play Parchesi with her later in the day, and then he grasped Emma brusquely and took her off to an empty carp pond and a splintered wooden bench.

"Your son came to see me in the night," he began abruptly. "He spoke to me in a tremulous voice, a voice that cracked, that sounded like a dish breaking."

"Yes," Emma said. "I know."

"Fine. Good. It's good to know where your kids are at night. Did he speak for you?"

"Now I'm in the pan," Emma said. "Now I'm frying."

"I see the shape of the debate. I have a practiced eye. Widows have wept in front of me, divorcées have wriggled, men on window ledges have grabbed hold of my tie. I'm a scholar of why and why not, a historian of yes and no. Don't be cowardly, Emma."

"I am."

"I'll have a kiss," he said furiously. "At least that." He came at her like a butting ram, bruising her mouth and then her nose, bending finally to her breast. Emma indulged herself shamelessly, greedily. She wondered briefly if they had an audience and then she thought of nothing but recklessness till he lifted his head.

"No more," he said. "I don't intend for you to enjoy yourself." His eyes reproached her. "You mean for me to be my own executioner — don't deny it. 'Humanist, doctor, romantic, he can hardly fail to see which way the wind blows,' says my Emma to herself. 'Didn't he tell me he loved his wife?' Most certainly he did that. 'Can I not make the case that had she lived he would never have looked at another woman — not at her ankles, nor her eyelashes?' You may make that case! 'Well, then,' says my Emma, 'I need only mention fidelity and he'll understand, and I can slip away. It's clear that this man grasps the meaning of continuity in love. He's been there himself, this Bartolome. He was married; he knew tenderness and tolerance; as I have, he suffered his mate's head colds, civic opinions, jokes, spiritual thrashings.' Mate. Helpmate. Mater. Matter. I have my own declensions. But to go on: 'He sees that I, Emma, am bound in old ties — to birth, to anniversaries, to hours in bed, to marathons of talk, to trifles. Look. The marks are on his wrists, too . . . still visible.' "

"Benjamin . . ."

"No. Let me spare you." He took the flower from his lapel

and laid it in her lap. "Let me applaud you. You are honoring your vows, very rare in these mendacious days. You are upholding society's standards — the family, obligations undertaken and so on — even rarer. You are being kind, forgiving, emotionally lazy, if I may say so. And, in addition, you're killing me, Emma."

She clasped his head to her. "Ah, Benjamin — if only I had two lives to live . . ."

He rose to his feet and towered over her, his eyes stormy. "Don't start in with "if only.' Did Abaham say 'if only' as he prepared to sacrifice his son? Did Job say 'if only' when he came down with boils? Kindly don't offer me your regrets."

"Charles is very dear to me. You're very dear to me."

"Your life, like your house, is too cluttered," he said. "Send something or someone to the Goodwill. It's over." He began to walk up and down in front of her, addressing her as if she were a jury. "I've talked to your husband. In other circumstances I'd call him a darling man. An odd soul but very charming. The minute I met him I knew it was over — that it was over before it began. I'm going to Europe to look for a mature Spanish widow. I'm going to make love with garlic from her paella on my breath. I'm going to put an earring back in this punctured ear lobe and live a wild life. I love you. I concede everything else. Good-by. Good-by, lovely Emma. Be off with you."

She dreamed of him. He flew over her head in an hallucinated sky, wearing a donkey's head, looking down at her with one invisible and one all-seeing eye, pelting her with roses and rainwater and his gorgeous crocodile tears. Upward and outward he soared, amid bouquets and stars and roosters in profile.

Good-by, Bartolome. Benjamin, Beniamino. Farewell. Adieu. You would scorn it — but accept my gratitude nonetheless. Good doctor. Your cure was green, fragrant, palatable. I taste it still. Watch me daydreaming and you will see yourself enshrined. No winter day will pass without some sample of you in its gray sky; no summer evening without your call in it; no spring without your beckoning. Take that — if not me.

All is easier now. There has been a refurbishing, a hem lifted here, a collar turned, a stitch caught in time. The garment will serve for several seasons more, I think.

The afternoon had the brightness of lemon peel. A primary sun washed the road and the beach with a rough thoroughness, like a housewife scouring in corners.

Cozumel was very nearly empty. The café where Charles and Emma sat had a whitewashed facade crazed with cracks. The floor was dirt, pounded and wetted, and three small tables sat on the narrow pavement. The road was a child's pencil mark running inaccurately to the horizon. The water of the bay was the brilliant blue of hair rinse; it seemed almost solid with its heavy, unmoving surface. In the middle of the plaza a food vendor cooked something pungent that drew two old men to the cart, one treating the other to lunch with consummate courtesy. In friendship, they waved the flies from each other's head and moved off arm-in-arm to eat under the trees.

An argument began inside the café. A fierce little Canadian in white duck pants, sockless in white shoes, was haranguing the waiter about the general uncleanliness of the bar, as if he were about to perform surgery on the zinc table and some patient's life was threatened by the thumb print on his glass. He went on and on, provoked by the waiter's uncomprehending smile, his voice scaling angrily upward like a toy flute. He looked like an attendant in an insane asylum with his white pants, his white shirt, his white temper.

Emma looked to Charles. "Stop grousing," Charles called over his shoulder to the intruder, and Emma was suddenly happy to be with him, happy that he drank boldly from a dirty glass, would take that and any and all other risks.

The tourist thrust his head out to look at them, took note of Charles's height and departed, leaving no gratuity except his absence. Emma drank her tequila and wrote in her notebook. There was always one in her bag, usually stained with spilled cologne or white with loose face powder. She bought them by the dozen, all red with spiral backs.

They could not be said to be diaries or journals; they were too random for that, full of directives: Buy Kotex. We're out of Scotch tape. Remember: read labels from now on; everything is full of poison. Call mother. Get raincoat cleaned; it smells of cat. Have oil filter changed if you want the car to start.

They also noted her astonishment: Mushrooms sprouted overnight on the lawn. My tonsils are growing back; is that possible? Bread can't be a dollar sixty a loaf — there'll be a revolution. Two stars fell in one night. Is that an omen? The Jerusalem tomato plant put out a blossom in the house. Unheard of.

She recorded what brewed in her head. Opinions: Everyone says I make snap judgments. Is that a bad thing? You can always change; you can change your mind. I don't think it's entirely necessary to tell the truth. There's always the question, Whose truth, yours or mine? If there is a God, will He answer my questions? Vision clears in old age. I think we must see things as they are just before we don't see at all. What if I'm wrong?

My, but I like Charles these days. He's full of improvisations and flourishes. He makes love before he brushes his teeth. He's grown tranquil. All my laundry is piled in the sink. He hasn't said a word.

I must meet generosity with generosity. I must listen to his inner voice — the one that whispers age coming, chances lessening, hurdles growing higher — and cluck away his aches and pains. There must be kisses offered with aspirin, a soothing hand for his migrainous forehead. I must not ask him to shave on Sundays. He need not give up his tweed rain hat. He need not silence his fears; he can name his desires. I will tell him I love him and not ask for extra household money before or after. I'm not a tart. In my own way I will forbear. He may put his sweaters in with my underwear. He may with impunity forget my birthday.

Notes for herself: I don't care about absolutes anymore. High time. Some philosopher, I can't think who, said we must moderate our expectations. I'm willing. I'd certainly like to be a reasonable woman. That above everything else. I don't think suffering ennobles. I'm going to be very careful about suffering. Only over momentous issues. If my mother dies. If, God forbid, I'm not a grandmother. I wonder if I can be silent if I have nothing to say. It's unlikely. Will I ever right a wrong? I'd like to. Do I want accomplices or friends? Which?

Resolutions: Try to be brave. Don't be afraid of cancer. Groan in the clothes closet with the door shut when you see signs of age. The second half of life is not the same as the first. Read Herrick for confirmation. Don't look back in anger. In fact, don't look back at all. Is wisdom totally unobtainable? If not, get some. Amass mental riches. Eat well. Death is final and boring; don't experience it in advance. Grow flowers. Watch chaffinches. Don't be calculating. Don't cause pain. It's not necessary to get fat.

And finally she set down her hopes: Will I live long enough? And her fears: I'll live too long.

"Emma?" Charles asked. "You're thinking very hard. Where are you?"

The question was a summons, one intimacy calling forth another. For a moment she was overtaken, recaptured; for one part of a moment, capricious. Then she stuck her pencil behind her ear, yawned, stretched, looked out at the improbable blue of the ocean.

"I'm here," she said mildly.

Charles looked at her. "And there," he added. "Tell the whole truth."

Her eyes were open, beautiful, indulgent. "Don't misjudge the distance," she said.

"No. I won't do that," Charles said.

Jessup appeared on the brow of a hill and started down the road toward them with a loping fox's gait. He was strangely dressed, wearing an orange serape, abused English tattersall trousers, a hat with holes in it for a burro's ears. He was strangely burdened, borne down with a heavy Arriflex camera strapped in a harness over his shoulder. Operating the camera, sandals flapping, he pursued a young Indian woman with a braid of hair like a bell-pull down her back and was followed at a run by a sound man, a grip, a best boy and Cleo, who carried a bottle of Puritas water and trotted lightly at his side.

"Hurry on, hurry on," he called to the woman. "He's waiting at the end of this road. His arms are outstretched — your heart stretches to meet him. Rush. Fly. Good, good, quicker, quicker, as fast as you can go. Don't feel the rocks, don't feel the road, don't stop."

His camera whirred like a bird; his eyes, bird bright, wept his pleasure at the image he had sculpted, hand made. At the end of the road two figures met and clung to each other, held, cleaved. He staggered toward them, the cyclopean eye of the camera coming nearer and nearer, taking them into its unblinking stare, adopting them. They were his for a long moment, and then he took his eye away from the lens and whispered, "Yes. Oh, yes. Cut."

He turned to a barefooted, gap-toothed youngster holding a microphone on a boom. "All right for sound?"

"There's a lot of wind, Mr. Jessup."

"There's a lot of truth. A little wind over it won't hurt." Then he sank to his knees in the road, bowed his head and panted like an old dog, his chest heaving, his nostrils stirring the dust, his old tattersall-covered backside offered up to God and art. His crew gathered around him.

Then he lifted his rapt and wicked face and brought his hands together in applause. The others joined. The sound of clapping hands was like rain spattering.

"It's a wrap," he said. "We're finished. We're out of wages, out of work, dysenteric, disgruntled — but, oh, my dears, not disgraced."

Cleo advanced on him, a towel in hand. "Dry off," she said,

and caught the runnels of sweat as if they were sacred fluid wrung from a saint.

But Jessup would have his moment. He knotted the towel into an ascot, showed his audience the noble bridge of his nose, the regal set of his burro's hat. "Out of the ashes, the phoenix," he said. And while his crew shifted from one leg to another, consumed with boredom and a desire for beer and bimbos, he spoke an epilogue.

"What have we done here, in this remote place? It's quite simple. We've found our way, amid impossibilities, obstacles and difficulties to health, to reality, to love. Health, because it's ethical to do what one believes in. Reality, because there's no jiggery-pokery here — this is the story of a real woman and her husband and their life. Love, because I do nothing without it. Yes, I know. I hear you saying, 'Listen to the old prick who has chewed us out, abused us, humiliated us.' Well, I'm always angry. I don't apologize. I need to be angry. I don't need to justify myself in any other way than by my work. If you want to eat some food, come to my house. If not, good-by."

The company disbanded hurriedly, leaving cans and litter and cigar butts among the flowers in the grass.

Jessup remained where he was, the sea breeze lifting his white hair. His face had a pointed, muzzly look, like an animal delicately sniffing the air for its food, its survival. He swept the landscape. Far away he saw two figures in a café, a man and a woman. He lifted his hands as if he were elevating a chalice.

"Who are they?" he said. "Why are they here? What will become of them?"

Already, in his magician's mind, he began the answers.

## DATE DUE

| | | | |
|---|---|---|---|
| DEC 0 7 1984 | | | |
| NOV. 1 4 1986 | | | |
| NOV 2 2 1996 | | | |



Frank, Harriet
Special effects